Getting Under the Skin

The Body and Media Theory

Bernadette Wegenstein

The MIT Press
Cambridge, Massachusetts
London, England

MIT Press books may be purchased at special quantity discounts for business or sales promotional use. For information, please email special_sales@mitpress.mit.edu or write to Special Sales Department, The MIT Press, 55 Hayward Street, Cambridge, MA 02142.

This book printed and bound in the United States of America.

Library of Congress Cataloging-in-Publication Data

Wegenstein, Bernadette
  Getting under the skin : the body and media theory / Bernadette Wegenstein.
    p.   c.m.
  Includes bibliographical references and index.
  ISBN 0-262-23247-2
  1. Body image.   2. Mass media.   I. Title.

BF697.5.B63W42 2006
306.4613—dc22

2005052045

10 9 8 7 6 5 4 3 2 1

Of the Despisers of Body

"It is unto the despisers of body that I shall say my word. It is not to re-learn and re-teach what I wish them to do; I wish them to say farewell unto their own body—and be dumb.

'Body I am and soul'—thus the child speaketh. And why should one not speak like the children?

But he who is awake and knoweth saith: 'Body I am throughout, and nothing besides; and soul is merely a word for a something in a body.'

Body is one great reason, a plurality with one sense, a war and a peace, a flock and a heardsman. . . .

I go not your way, ye despisers of body! Ye are no bridges to beyond-man!"

Thus spake Zarathustra.

—FRIEDRICH NIETZSCHE, *THUS SPAKE ZARATHUSTRA: A BOOK FOR ALL AND NONE*

Contents

Foreword

Mark Hansen

According to historian Bernard Andrieu, the trio of phenomenology, psycho-analysis, and cognitive science/artificial intelligence has yielded—as the twenti-eth century's legacy to the history of the body—an "epistemological dispersion of the human body." Through their cumulative impact, these disciplines have challenged prevailing conceptions of the body as an integral organization that is bounded by the skin and differentiated systemically from the environment, offering instead a picture of the body-in-pieces. While this revolution in the conception of the body—together with the invention of what has been called "body criticism" (Stafford)—picks up on a long-standing history of body frag-mentation dating back at least to the invention of modern anatomy in the six-teenth century, it is only in the twentieth century and, indeed, in the wake of these above-named disciplinary inventions, that the concept of body fragmen-tation can be integrated into a holistic body concept, producing a new and finely nuanced conception of the body as a complex form of mediation or, better, as the potentiality informing mediation per se.

In *Getting Under the Skin: Body and Media Theory,* Bernadette Wegenstein ex-tends the scope of Andrieu's suggestion by laying out the gradual process through which the body, itself subjected to radical mediation, ultimately is ex-posed as the general potential for mediation at the end of the twentieth century. Through a keenly balanced mix of theoretical argumentation and exemplifica-tion, Wegenstein demonstrates both how the reconciliation of fragmentation and holism under the banner of Andrieu's disciplinary trio offers a new under-standing of embodiment (distinct from the static body) as a dynamic process encompassing alterity, and also how the advent of new media has intensified the dispersion of the body to a critical point. At once a genealogy of mediation and a status report on contemporary media, Wegenstein's study performs the crucial task of filling in the historical void that has functioned in criticism over the last decade to disjoin the study of modernity, now vastly expanded in scope, from explorations of the so-called new media revolution. In the process, *Getting Under the Skin* foregrounds the continuity of the latest digital technologies, together with the cultural and artistic practices they support, with the history of Western society in the modern period.

Its broad scope and evenhanded tone may make *Getting Under the Skin* the book that can heal the divisions and disjunctions between die-hard modernists (and there are certainly more of these today than ever) and those of us, myself included, who feel that keen attention to the technico-material conditions of life and of knowledge production—which today means, above all, the digital computer—constitutes nothing less than the very basis for critical analysis of culture, be it historical or contemporary in scope. By focusing her study of mediation on the history of the human body, Wegenstein is able to highlight both the continuity and the novelty of the digital in relation to prior technical regimes. For this very reason, her study is perfectly positioned to forestall reactions, which are all too common to those of us working in the area of new media, that accuse us critics—and the artists and practitioners about whose work we write—of reinventing the wheel and of ignoring the precedent of history. In this sense, Wegenstein's explorations of 1960s body art or Dada performance or sixteenth century anatomical treatises are every bit as important to the argument of *Getting Under the Skin* as is her analysis of contemporary media art and architecture practices; insofar as they do stand on their own, these explorations make forcefully clear the contention here advanced that the digital cannot be understood in a historical vacuum. And while contemporary media practices may indeed mark a revolutionary moment in our understanding of the body, they do so only as contributions to a broader legacy; they carry out a transmutation that has been prepared by—and thus continues to depend on—a long gestational process. At the same time, however, it must be said that Wegenstein's appreciation for these historical stages in the history of the body as a history of mediation is uniquely informed by the digital revolution, and justly so; thus, a sense that the boundedness of the body has given way today to a bidirectional informational flow that makes the body an "organ instead of a body" (OiB) flavors Wegenstein's revaluations of these earlier moments, giving a structure if not a telos to the entirety of the twentieth century's complex reconciliation of fragmentation and holism.

Wegenstein's conceptual differentiation of embodiment from the body perfectly exemplifies the advantages of focalizing an expansive history of the body through the contemporary intensification of mediation. While the trope of embodiment (and disembodiment) has pervaded recent discussions of digital media (most notably forming the core of Kate Hayles's groundbreaking critical reconstruction of "how information lost its body" in the postwar articulation of cybernetics), it has not been differentiated categorically from the body, but rather has been positioned so as to denote a broader slice of materiality than the body narrowly considered. Thus, the burden of Hayles's argument is to demonstrate the impossibility of a disembodied instance of information, since the latter always must take on some concrete material form (even where this remains—from the technical standpoint at least—contingent in relation to informational content). On this line of argument, the irreducible embodiment of information remains of a piece with the human as a concrete embodiment of information, despite the radical differences in the respective materiality at issue in the two cases.

Precisely by urging a conceptual differentiation of embodiment from the body, Wegenstein manages to move beyond the impasse that Hayles's work has seemingly bequeathed to cultural studies—namely, the opposition of embodiment and disembodiment. Rather than expanding discussions of how humans are now "seamlessly articulated with" computers (Hayles) or how humans retain a distinct form of embodiment that differs categorically from the materiality of computers, even though the two can be "interactively coupled" through "indirection" (Varela, Hansen), Wegenstein here charts her own course: specifically, by welcoming the capacity of the (human) body to disappear, while insisting on the incapacity of (human) embodiment to do likewise, Wegenstein embraces a dimension of contemporary cyber-culture (the virtualization of the body) without taking on its more suspect tenets (radical freedom from constraints of embodiment, possibility for downloading consciousness onto computers, etc.). In this way, Wegenstein is able to "listen to" contemporary culture in what I consider to be an exemplary fashion: for if some dissolution of bodily boundaries seems to be an undeniable fact of our contemporary experience (and this is a claim that finds ample substantiation in many domains, from marketing to psychoanalysis), then the critical problem to be addressed must be that of rethinking what the experience of human embodiment—the experience of embodiment that is constitutive of the human—is in our world today. And this is just the critical injunction to which Wegenstein's janus-faced, bidirectional genealogy of the body as mediation answers.

Although prepared for by the explorations of the first three chapters—focusing on the development of body criticism from sixteenth century anatomy to the twentieth century, on body performances in art from the 1960s to the 1990s, and on the rhetoric of the skin as body boundary—the theoretical payoff of *Getting Under the Skin* comes in the final chapter, where an analysis of contemporary media converges with a rehabilitation of certain strands in phenomenology, psychoanalysis, and feminism in order to generate a powerful conceptualization of the human as a form of distributed embodiment, an "organ instead of a body," that does not so much demarcate itself against an environment as extend seamlessly and robustly into the now ubiquitously digitized technosphere. Having traced the conversion of performativity and medical visualization technologies from an obsession with the body as interior to an expansion of the body into the exterior environment, Wegenstein is well positioned to bring home the revolutionary impact of digital technology, namely, the way in which the medium has become the body, and body criticism has become media criticism.

On her argument, new media comprises a twenty-first-century intensification of the dispersion of the body begun and substantially accomplished in the twentieth century: New media artworks and architectural practices have literally "gotten rid of the body," leaving in its place a merger of "the flesh of technology with that of the interacting viewer-participant." Likewise, "current body discourse has 'gotten rid' of the body insofar as the medium has become corporealized itself." What is thereby revealed is a constitutive parallelism—indeed, a transduction (following Gilbert Simondon's conception of a relation that is primary in relation to its terms)—between body and medium. Expanding on Wegenstein's deployment of the retroactively disclosive function of the contemporary perspective, we might go so far as to say that the current state of new media exposes a mediating function of embodiment that has always constituted the human, even in the (long) period where this function coincided, more or less comfortably, with the particular organization known as the (organic) body. This is a point that resonates with her own conclusion, even as it moves beyond the terms of convergence foregrounded by her study. Thus, she can insightfully claim that "the holistic discovery of the body as constitutive mediation has converged with an age of mediatic proliferation, such that what we are in fact witnessing in the apparent continuing fragmentation of the body is the work of mediation itself *as* the body." In a move that ties all loose threads together, Wegenstein here clarifies exactly how the terms for the holism or integrality of embodied function now coincide perfectly with the radical fragmentation of the body: In the digital age such coincidence—the double consequence of mediation—simply is the condition of (human) life as such.

Getting Under the Skin is not without debts to previous scholars of embodiment, media history, and new media. Beyond a willingness to recognize these debts, Wegenstein's method is characterized by, in my opinion, a particularly productive manner of working off of and through the conclusions of others. I already have mentioned one instance of this procedure, namely, Wegenstein's qualified embrace of certain aspects of contemporary posthumanist discourse, but the example perhaps bears further development, since what is at stake in Wegenstein's embrace is a reorientation of posthumanism back toward an (admittedly revamped) humanism. Not afraid to entertain arguments concerning the suborganic, processural, and distributed modes of agency that have been theorized by cognitive scientists such as Edwin Hutchins, biologists such as Richard Dawkins, and (perhaps most notably) by Deleuze and Guattari in their infamous reconceptualization of Artaud's "body without organs," Wegenstein offers a picture of the human that may be unsettling to many card-carrying humanists, but that is all the more urgent because of its effort to address the contemporary stage of our technogenesis (our coevolution, as a living species-being, with technics). What Wegenstein is telling us is that the human today is a being whose integrity as a being comes from its utter dispersion; the potential indifference between body and environment that has always informed the concept of mediation, of embodiment as mediation, now has been brought to the fore, revealing the deep-seated and "essential" transduction of the human with technics, and giving it the particular configuration of an "organ instead of a body," an always temporary, though temporarily autonomous, coding of the body by a specific "organ," here meaning a conjunction between a bodily potentiality and a technical "-ibility" or affordance.

What is most striking about this argument is the way that Wegenstein comes to it: namely, by embracing—experimentally as it were—the disembodiment thesis (or rather, the part of it that upholds the disappearance of the body in our contemporary technoculture). This experimental embrace of disembodiment allows her to clear the ground for rethinking embodiment in general, and for revaluing the role of the female body in particular. Thus, while Wegenstein follows feminists like Butler and Grosz (not to mention Irigaray and Haraway) in attempting to revaluate the identification of the feminine with the mute body, with embodiment as mere (formless) matter (*hylé*), her argument does not yield a defense of female embodiment so much as a repositioning of the feminine at the vanguard of a mediatic regime of embodiment, where the latter is neither anchored in the flesh of the body nor opposed to disembodiment (understood as a break with the longstanding bio-cultural organ-ization of the body). In this way, Wegenstein is able to put to (new) use the qualified embrace of disembodiment that, she rightly claims, was and remains central to feminist efforts to "produce the 'surplus' of gender"; in her new use, however, this surplus opens the possibility for a new collective (and no longer "essentially" gendered) experience of embodiment-disembodiment, one that is, to be sure, lived singularly by differently individuated beings. In the new mediatic regime, disembodiment comprises an opportunity to experiment with what the body can do, which means that, in accordance with the Spinozist-Deleuzian paradigm she here adopts, disembodiment itself paradoxically becomes an irreducible dimension of embodiment.

In a similar vein, Wegenstein's insightful and original claims regarding the body *as* mediation serve to differentiate her argument from Friedrich Kittler's radicalization of McLuhan's media-theoretical paradigm shift (the medium is the message) into a "science" of media proper (with science here intended to oppose the relativity of all hermeneutics). While her evolutionary conception of mediation bears certain affinities with Kittler's own genealogy of media forms (affinities that are buttressed by her qualified, experimental embrace of certain dimensions of posthumanism), her argument remains resolutely and strongly culturalist. Indeed, the force of her exploration of avant-garde performance from the early-twentieth-century experiments (futurism, Dada, etc.) through the 1960s' body art and happenings to the work of the 1990s stems from its detailed inventory of media-related tropes actualized, in divergent ways, through the work of the body. (And something similar could be said for her analysis of the rhetoric of the skin in medical visualization technologies and recent popular culture.) Not only do these artistic movements (and these imaginings of the skin boundary) mark stages in our culture's ongoing correlation of the body and media, but they have prepared the ground for the digital revolution itself, insofar as this is—necessarily—a revolution first and foremost in our own experience of (dis)embodiment, in the experience that is, literally, constitutive of the human in its current, technogenetic configuration. In a certain sense, then, Wegenstein's argument marks a triumphant return to McLuhan's understanding of media as prosthesis to the human body, an understanding that has yet to exercise its full force and significance. Her conception of human embodiment as distributed, temporary, and organ-centered (in the sense discussed above) manages to reconcile the humanist dimensions of McLuhan's thesis (those dimensions most distasteful to Kittler) with a posthumanist conception of technics, demonstrating in the process (and *pace* Kittler) that technical autonomy need not come at the expense of human perceptual ratios. Given the profound extent to which human life is now imbricated with technics at an increasingly fine scale, such a reconciliation is not only unavoidable but utterly necessary. It forms nothing less than the inaugural move of any effort to think of the human in the media age, and correlatively to think of the media age as a concrete stage of human technogenesis.

As I hope I have indicated in my remarks here, Wegenstein's procedure in *Getting Under the Skin* greatly benefits from her facility in reading against the grain of received critical *doxa*. Not only does this procedure permit her to capitalize on extant critical discussions of media, embodiment, and culture without assuming the baggage of their (inter-)disciplinary heritage, but—even more significantly—it makes possible the discovery of new avenues of thinking, avenues that would remain unthinkable for many if not most of Wegenstein's contemporaries, not to mention prior generations of media scholars. One striking example comes by way of Wegenstein's assimilation of the phenomenology of the body (Merleau-Ponty, Barbaras) into a program, influenced by the qualified feminist embrace of disembodiment and by Deleuze and Guattari's critique of organic embodiment (organ-ization), that would seem to be at odds with the grounding commitments of phenomenology, even one as advanced in its reckoning with dualism as Merleau-Ponty's. Rather than getting hung up on the apparent incongruities between these diverse schools of thinking, Wegenstein allows her topical focus—the revaluation of the body *as* medium that is taking place in our technical lifeworld today—to form a bridge between them. In this way, we are again allowed to glimpse a reconciliation, beyond the point of impasse, between the most powerful approach available today for thinking the fundamental (human) experience of embodiment and equally powerful, indeed inescapable, critical assessments of how media culture has deterritorialized—and is currently in the process of reterritorializing—the body.

As I see it (and I think Wegenstein's analysis of advertising culture in chapter 3 speaks eloquently to this point), any hope we critics, artists, and twenty-first-century citizens may have of influencing how this reterritorialization takes place will depend on our ability to intervene by reasserting the agency of embodiment and by reconfiguring it for (admittedly) radically altered living conditions. On this front, it is heartening to see Wegenstein praise phenomenology (along with psychoanalysis) for its constitutive effort to separate and champion a "subjectivity" of the body from the relentless objectification imposed on it by contemporary capitalist culture. In this deployment, phenomenology would form part of a defense of the "operational perspective" of the (human) body that, no matter how fragmented and distributed (indeed, disembodied) it might become, must remain the focus for any effort to think about human technogenesis in its contemporary stage, which is to say, in an age that is witnessing, in one and the same moment, both the radical exteriorization of the human into a convergent media platform and the massive infiltration of technics into the most intimate interiority of the human being as we have hitherto known it.

If this double assault on the "integrity" of the human body marks our moment as a particularly rich and complex one, it also for this very reason calls for new methods of thinking, methods that can help us think beyond the impasses which continue to hobble even the most enlightened and well-intentioned interdisciplinary ventures. Bernadette Wegenstein's *Getting Under the Skin* furnishes an exemplary instance not just of such a thinking, but *of the very process through which such thinking becomes possible.* Her careful genealogy of the correlation of the body and media prepares the way for a theorization—of the body as the potentiality informing media—that cuts across all disciplinary divides preventing an embodied phenomenology of the radically dispersed contemporary body, of the body as medium. In the wake of this accomplishment, there simply is no longer any point in rehashing tired claims concerning the implicit anthropomorphism of the flesh or the ineliminable dualism of intentionality; in effect, the resources of phenomenology have already been secured for a new conceptualization of the flesh, one that is perfectly compatible with the virtual media environments now ubiquitous in our contemporary lifeworld. As a contribution that draws much from recent work at the crossroads of media, embodiment, and culture, *Getting Under the Skin* will undoubtedly provide much to draw on in its turn: specifically, by showing the path beyond the disembodiment-embodiment impasse, it will help liberate today's generation of cultural critics from unnecessarily constraining and counterproductive critical commitments and will thereby take critical thinking about embodiment and media into a new frontier, one where the conjunction of these latter will have to be rethought as transduction, as a relationality that remains primary in relation to the terms it relates.

Preface

It was during the research for my dissertation, *The Representation of AIDS in the European Media,*[1] that a deep interest in the body as culture stirred in me. Specifically after having read such books on the body in the field of literature and science as N. Katherine Hayles's *How We Became Posthuman* (1999), I knew that there was something of deep importance *happening* to the body. After visiting Gunther von Hagens's controversial *Körperwelten*[2] (*Body Worlds*) exhibit in Vienna in early 1999, in which I witnessed plastinated cadavers posing as chess players or pregnant women, I decided to study this body discourse that had very literally and obviously *gotten under the skin.* Thus began my journey into body criticism, which very soon brought me to cognitive science, media theory, phenomenology, philosophy, psychoanalysis, as well as science and literature studies, and more practically to the study of popular culture such as advertisement, as well as to architecture and new media art. First, however, the journey into body criticism brought me back to the invention of anatomy and of the female sex and sexuality in early modernity.

Chapter 1, Making Room for the Body, examines current body criticism by way of its key concepts, which serve as paradigms for the applied analyses throughout the remainder of the book. This introductory chapter describes how the body became an object of critical study from early modernity's anatomical practices to twentieth-century thought, taking into consideration phenomenology, psychoanalysis, cognitive science, and feminist theory, and their specific contributions to a new body concept. Different factors have played an important role in the redefinition of subjectivity and individuality (as well as in the various reports of their demise) within this body discourse: the discovery of the unconscious, specifically Lacan's fractal body image in psychoanalysis; new biomedical technologies (for example, of reproduction), and new medical visualization practices of screening the body; discussions in gender studies and feminist theory on what or who the body is; as well as the rise of new media. Chapter 1 has two main theses, which form the basis for *Getting Under the Skin:* The first thesis is that the history of a body-in-pieces is a history of a struggling relationship between a fragmented and a holistic body concept, for which the rest of the book delivers a body of evidence; the second thesis is that, despite the body's capacity to "disappear" (as, ostensibly, with the digital image), embodiment cannot. The experience of being-in-the-world and of thought is therefore an experience of embodiment. Moreover, embodiment—being akin to articulation—is inherently performative, which leads to the next chapter on the history of performance art throughout the twentieth century.

Chapter 2, Body Performances from 1960s Wounds to 1990s Extensions, shows how throughout the rise of the mediatized environment of the twentieth century, and especially under the influence of the early Avant-garde (for example, Futurism), performance art first collapsed into the body and, during the last decades, extended itself more and more into new digital spaces. The claim is that the blurring of the differences between the environment and its content, materialities and their use, process and product have been inspired by an augmented awareness and production of mediation. After situating body-oriented art in the late twentieth century, chapter 2 discusses the body as *raw material* performed in 1960s Wounds, and the body experiments and their relationship with technology in 1990s Extensions. The third chapter, How Faces Have Become Obsolete, describes popular medical techniques for visualizing the human body and the attempt to control and dominate the body's interior. Furthermore, it studies the abundance of organ images and other penetrations of the skin in today's popular culture, and the resulting strategies of *getting under the skin.* The examples used in this chapter stem from advertisements, high fashion, film, and other popular domains, and show how the skin and other organs have been "freed" and separated from the idea of an entire body, as well as how these freely floating body parts have taken on the role of pure mediation, of flat screen, of the *sur-face* on which the body as such is produced. For this move to happen, the face as principle mediator of the soul had to become obsolete, a fact that the philosophers Gilles Deleuze and Félix Guattari, whose theory of the body is discussed in this chapter, had foreseen long before. The fourth and final chapter, The Medium is the Body, argues by way of an analysis of current trends in architecture and new media art that the discipline of body criticism is in fact deeply connected and indebted to the discipline of media criticism. Chapter 4 invokes a neophenomenological critique of the digital image, explaining its development into affectivity (Hansen) and corporealization. This new approach to body criticism has literally replaced the study of the semiotics of media, as the body is no longer allowed merely to stand in for something else (as in Nietzsche's metaphorical concept discussed in chapter 1), but rather the medium has *become* the body. This move was facilitated by the advent of new media in the twentieth century, since through new media's new logic of dispersion the body could free itself from its inner universe and its organs (Deleuze), the inside merging with the outside and the very body surface or skin collapsing and flattening out. In conclusion, both theoretical insights and practical examples are brought to bear in arguing that the history of the body is a history of constitutive mediation in which both fragmentation and holism were, and are, indispensable modes of imagining and configuring the body.

Acknowledgments

Thanking people and institutions is not an easy task for somebody who believes that life is contingency. I could go back to my high school teachers in Vienna, Hilde Aigner (Ancient Greek and Latin) and Herwig Raupp (English), who stirred my interests in linguistics as well as in media besides their main task— turning us teenagers into decent human beings. I am indebted to my dissertation advisor in Romance Philology from Vienna University, Michele Metzeltin, who believed that I should become a scholar, and whose intuition I followed.

However, contingencies aside, this book would not have been possible without the input, scholarly discussions, and help of many friends and colleagues. I want to mention Jim Bono (The University at Buffalo), Mark Hansen (The University of Chicago), Stuart Murray (University of Toronto), and, above all, Tim Lenoir (Duke University) for their support and interest in my work. For her input on earlier versions of the book and her positive feedback I want to thank Liz Grosz (Rutgers University). I also want to thank the anonymous reviewers at The MIT Press for their constructive and detailed suggestions, and, especially, my editor Douglas Sery for his cheerful and always positive and immediate response to the various stages of the book. I also thank production editor Mel Goldsipe, copy editor Suzanne Stradley, designer Yasuyo Iguchi, and production coordinator Janet Rossi at The MIT Press for shepherding my book along the way. For financial support I am indebted to the Austrian Fonds zur Förderung der wissenschaftlichen Forschung and their generous Charlotte Bühler habilitation grant for women (1999–2001), thanks to which I could start my research project and at the same time become a mother. I am grateful to the University at Buffalo and in particular the department of Media Study, who have supported my research in many ways: first and foremost my department chair Roy Roussel who gave me research time off whenever possible, my colleagues for substituting for me in many meetings, the Julian Park Publication Fund for financing the diverse image editing costs, and not least the generous Dr. Nuala McGann Drescher Affirmative Action/Diversity Leave Program (2005), without which I could not have finished the book. I owe special thanks as well to Sepp Gumbrecht (Stanford University) for inviting me as a visiting scholar to Stanford, and hence for having changed my life, as it was during my stay at Stanford in 1998 and 1999 that I started not only this book project, but also decided to stay in the North American university sphere. However, it is to my husband Bill that I am indebted more than anybody else for having been able to write *Getting Under the Skin:* thanks to him as a colleague, a friend, a critic, an editor of my (often very German-sounding) English, and a partner in life and love, I was able to keep going through the ups and downs of the book. It is no exaggeration to say that without Bill *Getting Under the Skin* would not exist. I don't want to miss including our children Alexander and Charlotte into the list of people to thank, for their patience with a mother who is "always writing books," as they put it. I hope that their exaggeration will come true!

Thanks also to all the babysitters and friends, and again to Bill, who took care of the children while I worked on the book over the last years: Alessia Giangrande, Christina Kaulbach, Hedva Krauze, Mary Kervalage, Olivia Maginley, Melissa Matschke, Claudia Mödinger, Siobhan Mulvey, Hanna Stepanik, Meghan Sweeney, Josie Stott, Kristen Venditti, and Carisa Weaver. Thanks, finally, to my student assistants and careful editors of the final stages of the book: Christopher Galbraith, Eric Albright Mills, and Lisa Rooth. I also thank all agencies, architects, artists, and their representatives who were helpful in providing me with images, material, and feedback.

This book is dedicated to my mother, Elisabeth Habietinek Wegenstein (1934–2002), who taught me how to think, speak, and write, be intuitive and passionate, and create my own "house of being." Above all I want to thank her for teaching me not to make any concessions when it comes to my heart.

1

Making Room for the Body

the internal nothingness
of my self

which is night,
nothingness,
thoughtlessness,

but which is explosive affirmation
that there is
something
to make room for:

the body.[1]
—ANTONIN ARTAUD, "TO HAVE DONE WITH THE JUDGMENT OF
GOD, A RADIO PLAY"

According to French historian Bernard Andrieu, the twentieth century has been characterized by the "epistemological dispersion of the human body."[2] According to his thesis, it is only since the approach and methods developed by the *Nouvelle histoire* (New History)[3] in the middle of the twentieth century that the body became an object of intense investigation. In the introduction to his *Feudal Society* (1949), Marc Bloch[4]—one of the cofounders of the new historian journal *Annales*—wrote that "the task of the historian is not to exhibit an uninterrupted chain of connections linking the patterns of the past . . . but rather to understand the infinite variety and richness of the past in all its combinations."[5] It is in this spirit that Jacques Le Goff suggests rewriting history with a small *h,* as a history "lived by people,"[6] a perspective that emphasizes what he terms the *Zusammenhänge,* the connections between historical events, their context, and the materiality under investigation. No entity would better offer itself to this new-historical approach than the human body. As British sociologist Bryan S. Turner states, the usefulness of the body to critical analysis lies in the fact that we both are and have bodies. Or, to put in the terms of Le Goff, we experience our own body as well as the bodies of others: "The body is a material organism, but also a metaphor; it is the trunk apart from head and limbs, but also the person [as in 'anybody' and 'somebody']. . . . The body is at once the most solid, the most elusive, illusory, concrete, metaphorical, ever present and ever distant thing—a site, an instrument, an environment, a singularity and a multiplicity."[7] In the aftermath of this approach to questions of epistemology and historical progress, the last decades have seen an ever-increasing number of studies about the human body, representing a bewildering array of perspectives and approaches. Today we know the histories of a sexual body, a female body, a pregnant body, a Greek body—to list but a few of innumerable examples—as well as the histories of a body-in-pieces; in other words, of certain organs and body parts in their specific cultural, historical, and geographical configurations.

One of the most prominent attempts to tell a history of the human body— albeit, as his title says, in fragments—is the multivolume work edited by Michel Feher.[8] In this work more than forty authors present various aspects and moments of the human body and its parts. The first volume, the "vertical axis,"[9] explores the relationship of the body to the divine, the bestial, and the machinic or "monstrous doubles of the human body."[10] The second volume, or the "psychosomatic approach,"[11] provides cross-disciplinary and diachronical studies of the manifestation and production of the soul through emotions evoked by such phenomena as pleasure, sufferings, and death. The third volume, which goes farthest "under the skin," studies the "uses of certain organs and bodily substances as metaphors or models of the functioning of human society, on the one hand, and, on the other, [describes] several remarkable characteristics attributed to certain bodies because of the status of the individuals they incarnate, that is, the position they occupy in a certain conception of the social body, or even of the organization of the universe."[12] Examples from this volume revolve around such body parts and substances as sperm, breast milk, and blood, the clitoris, and the vagina.[13]

The dispersion of the body and the resulting invention of a cross-disciplinary approach to studying the body critically has to do with the redefinition of the body and its functions in several areas of study and research throughout the twentieth century. According to Andrieu, it is because of the realms of psychoanalysis, phenomenology, and cognitive science or artificial intelligence that we are facing an epistemological shift that has, over the last century, opened up new and old interests in the body in all its concreteness as well as in its symbolic value—from philosophy, feminism, and gender studies in general, to the studies of performance art and media art in particular. It is not an exaggeration to say that, throughout recent decades, the study of the body has dominated many critical disciplines in the humanities to the extent that a new discipline has arisen: what Barbara Maria Stafford has coined *body criticism* (1993). This first chapter investigates how and why these disciplines have opened themselves to questions surrounding the body, thus making room for a new body discourse, and what kind of body concepts result as a basis for bodily installations and configurations in popular culture, media art, and architecture at the turn of the millennium. The thesis of chapter 1, and the basis of the chapters to follow, is that the history of a body-in-pieces is a history of a struggling relationship between a fragmented and a holistic body concept. What I mean by holism is "the view that parts of a system have significance mostly in virtue of their interrelations with other parts."[14]

Throughout this chapter I show how the concept of bodily fragmentation, in circulation since the sixteenth century, has, in the twentieth century, been integrated into a holistic body concept—a concept that reveals the history of the body to be, in fact, a history of mediation. As shown throughout the following chapters, the history of the body is a history of constitutive mediation, for which both fragmentation and holism are indispensable modes of imagining and configuring the body. However, as I explore in greater detail in chapter 4, it was not until the turn of the millennium, and the digital revolution, that the body was able to show best its *real face:* mediality.

Historical Fragments of the Modern Body-in-Pieces

In the following, I summarize certain fragments of the history of the body, without which we cannot fully grasp the current body concept in question. Of course, body criticism did not emerge *ex nihilo* in twentieth-century thought. There is a long history of the body—one as long as bodies have existed. One of the crucial moments for the transformation of the body concept from a more unified perception of the body to a body-in-pieces was high modernity (that is, eighteenth and late nineteenth centuries). According to Bryan Turner,[15] modernity constitutes the beginning of a "somatic society," a society within which major political and moral problems are both articulated in respect to the body and expressed through it. Socioeconomic changes in Western culture—such as the liberation of the body from explicit economic and political bondage to supra-individual power structures (political liberalism, the theorization of privacy, etc.); the secularization of church, and hence the loss of a publicly accepted pedagogical religious discourse; the emergence of a postindustrial society organized around the control of communication; the ever-growing domination of consumer society; and the consequent emphasis in late capitalism on hedonism, desire, and enjoyment—have conspired to create a "new" human body. The new body has a higher expectation of longevity and rejects death from daily experiences. Social reforms of working conditions, such as early retirement, have increased the opportunities for bodily focused leisure activities (hence the importance of sports and keeping fit). A specific focus on the beautiful body has been promoted through Hollywood and the norm-regulating media of mass communication.[16] Finally, the body experience has penetrated fields from the performing arts to adolescent culture, with activities such as piercing and tattooing becoming a collective symbol of almost tribal belonging.

For Turner, the socioeconomic changes have to be seen in relation to a society of rapidly expanding technology as well as in relation to some significant recent developments in medical technology—for example, reproductive technologies such as artificial insemination, in vitro fertilization, xenotransplants, and microsurgery and nanosurgery. The scientific advances associated with new medical technologies have raised major philosophical, ethical, and legal issues in contemporary society, issues ultimately related to the nature of personhood, identity, and individualism.

The British sociologist Anthony Giddens[17] has described the changes as a result of the dissolution of the relation of property between the state and the individual in the period of late or high modernity. Nevertheless, the German historian Norbert Elias[18] argues that the individualization of the body already had begun to take place in early modernity, a process consisting of the separation and differentiation of individuals from the social body. As the autonomous individual begins to take on responsibility for his or her own body, emotion, nonutilitarian trust, and interpersonal intimacy become the principal criteria of self-realization. The individual body no longer is defined by its dependence on an external power; rather, the body is defined by the activities in which it engages. As a result, the body has become a "project" to be worked on and accomplished as a fundamental aspect of the individual's self-identity. In twentieth-century self-care, responsible living, organic food, and fitness are just some of the slogans that helped proliferate self-realization and, as a result, a fully dominated and controlled body.

In the aftermath of high modernity the health, hygiene, shape, and appearance of the body have become among the most important expressions of an individual's identity.[19] This bourgeois body has become an individual property and a personal construction; conflicts that once occurred *between* medieval bodies now take place *within* modernity's embodied and self-aware individual. A current example of such a conflicted body is the AIDS body. The AIDS-discourse universe[20] expresses precisely the tendencies toward the separation—and hence loneliness—of modern embodied experience. The French AIDS nurse Françoise Baranne, for instance, talks about her experience with AIDS as if she had entered another universe: "I am nothing but an immigrant making do uneasily in the country of AIDS, and who doesn't dare to return home for fear of not being admitted anymore."[21] This local abstraction of an *AIDS country* has its universal correlate in the symbolization of the HIV virus as a spiked globe, an association that originally comes from an aestheticized microscopic image of the virus. The spikes often are portrayed as screws glimmering in outer space, in an obvious representation of war. The symbol of the spiked globe can be seen as a metaphor for the danger of AIDS itself, but also for the tendency of the infected and affected to inhabit such a separate universe as described by the French nurse, as a manifestation of bodily and hence physical differentiation. Baranne does not want to confront the illness of the body (that is, of her patients), but rather wants to fight in a country where there is only AIDS and nothing but AIDS, a country in which the distinction between healthy and ill no longer would exist. To return to Elias and Giddens, then, there is no longer an externally imposed conflict between bodies in the AIDS-discourse universe.[22] Instead, the conflict between bodies has metamorphosed into a conflict within bodies, embodied individuals living separately in ghettos on the AIDS globe.

The modern body has been theorized by cultural historians (Michel Foucault and Barbara Duden), historians of art (Barbara Maria Stafford), historians of medicine (Jonathan Sawday), historians of science (Thomas Laqueur, Bruno Latour), and sociologists (Anthony Giddens). As it would be impossible to summarize all of these important theories of the modern body, in what follows I discuss only a few of the milestones these theories represent.

In her study of the eighteenth-century German physician Johann Storch and his reports on the medical history of eighteen hundred women of all ages in Eisenach, Germany, the historian of the female body Barbara Duden identifies a "new kind of discrete object" that the modern body has constituted since the late eighteenth century: "This isolated, objectified, material body was seized by a dissecting gaze that embraced not only the entire body, not only its surfaces, but also its recesses and orifices. It penetrated inquisitively into the inside, evaluating the palpated organs and relating them to a visual image of organs and cadavers. This gaze turned the body, and with it the patient who possessed it, into a new kind of discrete object."[23] The process by which the body was objectified and isolated through the practice of anatomy already had begun in the fifteenth and sixteenth centuries, producing what we could call the *scientific fragmentation* of the body. As a result of these practices, not only did an objectified, materialized body-in-pieces present itself to a new gaze, but also through the practice and theory of dissection, the female body, as such, emerged with the "discovery" of female anatomy. During antiquity and the Middle Ages a gender paradigm of mimicry had been established between the sexes in which the female body was seen as the inversion[24] of the male body, and both female and male bodies were perceived as an inseparable unit mirroring nature and ultimately God. With the "discovery" of female anatomy and the "creation" of *woman* as a biological category, female and male bodies started to be seen as disconnected entities, or isolated bodies. As historian of the sexed body Thomas Laqueur points out: "In the one-sex model that dominated anatomical thinking for two millennia, woman was understood as man inverted. The uterus was the female scrotum, the ovaries were testicles, the vulva a foreskin, and *the vagina was a penis.*"[25] Among other examples of society's preference for the male body were, on the one hand, the domination of male sperm and its historical representation in medicine over the representations of female breast milk and blood; and, on the other, the strict separation of femininity and maternity according to which it was believed that, due to a maturation process, the female orgasm ended in marriage, because the locus of pleasure, the clitoris, shifted to the reproductive locus, the vagina.

The new sex paradigm of high modernity presented the female body as no longer subordinated to the male body in an inverted (and hence hierarchical) way. Instead, woman now became the locus of difference per se, the *other body.* We shall see later in this book how the concept of female *otherness* was no less problematic for the development of a female subjectivity, and how it has been reformulated in recent feminist thought.

As stated above, if we look at the history of a body-in-pieces, we find that it is a history of a mediated body. This underlying *dynamic anatomy* is promoted by a movement that unravels itself throughout the history of the body. Thus, the fragmented body as we have known it since early modernity has not simply been replaced by a holistic body concept; rather, fragmentation has been revealed as the stratification of a body concept that, from the holistic perspective, can be grasped as constitutive mediation. Fragmentation and wholeness are, in other words, part of the same process: the process of mediation. Jean-Luc Nancy has formulated this circumstance as follows: "The parts of the corpus do not combine into a whole, are not means to it or ends of it. Each part can suddenly take over the whole, can spread out over it, can become it, the whole—that never takes place. There is no whole, no totality of the body—but its absolute separation and sharing."[26] In *Corpus* Nancy emphasizes the body's relation via sharing with other bodies, and the impossibility of thinking of the body outside of this relationship. Bodies are first and always *others*. The other is a body because only a body is other, Nancy argues. At first glance this might seem a tautology, but the inherent alterity of any body is the *conditio sine qua non* of being as such, of being a particular body—a body that is exposed to its own extremities.[27]

Symbolically fragmented body parts have been important since the dominant Galenic view of the body[28] in antiquity, in which all parts were perceived as if in perfect harmony with each other, reflecting, above all, the inner harmony and health of the individual. The individual's health was perceived as a reflection of the higher harmony of nature, which in turn was a reflection or mimicry of divine harmony. To cite just one example of how, in Galen's view, health, harmony, and the "usefulnesses" of body parts were linked together, the brain was thought to possess the psychic faculty; the heart, the vital faculty; and the liver, the natural faculty; together forming a health-inducing triad.[29] The most important distinction between the Galenic fragmentation of the body and the current body-in-pieces is that today's body parts can constitute their own biotopes, can function independently from each other: "usefulness" has become self-referential, a usefulness of body parts that are conceived and represented as independent and autonomous from the unity of the body (chapter 3 examines this further).

The anatomical fragmentation of the body is a phenomenon dating from the fifteenth and sixteenth centuries. Thus, the body-in-pieces has existed as a topical, hence spatial, trope even outside the realm of medicine since early modernity. In this respect, it is worth mentioning the contemporary rise in the courtly tradition of the textual genre of *blazon*. The blazon has been described as a "poetic fantasy of male surrender to female dissection"; it "formed a significant part of the culture of dissection which produced the partitioned body."[30] The elevation of the fragment to a position of central significance and the rejection of totality thus are not inventions or novelties of postmodernity; rather, "early moderns, no less than postmoderns, were deeply interested in the corporeal 'topic.'"[31] It is modernity's "impulse to distinction and individuation"[32] that helped form the "age of synecdoche,"[33] an age in which parts are imagined as dominant vehicles for the circulation of cultural goods and for the articulation of culture *tout court.*

The term *topical* (from *topos,* the Greek word for place) meant, "of or applied to an isolated part of the body," before it came to mean "of current interest, contemporary," as it still is used in today's language. In other words, it was the spatially imagined body that—as pointed out by Hillman and Mazzio[34]—was the most common vehicle for the making of social and cosmic metaphors in early modern Europe.[35] This discovery of a spatially imagined body also has to be seen as a result of the conquest of the inner body as a locus of anatomy. From the beginning of the fifteenth century, the revival of anatomy influenced and determined the representation of the human body in the applied arts and in architecture. Moreover, with the novelty of perspective a desire for immediacy could be expressed, a desire to put the spectator right into the depicted world. No doubt the early modern desire for immediacy can be seen as a precursor for our current fascination with virtual reality, our 3-D animation in a so-called simulation culture. As the media theorists Jay David Bolter and Richard Grusin point out, this desire for immediacy "has been a defining feature of Western visual (and for that matter verbal) representation."[36]

If we accept the proposition that the body was "opened up" through the event of anatomy in early modernity, its subsequent history can be seen as an ongoing and accelerated process of fragmentation and decomposition into smaller and more controllable units. The skin, having increasingly given up its quality of a human border or natural frontier, no longer is an obstacle for this process of decomposition. German historian Claudia Benthien argues that the loss of the skin as border in such cultural contexts as the multicultural societies of North America has to do with the importance of the skin in the new world (racial and ethnic segregation), and the resulting wish of individuals for such modifications as tanning, cosmetic surgery, or the wrinkle-reducing botulin toxin (Botox) injection.[37] However, techniques and technologies of bodily fragmentation have not only revolutionized the outer appearance; what modern medicine's exploration of the twentieth-century body has shaped most drastically is the very meaning of that body for our culture.

From current first world medicine's perspective, the only bodily unity that still remains "undiscovered" is the brain[38] as the seat of thought and intelligence.[39] The next section investigates the area of the brain, and how the disciplines of artificial intelligence and artificial life are not only a natural consequence of the body-in-pieces, but have introduced bodily fragmentation and disembodiment into the order of twentieth-century discussions of thought.

(Dis)embodiment and Artificial Intelligence or Artificial Life

In his essay, "Can Thought Go On without a Body?"[40] the French philosopher Jean-François Lyotard brings in the important (and inevitable) question of gender and the gendered body in connection with the separability of thought from the phenomenological body of perception: "Thought is inseparable from the phenomenological body, although the gendered body is separated from thought, and launches thought."[41] It is precisely in this very difference that Lyotard sees a "primordial explosion" comparable to a solar catastrophe, and it is this question of the inseparability of body and thought that will be at the core of cognitive science's preoccupation. In fact, this question already had surfaced thirty years earlier when the British mathematician Alan Turing implicitly demonstrated, with his acclaimed Turing test,[42] that investigations about the nature of thought could not be answered simply in abstract terms, but only with respect to the concretely gendered embodiment of thought.

In his thought experiment, Turing literally embodies the question of whether machines can think by replacing the question with whether or not we can tell the difference between when the machine is imitating a woman or when a man is doing the imitating. In other words, he replaced the original question of whether machines can think with a gender-sensitive "imitation game":

It is played with three people, a man (A), a woman (B), and an interrogator (C), who may be either sex. The interrogator stays in a room apart from the other two. The object of the game for the interrogator is to determine which of the other two is the man and which is the woman . . . . We now ask the question, "What will happen when a machine takes the part of A in this game?" Will the interrogator decide wrongly as often when the game is played like this as when the game is played between a man and a woman? These questions replace our original, "Can machines think?"[43]

The question for Turing, then, is not *what* is thinking but *who* is thinking, for thought—as it turns out—is a much broader cognitive function than a mere mechanism that a machine can imitate. The outcome of Turing's test is that thought is interdependent with consciousness and the question of intentionality, both concepts that presuppose subjectivity and body images, hence a gendered, sexual, aged, and racial being-in-the-world (possibly incorporating symbols of class, caste, or religion as well). In other words, as long as we cannot *be* machines, the question of whether machines can think is obsolete.[44]

Nevertheless, there are a variety of reasons why we actually could address these questions against the background of recent achievements in technology, robotics, and artificial intelligence, which have made for a reconsideration of what it means to be human. In fact, some theorists claim that we no longer are humans, but rather *posthumans* ever since we have started to merge with machines.[45] According to N. Katherine Hayles,[46] the posthuman is not a *being,* but a point of view that privileges informational pattern over material instantiation, that views consciousness as an epiphenomenon rather than the seat of human identity (a perspective similar to that of Friedrich Nietzsche or Martin Heidegger), that considers the body as an original but replaceable set of prostheses, that—most important—is capable of seamlessly articulating humanness with intelligent machines. For Hayles, the "posthuman subject is an amalgam, a collection of heterogeneous components, a material-informational entity whose boundaries undergo continuous construction and reconstruction."[47]

Hayles's investigation into the nature of the posthuman unfolds the history of cybernetic technoculture of the twentieth century, a culture that has constructed the figure of the *cyborg*[48] as a cultural icon in the postwar era. One of Hayles's major theses in *How We Became Posthuman* is that since the 1940s information has lost its body in three waves of cybernetic configurations: first, *homeostasis,* starting from 1945 (Macy Conferences), when information was considered a quantifiable signal that could be transformed into other measurable codes; second, *reflexivity,* in the 1960s, when the process and the autopoiesis of information, as well as the system-environment (observer and system) and the analysis of the information context, were stressed at the same time that an interdependent relationship was established between the microcosm (human) and the macrocosm (world); and third, *virtuality,* since the 1980s, when information has been embedded entirely within the spiral-computer universe, handing it over to the disembodied realm of new media, in which data has become flesh, and from which the system can evolve into any direction (no hierarchy, origin, or given directionality).[49]

At this point, it is worth looking into the history of the very notion of embodiment and its proclaimed disappearance. However, we need to distinguish carefully between the disappearance of the body from that of disembodiment—

in fact, it is the latter that is at stake for our current concerns. As Hayles points out, embodiment always outlives the body in that it can be performed in the body's material presence or absence. This is precisely why Turing opted for the analysis of concrete gendered embodiment when analyzing the machine's capacity to think.

According to French media philosopher Jean Baudrillard's critique of the television image and the interconnected loss of public space in which "the body, landscape, [and] time all progressively disappear,"[50] the postmodern body has long been swallowed up by the screen and network, which themselves replaced mirror and stage in their mediating function. Similarly, media theorists Arthur and Marilouise Kroker question if our fascination with the body is nothing else than the celebration of its disappearance.[51]

To stretch the provocation even further, one might argue that the body's "death" and "death declaration" have been upon us ever since Descartes split the body and mind into an extended substance, the *res extensa,* and a thinking substance, the *res cogitans.* Since then the Western world has tended to think of the brain as the seat of knowledge, which has been traditionally associated with men, whereas the bodily functions (for example, giving life) have been related to women. Despite the fact that the Cartesian tradition has been more influential than any other tradition in modern philosophy, there exist other philosophical paradigms, such as the monism formulated by Spinoza, that reject Cartesian dualism, and that have been of great importance to the feminist thought revolution at the turn of the millennium.[52]

One factor common to various attempts, feminist and otherwise, to problematize the mind/body distinction at work in the sociocultural field is a debt of influence to Michel Foucault, who saw the "end of man" as a condition that announced itself in the era of high modernity:

As the archaeology of thought easily shows, man is an invention of recent date. And one perhaps nearing its end. If those arrangements were to disappear as they appeared, if some event of which we can at the moment do no more than sense the possibility—without knowing either what its form will be or what it promises—were to cause them to crumble, as the ground of Classical thought did, at the end of the eighteenth century, then one can certainly wager that man would be erased, like a face drawn in the sand at the edge of the sea.[53]

The erasure of man, as Foucault puts it, also can be understood as resulting from the attempt to objectify the ultimately unruly assemblage of practices that humans engage in into a set of manageable, measurable data—an attempt that finds its correlate in the search to replace or at least imitate the human with pure and disembodied *res cogitans,* that is, smart machines. Some of the hard-core representatives of that angle within today's theory of disembodiment go so far as to maintain that intelligent machines will replace and outlive humans. Of course, this proposition does not stand in isolation but emerges out of current narrative forms such as science fiction and cyberpunk,[54] as well as advertisement and other realms of popular Western culture,[55] in which the desire for immortality and its resulting myths are widely represented.

In her important study of the posthuman, Hayles analyzes and interprets the three waves of cybernetics with and against science fiction narratives by Philip K. Dick, Neal Stephenson, and many others to show that science and literature are always interrelated and that the concept of the posthuman is neither a scientific construct nor fiction, but rather emerges out of a cultural moment of progress and invention that is manifest in the pores of our turn-of-the-millennium culture. In fact, when one hears scientists speak about the possibilities of intelligent machines and artificial life, one often gets the impression of listening to science fiction authors, if not to the preamble of *Terminator,* as in the following quote by Warren McCulloch:

As the industrial revolution concludes in bigger and better bombs, an intellectual revolution opens with bigger and better robots. The former revolution replaced muscles by engines and was limited by the law of the conservation of energy, or of mass-energy. The new revolution threatens us, the thinkers, with technological unemployment, for it will replace brains with machines limited by the law that entropy never decreases.[56]

McCulloch—who was born at the end of the nineteenth century, studied medicine and mathematics as well as philosophy and psychology, and ended his career in the field of physiology experimenting with the functional connections in the cerebral cortex—was driven by two questions: "how [do] we know anything about the world[?]" and "why [do] we desire anything[?]"[57] The answer to these questions for McCulloch, the thinker, are to be found in the nervous system, "a logical machine," a part of the body he describes as "stuff and process,"[58] as opposed to the mind, which stands for ideas and purposes. McCulloch's enthusiasm for intelligent machines and the replaceability of the human brain, however, does not differ much from such contemporary techno-euphoricists as Ray Kurzweil (*The Age of Spiritual Machines: When Computers Exceed Human Intelligence,* 1999), robotics theorist and practitioner Hans Moravec (*Robot: Mere Machine to Transcendent Mind,* 1999), or MIT Media Lab cofounder Nicholas Negroponte (*Being Digital,* 1995)—a group of male futurists who are all expecting to be able to download "information" from the brain into the computer in the near future. Human beings, in these views, are nothing else than very complicated machines, or as the builder of the first neural network simulator, Marvin Minsky (*The Society of Mind,* 1986), puts it: "A person is a very large multiprocessor with a million small parts, and these are arranged as a thousand computers."[59]

Anthropologist Stefan Helmreich's ethnographic research at the Santa Fe Institute,[60] a major U.S. artificial life lab, discloses the viewpoint of scientists for whom not only is the human a multiprocessing machine, but the machine itself has become the model for understanding the human. The artificial life (AL) researchers at the Santa Fe Institute believe that a computer program is not a simulator of intelligence or of the human brain, but indeed in capable of creating actual life-forms. Developers of AL applications, in other words, see reality as the product of information codes.

Of course, many criticize the notion of the *disembodied cyborg* or *posthuman.* Their main point of criticism is the very notion of a disembodied being (that is, the mind/body split), as had been discussed already in Lyotard's philosophy. Such theorists of cognitive science as George Lakoff and Mark Johnson, for instance, adhere to this kind of criticism. In their interdependence theory between reason and the body, they argue against the possibility of disembodied reasoning. In the introduction to *Philosophy in the Flesh* they write: "Reason is not disembodied, as the tradition has largely held it, but arises from the nature of our brains, bodies, and bodily experience. This is not just the innocuous and obvious claim that we need a body to reason; rather, it is the striking claim that the very structure of reason itself comes from the details of our embodiment."[61] Similarly, for philosopher Hubert Dreyfus, "what distinguishes persons from machines, no matter how cleverly constructed, is not a detached, universal, immaterial soul but an involved, situated, material body."[62] Toward the end of this chapter we see how this very argument has its roots in psychoanalytical and phenomenological definitions of the body and the development of those definitions since the early twentieth century.

Ever since the 1960s, we have been inundated with cyborg and posthuman definitions. One of the most critical and influential of these (especially for cyberfeminism) was given by cultural theorist Donna Haraway, who described cyberspace as a realm of hybrid potential in her socialist-feminist reading of the cyborg. "A cyborg is a cybernetic organism, a hybrid of machine and organism, a creature of social reality as well as a creature of fiction . . . . Contemporary science fiction is full of cyborgs—creatures simultaneously animal and machine, who populate worlds ambiguously natural and crafted," she writes in her legendary "Cyborg Manifesto."[63] In her *Modest_Witness@Second_Millenium.Female-Man©_Meets_Oncomouse^TM: Feminism and Technoscience,* Haraway gives an even more categorically dispersed description of the cyborg as an end-of-the-millennium figure. This cyborg's flesh literally has merged with her environment—both physical and psychological. Haraway writes, "Cyborg figures—such as the end-of-the-millennium seed, chip, gene, data-base, bomb, fetus, race, brain, and ecosystem—are the offspring of implosions of subjects and objects and of the natural and artificial."[64]

The turn of the millennium, thus, not only produced the field of body criticism, but also the emerging field of posthuman studies, within which the term *cyborg* has been replaced with the term *posthuman.* As Robert Pepperell points out, this field is concerned with a new "self-awareness of the human condition that owes something to our anxiety about, and our enthusiasm for, technological change, but is not entirely determined by it."[65] Pepperell himself examines a number of posthuman technologies that are responsible for this new condition (for example, nanotechnology, prosthetics, robotics), and the emerging questions concerning and resulting from the blur between the real and the artificial.

At the end of Hayles's investigation into how we became posthuman—one, if not *the,* major contribution to the field of posthuman studies—she states that the event of cognitive systems distributed in cyberspace has revolutionized the very idea of "thinking." Thought, as Haraway and others have pointed out, no longer is the domain of humans, but of machines as well, and I might add that it is especially the linguistic notion of thought that has been expanded. We use the word *thought* for information processing in both humans and machines because we do not have another language available to describe these processes. As we see in Minsky's analogy, humans are *like* machines, and vice versa. We describe them as such because we are trying to learn from them in order to build better machines, and—as the researchers at the Santa Fe Institute believe—we are learning from the machines in order to understand ourselves better. An example from popular culture shows this dilemma in an aesthetically engaging way: in the Icelandic singer Björk's music video "All is Full of Love" (1999), directed by Chris Cunningham, robots with interfaces resembling Björk (figure 1.1) interact with each other erotically in a human, lesbian way. The robots,

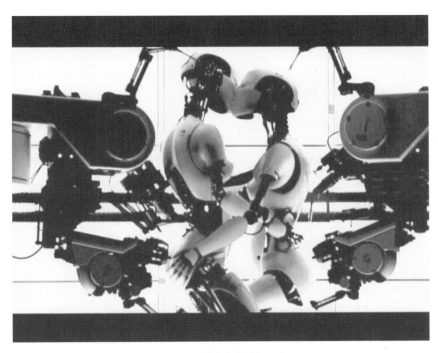

Figure 1.1. Björk. Still of music video, "All is Full of Love," 1999.

in other words, behave humanly, but are themselves built according to the image of the posthuman.[66]

Another example of cyborg criticism, this time from a performance artist, is the Korean artist Lee Bul's feminist cyborg installations (figure 1.2), which she produced in the late 1990s. These sculptures—made of silicone and white porcelain—"feature fragmented, often headless, one-legged and one-armed bodies with the voluptuous proportions typical of Western women as depicted in sexually loaded Japanese comics and animation."[67]

Whereas Björk's robots seem to transcend humanity, Lee Bul's cyborgs can be read as a criticism of the projection of ideals onto the female body, whether this be a human body or a cyborg. Critics of the cyborg figure, however, seem to agree in their observations that the body is a holistic entity, inseparable from its environment: it produces culture at the same time as culture produces it. This postmodern critique is what unifies the myriad positions against AI and AL, and ultimately against the Cartesian mind/body dualism.

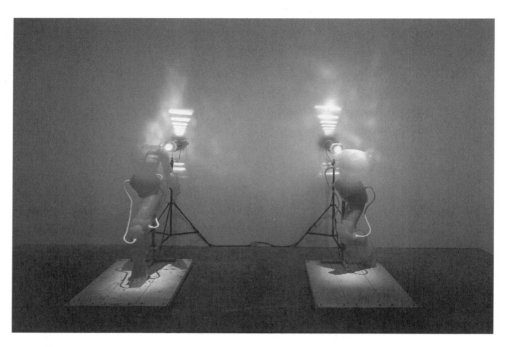

Figure 1.2. Lee Bul, *Cyborg Red and Cyborg Blue,* 1997–1998. Cast silicone, paint pigment, steel pipe support and base, each 160 × 70 × 110 cm. Installation view, Le Consortium, Dijon, 2002. Collection of Ssamzie Foundation, Seoul. Photo by André Morin. Courtesy of Le Consortium.

The critique of the mind/body dualism also revolutionized the rethinking of body and gender issues in current corporeal feminism. What becomes clear from this reopened discussion about the body and the human condition is that *despite* the additional knowledge of the body and its possibilities, we still do not know what the body really is. Expanded or shared cognition therefore may be innovative, but it apparently is not the ultimate way to explain the *posthuman condition* either. It is precisely in this sense that I would like to reemphasize Hayles's final remark that we must see the discourses of disembodiment not merely as a "loss" of the body, but as surplus or excess, in that "human functionality expands because the parameters of the cognitive system it inhabits expand."[68] Accordingly, it is more than a question of "leaving the body behind" in the fantasies expressed by the (male) techno-euphoricists; this very question has made room for certain underevaluated bodies—the body that since its birth in high modernity has been identified as *other,* namely the female body.[69]

Nature versus Nurture: What or Who Is the Body?

> It is true that one cannot think the body because we still don't know what the body is, or what it is capable of doing, what its limits or its capacities are. More than that, we don't know what a body is because a body is always in excess of our knowing it, and provides the ongoing possibilities of thinking or otherwise knowing it. It is always in excess of any representation, and indeed of all representations. This is part of Deleuze's point: that we don't know what a body can do, for the body is the outside of thought, which doesn't mean that it is unthinkable but that we approach it in thought without fully grasping it.[70]
>
> —ELIZABETH GROSZ, *ARCHITECTURE FROM THE OUTSIDE*

Hayles has pointed out that the boundaries of the posthuman are under permanent construction and reconstruction. In the above quote by feminist philosopher Elizabeth Grosz, we learn that the body is always in excess of our ability to know its capacities and possibilities, and that when we try to approach the body, we can do this only rudimentarily. One consequence of this posthuman condition is that it is only through the analysis of one bodily aspect or another that we can reveal some truths about it. This consequence is precisely why we have to turn to the more concrete question of embodiment or—with Hayles—disembodiment, and ask concrete questions concerning concrete bodies.

In our reading of the Turing test, Turing's quest to answer the question of whether machines can think revealed an implicit dependence on human categories of gender, which goes to show that a human body is in some sense always a gendered biotope (it is thrown into gender, as well as into race, religion, class, etc.). To paraphrase Grosz, making sense of the consequences of this is a highly speculative endeavor. Grosz had contemplated the difference between the sexes already in her earlier psychoanalytical criticism, stressing the importance of thinking of subjectivity "not in terms of the domination of the characteristics of mind, the mental sphere, or the psyche, but in terms of bodies."[71] She thus brings the focus back to the real, actualized body—understanding subjectivity as "a living-out of the specificities of the body," that is, the sexed body.[72]

The sexed-body paradigm, however, automatically brings with it a large problem: it follows the masculine norm, a norm that enjoys the privilege of being marked or not. In other words, when the body was actually taken into account throughout the history of philosophy, it was not according to two sexes, but according to a male norm (for example, Freud, Husserl, Bergson, Merleau-Ponty, Heidegger, Foucault, Lacan, Deleuze, Guattari).[73] Femininity, on the other hand, is not only subjected to that male norm in a hierarchical and patriarchal sense; the problem also is that, since high modernity, femaleness has been identified as *otherness,* an otherness that is a priori sexed. Unlike the case of men, there is no asexual being. Or, to borrow Ann Cahill's phrase, without taking into account the role of the body, the justification of women's inferiority would have lacked its entire argument.[74] This *somatophobia* for the female body can be traced back to the beginning of Western philosophy. Take Plato, for example: "In the *Cratylus,* Plato claims that the word body (*soma*) was introduced by Orphic priests, who believed that man was a spiritual or noncorporeal being trapped in the body as a dungeon (*sêma*)."[75] A binarization and dichotomization of the sexes into mind (male) versus body (female) occurred long before 1641 when René Descartes institutionalized this split in his *Meditationes.* In Christianity, in fact, the mind/body split corresponds to the fundamental immortality/mortality separation, with Christ as the example par excellence—his body human, his soul divine. Grosz points out the clear privileging of the sphere of the mind in philosophy, a sphere that is beyond consciousness and even beyond nature. For Descartes, for instance, only the body is part of nature, a functional device, and a "self-moving machine," whereas the mind inhabits the realm of God.

The different feminist approaches to the body can be seen as answers to the problematic that attributes the mind to men and the body to women before feminism began to move beyond the mind/body split. Corporeal feminism itself can be seen as a direct response to a shift from a somatophobic philosophy to a philosophy of the body, which is at the same time almost paradoxically a "female philosophy" to the extent that the body—the *res extensa*—has been left out in earlier male-dominated body theories.

To begin with, the *ecofeminism* of the 1970s—which defines the body as a unique means of access to knowledge and ways of living—wanted to protect the realms of femininity. Ecofeminism is thus very concerned with maternity, as this is a realm of femininity that proves the attachment to nature better than any other.[76] For liberal feminists of the 1970s, in contrast, political inclusion of women into the decision making process in modern democracies was the main issue (for example, U.S. feminist activist group the National Organization for Women, founded in 1966). However, the very questions of maternity and reproductive rights stood in the way of an easy solution to the political status of women in egalitarian societies. The problem thus lies in the very nature of reproduction, in overcoming it without depriving women of the specificity of pregnancy and maternity. As Barbara Duden points out in her *Disembodying Women: Perspectives on Pregnancy and the Unborn* (1991), the problem of the female body and its pregnant anatomy is that, from the beginning, the womb has been conceived of as a miraculous machine made and used by nature. It is hence no wonder that this concept has been one of the hardest for women to free themselves from:

From the historical beginnings of western medicine, the womb has been seen as a two-handled vessel used by nature for cheese making. When it is stirred and the rennetlike seed is deposited in it, its contents, menstrual blood, curdle. Aristotle provides the classical formulation: "The action of the semen of the male in 'setting' the female's secretion in the uterus is similar to that of rennet upon milk. Rennet is mild, which contains vital heat, as semen does."[77]

As a consequence of the female-body dilemma that liberal feminism was trapped in, some feminists have opted for a "move beyond the constraints of the body,"[78] stressing the conflict between the female role of the mother and equal participation in the workplace and other public domains. These feminists started to support in vitro fertilization programs, as it is not from men that women have to free themselves, but from their objectified bodies.

Social-constructivist feminism (going as far back as Mary Wollstonecraft's *Vindication of the Rights of Women,* 1792), however, offers an approach to the female body that translates the mind versus body opposition into a biology versus psychology opposition. Representatives of this approach within psychoanalysis, such as Juliet Mitchell and Julia Kristeva, "believe that it is no longer biology per se but the way in which the social system organizes and gives meaning to biology that is oppressive to women."[79] Their project is, therefore, "to minimize biological differences and to provide them with different cultural meanings and values."[80] This kind of feminism is particularly concerned with the female figure of the mother. Following the French psychoanalyst Jacques Lacan, who said that woman only figures in the sexual relation as mother,[81] the linguist and psychoanalyst Julia Kristeva claims that we cannot say of a *woman* what she *is,* except when referring to the mother, the only woman, the only *other sex* we know.[82]

With the discovery of this *other sex,* a power-discourse began to be installed—one that turned the formally demonized female body (for example, witches), as holder of magic and supernatural wisdom (for example, birth giving), into a reproductive organism in which reproduction became merely a function of the body. Thus, control over the female body through the development of medicine has been at stake ever since the eighteenth century. From inversion to difference, the category of woman comes into being through the isolated, fragmented body of modernity.

As Toril Moi points out in *What Is a Woman?,* the linguistic differentiation between gender and sex—common in the English language, but uncommon in many other Indo-European languages—has not necessarily done any good for the theorization of gender, at least not in its attempt of "producing a concrete, historical understanding of what it means to be a woman (or a man) in a given society."[83] For the task of understanding gendered subjectivity Moi suggests a different approach, one that—following Simone de Beauvoir's *Le deuxième sexe* (1949)—understands the body as *situation,* our "grasp on the world and a sketch of our projects."[84] Moi stresses that for de Beauvoir, having or being a body is not a matter of destiny (an argument for which she was, however, well reproached by many feminist thinkers), but a matter of a "fundamental kind of situation, in that it founds my experience of myself and the world."[85] The body-as-lived-experience in question is indebted to de Beauvoir's reading of the French philosopher Maurice Merleau-Ponty's *Phénoménologie de la Perception* (1945), which is discussed in the following section, From Fragmentation to Mediation. In de Beauvoir's existentialist interpretation of the body, there remains no room for any separation of the body from its world—which is not to say that the body is a mere product of its situation, its context (as in a social constructivist account), but that there simply is no looking at and into the world without a body, be it male or female.

However, neither ecofeminism, liberal feminism, nor social constructivism were able to account for a female subjectivity that does not implicitly or explicitly rely on a male and hierarchical gender model. Even difference and otherness are categories trapped within a dualistic and oppositional gender paradigm. Therefore, for a new generation of feminist thinkers the problem of duality itself had to be redefined. It was not until such monist thinkers as the Dutch philosopher, and contemporary of Descartes, Benedictus de Spinoza were rediscovered by Deleuze[86] that a possibility of bypassing the dualist paradigm with a nonoppositional notion of difference[87] appeared.[88] Feminist theorist Moira Gatens sums up the importance of the rediscovery of the Spinozist body concept as follows:

The Spinozist account of the body is of a productive and creative body which cannot be definitely "known" since it is not identical with itself across time. The body does not have a "truth" or a "true nature" since it is a process and its meaning and capacities will vary according to its context. We do not know the limits of this body or the powers that it is capable of attaining. These limits and capacities can only be revealed in the ongoing interactions of the body and its environment.[89]

With this new emphasis on the materiality of the body and the body's inter-action with its environment, sexual difference reemerged within subjectivity studies in a radically different way. No longer a place of exclusion and sexual-ization, female *bodies* (and I emphasize the plural) can now be described as the accumulation of different layers of media. In this model of subjectivity, iden-tity is a process that never comes to a halt, as bodily layers can be taken off one by one and rearranged anew.[90] Femininity and masculinity are now strata that are neither stuck in the prisons of essentialism or social constructivism, but are free-floating, nomadic, volatile, performative markers of gender and identity. Feminist thinkers from Donna Haraway, Judith Butler, and Rosi Braidotti to Elizabeth Grosz, Moira Gatens, and Luce Irigaray are part of this new approach to the body, an approach that first needed the fantasies of disembodiment de-scribed by Hayles to produce the *surplus* of gender.[91]

In this kind of philosophy, "the body is no longer understood as an ahistori-cal, biologically given, acultural object."[92] Rather, what is at stake now is the lived, experienced body and its actualizations, for instance in language, as in Iri-garay's feminism of the "sex which is not one": To *speak woman* is not the same as speaking of woman. It is not about producing a discourse of which woman would be the object or the subject. That said, in speaking woman, one might attempt to make room for the other as feminine.[93] This notion of a fundamen-tal, irreducible difference between the sexes, which puts the emphasis on cul-tural marking and inscription, has been called *deconstructivist,* and is a core part of the revolution of body criticism within feminist philosophy. In this move, the very notion of gender versus sex is erased, and the dualist dichotomy is under-mined. Now the body becomes a socially discursive object, "the site of contes-tation, in a series of economic, political, sexual, and intellectual struggles."[94]

In this very spirit, the philosopher and gender theorist Judith Butler deconstructed the categories of sex and gender by pointing out that sex itself already is a gendered category, and that there is no genderless body to begin with:

Gender ought not to be conceived merely as the cultural inscription of meaning on a pregiven sex (a juridical conception); gender must also designate the very apparatus of production whereby the sexes themselves are established. As a result, gender is not to culture as sex is to nature; gender is also the discursive/cultural means by which "sexed nature" or "a natural sex" is produced and established as "prediscursive," prior to culture, a politically neutral surface *on which* culture acts.[95]

This brings us finally to Grosz's approach to the body, which unites a deconstructivist feminism with a feminism of sexual difference. Gender is now defined as both inscription and production of the sexed body, putting the emphasis on the materiality of gender for the creation of the body image. Grosz writes that:

an argument could be made that the much beloved category of "gender" so commonly used in feminist theory should be understood, not as the attribution of social and psychological categories to a biologically given sex, i.e. in terms of mind/body split, but in terms that link gender much more closely to the specificities of sex. Gender is not an ideological superstructure added to a biological base; rather gender is the inscription, and hence also the production, of the sexed body.[96]

Grosz makes room for a body concept that goes beyond the question of gender and therefore beyond the question of nature versus nurture. In her fluid body concept, the body becomes an "open-ended, pliable set of significations, capable of being rewritten, reconstituted in quite other terms than those which mark it, and consequently the form of sexed identity and psychical subjectivity at work today."[97] As Grosz further points out, the body has become a sphere of multidirectionality: human bodies have gained the capacity of producing fragmentation, fracturings, and dislocations that orient bodies and body parts toward other bodies and body parts. Grosz develops a beautiful metaphor for these new body movements that not only relates different body parts to others but by envisioning a body that is made from "the outside in," overcomes the binary opposition of inside versus outside. The exterior and the interior of the body merge into the figure of the Möbius strip, through which "interior aspects of the subject lead inextricably to the exterior surfaces of the body."[98] This new body concept breaks down all possible binary oppositions, from the subject-versus-object to the inside-versus-outside and the mind versus body distinctions:[99]

The Möbius strip model has the advantage of showing that there can be a relation between two "things"—mind and body—which presumes neither their identity nor their radical disjunction, a model which shows that while there are disparate "things" being related, they have the capacity to twist one into the other. This enables the mind/body relation to avoid the impasses of reductionism, of a narrow causal relation or the retention of the binary divide. It enables subjectivity to be understood not as the combination of a psychical depth and a corporeal superficiality but as a surface whose inscriptions and rotations in three-dimensional space produce all the effects of depth.[100]

Only on the basis of this new paradigm of sexual difference has recent feminist theory been able to think of sex and gender in a nonoppositional, nonhierarchical (that is, patriarchal) way—a way from which a new model of subjectivity in a variety of configurations has emerged, and which is studied throughout the remaining chapters of this book. In this new understanding of bodies, *female* bodies (along with other minority bodies) no longer need to be defined in terms of lack and absence (castration); rather, to use Grosz's terms, the female body can now start to be rewritten as a positivity.

Returning to the initial questions of nature versus nurture and what or who the body is, we can say now that while these recent theories of the body have not shown us what the body *is* but what a concrete body *can do,* what they do show is that, ultimately, the body is a multiplicity and a potentiality. This body concept owes its instability and redefinition not only to feminist body criticism, but to other influences as well. One of them is the philosophy of Deleuze and his influential rediscovery of Spinoza's body concept, which is discussed in chapters 3 and 4. Other important sources of influence for this unstable subjectivity concept emerging out of the stratified, dispersed body at the turn of the millennium are the psychoanalytic notion of the unconscious and the phenomenological investigations into human awareness.

Despite AI and AL theorists disagreeing with corporeal feminism theorists on the core question of embodiment—the first believing in the reproducibility and replaceability of the body, and hence in disembodiment, and the second holding this very mind/body split responsible for the crimes against women—they converge around the notion of instability and multiplicity of subjectivity. In the next section, I investigate how this model of multiple subjectivity was inspired by the fields of psychoanalysis and phenomenology.

From Fragmentation to Mediation

> And if such world affirmations or world negations tout court lack any grain of significance when measured scientifically, they are the more valuable for the historian and psychologist as hints or symptoms of the body, or its success or failure, its plenitude, power, and autocracy in history, or of its frustrations, weariness, impoverishment, its premonitions of the end, its will to the end.[101]
> — FRIEDRICH NIETZSCHE, *THE GAY SCIENCE*

As we have explored, the concept of the body from early modernity to high modernity underwent what could be described as a gradual process of objectification and fragmentation, and, in the case of the female body and philosophy, outright exclusion.

It is not until the end of the nineteenth century that an alternative to the objectification of the body appears: the attempt to reintroduce a holistic body concept into the human sciences, which in turn becomes characteristic of much twentieth-century thought. Holism—which I have defined as the interrelation of all (body) parts-in-pieces—slowly incorporates the discourse of fragmentation initiated in early modernity. One of the major forerunners of this return to a holistic body concept was Friedrich Nietzsche. In his second introduction to *The Gay Science* (1886), Nietzsche, who had just recovered from a severe illness, inquires whether it was not illness that originally inspired philosophy. He further asks if philosophy was not, in the long run, an interpretation of the *body*, whether it was not in fact the continually misunderstood interpretation of the body's symptoms. He argues that all metaphysical answers to the question of the *value* of life have to be seen as corresponding to the symptoms of specific bodies. In his desperation, Nietzsche waits for a "philosophical *physician*—one who has to pursue the problem of the total health of a people, time, race or of humanity—to muster the courage to push my suspicion to its limits and to risk the proposition: what was at stake in all philosophizing hitherto was not at all 'truth' but something else—let us say, health, future, growth, power, life."[102]

Nietzsche's body concept[103] is closely related to life, a unity of contradictory and multiple forces—no longer a simple product, but rather an organic animating relationship of forces.[104] As Eric Blondel points out, for Nietzsche images are metaphors of *the body;*[105] images, however, or even language for Nietzsche are mere (and ultimately unsuccessful) attempts to express what lies beneath the "truth," namely, that the body cannot be reduced to dualistic terms, but rather expresses a plurality of multiplicities that cannot be explained in physiological or spiritual terms. *Any* explanation, for Nietzsche, whether scientific or spiritual, is never factual, but always symbolic. Only philology, and precisely the act of interpretation, can attribute meaning to the body. Nevertheless, Nietzsche—as Blondel stresses—does not reduce the body to culture. His attempt is rather of a quasi-ontological nature in that, for him, everything begins through the body because prior to the body "there is no order or relation or text, and the world is the greatest possible multiplicity."[106] The body, according to Blondel, "is therefore an intermediary space between the absolute plural of the world's chaos and the absolute simplification of intellect."[107] Of course, the body serves as a metaphor here, a metaphor for an interpretative space within which the actual creation of meaning is an act of the will to power.[108]

The following section shows how some of the basic premises of Nietzsche's body concept were carried into the twentieth century, in particular into the fields of psychoanalysis and phenomenology and their definitions or approaches to the body. Finally, it looks at how these fields also have influenced the notions of the body that dominate at the turn of the millennium, and how the apparently divergent directions of fragmentation and holism can be understood as elements or perspectives within a greater horizon of mediation.

Psychoanalysis

The main impulse behind the psychological discussion of the body in the twentieth century is the advent of psychoanalysis early in the century and the resulting increase in medical consideration for the factor of sexuality in understanding the human psyche (Sigmund Freud, *Drei Abhandlungen zur Sexualtheorie,* 1905; Michel Foucault, *Histoire de la Sexualité,* 1984). Through psychoanalysis, the body has become increasingly diagnosed as a psychological entity. The key concept in this regard is the *image* of the body produced by the body itself (autoperception), hence the immediate perception of the world through one's own skin, the *moi-peau.*[109]

Psychoanalysis is less interested in the actual body than in the body image, which is considered a *representation,* that is, a construction that depends on how it is apprehended in external, social relations—an image that is created by the subject's perception of the outer world and the outer world's perception of it. The recognition of one's self in the gaze of the other is among the most fundamental concepts for understanding the meaning of subjectivity in the twentieth century.[110] Freud defined the ego as a corporeal projection, arguing that "the ego does not result from a preordained biological order, but is the result of a psychosocial intervention into the child's hitherto natural development."[111] Basing his psychoanalytical ideas on Freud's ego theory, the French psychoanalyst Jacques Lacan argued in *Le stade du miroir* (1936)[112] that the only way we can perceive our bodily selves is through a deceptive image that is framed by somebody else's gaze (in the beginning, the mother's or her substitute's), or by the frame of a screen or interface of some kind (mirror, computer interface, television screen, etc.). In this phase of the construction of the self, which takes place in the first six to eighteen months of a child's life, the child recognizes him- or herself in the mirror as a separate being from his or her environment (especially the mother). Through the recognition of his or her own *gestalt,* the child anticipates his or her corporeal unity, which is needed to build a proper ego. This results in the lack of an "original" bodily identity tracing back to *one* origin of a body image, such as the genetic mixture of the parents' bodies, and hence in the loss of a secure historical representation of the body, such as the presentation of a growing body in a child's photo-album. The stable concept of identity is replaced by what Lacan calls the *fractal body* (dispersed body), whose identity depends on a process of *inscription* and semanticization through an outside world. This fractal body, not responsible or even aware of the bodily images that it is producing, gives reason for a profound discussion and repositioning of subjectivity in the twentieth century.

In *The Ego and the Id* (1923) Freud talks about the body ego as a border surface, a *skin sack* or a *skin fold.* In other words, the skin for Freud is a psychic hull that constitutes the contact between the outer world and the psyche: "The surface of the body, the skin, moreover, provides the ground for the articulation of orifices, erotogenic rims, cuts on the body's surface, loci of exchange between the inside and the outside, points of conversion of the outside into the body, and of the inside out of the body."[113] For Freud the skin is what constitutes the ego: "the ego is ultimately derived from bodily sensations, chiefly those springing from the surface of the body. It may thus be regarded as a mental projection of the surface of the body, . . . representing the surfaces of the mental apparatus."[114]

Many definitions of the skin, and more generally of the human interface or surface, have been proposed since the beginnings of psychoanalysis; whether or not these attempts have taken into account a psychoanalytic key of analysis, all of them agree on the importance of the skin. The French dermatologist and philosopher François Dagognet, for instance, presents a physical anthropology in which any *interface* of the body is regarded as a region of choice.[115] For Dagognet, the skin obtains an incomparable importance over any other body part: in the skin the relation between outside and inside exists intensely. This definition clearly resonates with the analogy of the gendered body's inside and outside relationship as a Möbius strip, as described by Grosz.[116] In a later book, *La peau découverte,*[117] Dagognet characterizes the interdependency of the skin's "outside-inside" and "inside-outside" relationship as most relevant for the explanation of certain dermatological disorders such as acne, eczema, hives, and other skin diseases.

The *timeless timeliness* of our preoccupation with the skin is shown in Steven Connor's recent in-depth account of the skin's significance in its historical and cultural imaginary. In his *Book of Skin*[118] Connor reads the skin cross-culturally, diachronically, and synchronically. He points to the skin's importance from the Egyptian embalming practice to contemporary tattooing and piercing trends. Similar to Dagognet, Connor puts the emphasis on the skin as boundary zone and medium of passage: "The skin is the vulnerable, unreliable boundary between inner and outer conditions and the proof of their frightening, fascinating intimate contiguity."[119]

It is perhaps the post-Lacanian psychoanalyst Didier Anzieu[120] who has introduced the most useful notion for a psychoanalytical account of the skin, taking into account both *chrós* (Greek for body as a whole and skin) and *dérma* (Greek for fur, skin, leather). Anzieu's notion of the "skin ego" draws a comparison between the complexity of the skin and its different functions—that is, anatomical, physiological, cultural—and the complexity of the psychic ego. Of all our perceptive organs, as Anzieu points out, the skin is the most vital one: one could live blind, deaf, and lacking the senses of taste and smell, but without the integrity of the major part of the skin organ, one could not survive.[121] The skin has also the greatest mass (20 percent of the total body weight of a newborn, and 18 percent of an adult's weight), and occupies the largest surface (1800 sq. cm. of the newborn, and 2500 sq. cm. of the adult) of all our organs. The skin serves as an *interface* between *me* and the *other* by protecting the ego on the one hand like an envelope, and on the other hand dividing it from the outer world. The first skin that the baby recognizes as meaningful is that of its mothering environment. Thus it is not until the mirror and the Oedipal stages that the infant gets *into its own skin,* building up its ego on the basis of the (mis)recognition of itself in the mirror in the wake of a functional fragmentation, as shown by Lacan.[122] For Anzieu, the skin plays the most important role in psychic development because the ego can only be built on the basis of its experience of the sur-face of the (mother's) body.

For Freud, the relationship between the ego and the body image is libidinal, that is, constituted through a narcissistic investment during the oral stage when the baby is breastfed by the mother (autoeroticism). Freud clearly distinguishes the narcissistic libido (*Ich-Libido*) from the object libido (*Objekt-Libido*) that the child adopts later in his or her development; only the investment of a narcissistic libido can lead to a psychic unification of the body and the self. One of Freud's contemporaries, Otto Rank, finds in the phenomenon of paranoia the important topic of the projection of the self. In his book on the *Double* he states that it is in the shadow that the human being sees for the first time his or her own body.[123] Thus, paranoid anxiety points to a problematic or unsuccessful personification with the recognition of oneself in its shadow (double).[124] In the works of Freud and Rank, *paranoia* had become an important means for understanding the power of the image. Lacan points out that paranoid psychosis goes back to a broken genesis or development in the phase of a preimaginary reality, the stage that precedes mirror identification. Because of the possible threat of losing the unified body image and returning to a fragmented bodily experience, the psychological process of formatting an "Ego-Ideal" is accompanied by a feeling of anxiety. This feeling can return at any time during a paranoid psychotic experience, and in fact does come back in many different appearances. For instance, anorexia, hysteria, and other (often female) illnesses can be seen as mourning for the loss of a unified body image. Grosz sees anorexia in particular as a "mourning for a pre-Oedipal body and a corporeal connection to the mother that women in patriarchy are required to abandon."[125]

The genre of media performances discussed in the following chapters will suggest the relevance of these psychoanalytical insights into the formation of a secure body image and self. In chapter 3 we will further encounter several body artists who stage themselves in media performances. All these examples from contemporary art should be read against the Freudian, Lacanian, and feminist psychoanalytical theories developed during the twentieth century as a foreground for a new understanding of subjectivity and corporeality.

Phenomenology

Similar to psychoanalysis, phenomenology tries to separate the subject of the body (the world as perceived through one's body) from the objectified body (the body as it is perceived by the world)—a distinction between the subject of perception and the socially constructed body, between the psychoanalytical *I* and the *Me*.

The notion of the immediate perception of the world through one's own skin was promoted in the philosophy of the French phenomenologist Henri Bergson. For Bergson, the body image has two distinctive and somewhat paradoxically interrelated sides. On the one hand, *l'image du corps* is the way in which the subject perceives his or her own body, a perception corresponding to the Freudian psychoanalytical category "Ideal-Ego." The body becomes a necessary intermediary between the self and the unknowable outside reality of the body, organizing the relations to the outside through the mediation of images; the image one has of oneself is therefore the center of one's being and perception, a kind of interface to the world.[126] The other side of the interrelated body image, *l'image de corps,* indicates that the body itself is the perceptive apparatus through which the world is being processed. This means that the image is itself produced by the body (autoperceptive), the intermediary source of all images (corpocentrism). In other words, the body is at the same time mirror or screen for the images from the outside and the perceptive center; the body is "what takes shape at the center of perception."[127] Nevertheless, as Andrieu points out, this taking shape is constantly blurred by the motion of the body, because the Bergsonian body is "a moving limit between future and past."[128]

Unlike with psychoanalysis, for Bergson there is no unconscious, only an *unconsciousness.* In the Bergsonian notion of the body there is no rupture between events. Rather, all memory is related to the totality of events that precede it and that come after it. The unconscious mental state, hence, is nothing other than a never-perceived material object, or a nonimagined image.[129] The body (and not the soul) provides equilibrium, and is therefore the complementary pole to the mind, without which orientation toward the action would never be possible. For Bergson, matter is within space and mind outside of it. There is no possible immediate transition between these dimensions. Rather, the mind contacts matter through the function of *time.* The body in turn possesses the material capacity to translate the intensity of time into action. In this way the mind itself is not directly materialized, but rather becomes the body in action after first traversing the possible intensities of memory.[130] Bergson thus develops a theory of indirect unity, for it is neither in perception, nor in memory, nor in the activities of the mind that the body contributes directly to representation. The body is united indirectly with the spirit, and the markers of this unification are the image, on the one hand, and the skin (or a rethinking of that border zone), on the other.

The upshot of Bergson's contribution is the impossibility of thinking of consciousness outside of embodiment, because mind is only ever manifest in the actions of a body over time. Likewise, for Bergson's contemporary Edmund Husserl, the discipline of phenomenology Husserl founded sought the truth of consciousness in the ways the subject lives in his or her body. Whereas for Immanuel Kant phenomenology meant the study of empirical appearances, for Husserl phenomenology means the "science of essences" (*Wesenswissenschaft*).[131] At stake for Husserl are not real appearances, existences, things, or essences, but the intentionally conscious gaze onto the essences (*Wesensschau*). In other words, consciousness is always consciousness *of* something. Reality has no absolute or independent status, but is always presupposed as intentionality, or intentional appearance (*noema*). As a result, the body is no longer a symptom, a sign, or any other kind of manifestation or placeholder. Rather, the body becomes the presence in the world of an intentional subject and his or her phenomenal experience of the world. It is here that a body discourse can start to disperse the body by literally opening it to investigation. As Andrieu formulates it: "phenomenology opens the body trying to describe the various levels that constitute it: the body becomes flesh-body (*Leibkörper*) in order to demonstrate the lived incarnation of the subject, but without reducing it to its psycho-genetic stages."[132]

A generation after Bergson and Husserl, Merleau-Ponty dedicated his entire work to the problem of the lived (perceiving) body and its image, from his early *Phénoménologie de la perception* (1945) to the unfinished *Le visible et l'invisible* (1964).[133] In Merleau-Ponty's philosophy, the body (*Leib*) has become inseparable from the world it inhabits, for body and earth (that is, the body's environment) are related through the world's presence in the body: "the body not only flows over into a world whose schema it bears in itself but possesses this world at a distance rather than being possessed by it."[134] The "pragmatic turn" of this phenomenological approach lies in the fact that this body is only a body through its use by a subject, in other words through the way in which a subject's presence in the world embodies it.[135] Merleau-Ponty argues that the outer world is necessarily perceived through a lived body, hence, as Andrieu puts it, "I am susceptible to signify with my body the way in which I am conscious of the world."[136]

He thus founds a philosophy of embodiment and primordial presence that for the philosopher Gail Weiss constitutes the departing point in her analysis of the body image, leading her to develop a theory of embodiment as *intercorporeality:* "To describe embodiment as intercorporeality is to emphasize that the experience of being embodied is never a private affair, but is always already mediated by our continual interactions with other human and nonhuman bodies."[137]

Lacan had specified that a child always comes to its self-identity via a fundamental misrecognition of its own body. This concept of a body-in-pieces is, in other words, already distinctly phenomenological, in that the infant's own *experience* of itself prior to the organization of the image in the mirror is a body-in-pieces.[138] It is thus precisely in respect to the lived-body experience that Merleau-Ponty's thought converges with Lacan's notion of the mirror stage, in that for both thinkers the notion of an experienced embodiment goes along with a double alienation, the recognition of one's self in a deceptive image that is framed by somebody else's gaze, a mirror, a screen: "At the same time, this body image makes possible a kind of alienation, the capturing of myself through my spatial image. The image prepares me for another alienation, that of myself (as viewed) by others."[139] Indeed, as far as this aspect is concerned, Lacan's and Merleau-Ponty's explanations of subjectivity as it unfolds in the infant are very similar. As Weiss points out, they both emphasize "that it is this very schism that makes it possible for the child to project and extend her/his own bodily awareness beyond the immediacy of her/his introceptive experiences by incorporating the perspective of the other toward one's own body—a perspective one actively participates in—rather than having it thrust upon one from the outside."[140] In other words, the *inscription* and semanticization of the body through the outside world—as we described embodiment—is not a process that the subject undergoes, but on the contrary, one in which he or she is actively involved. Inscription does not occur without the subject's intercorporeal interaction providing an *outside-in* as well as *inside-out* perspective, to borrow Weiss's terminology.[141] What is more, with phenomenology the emphasis now lies on the production of images and no longer on the libidinal investments that in Freud's theory shift from the mouth to the anus and finally to the sexual organs. In fact, for the British psychoanalyst and Freud's contemporary Paul Schilder, "the object of the narcissistic libido is not the mouth, anus, penis, or clitoris per se, but the image of the body that arises out of the sexually pleasurable sensations associated with them."[142] The resulting "body image ideal" is—as Weiss formulates—"an internalized standard against which we continually measure our present body."[143]

However, as the Merleau-Ponty scholar Stuart Murray points out, Merleau-Ponty does not actually use the term *body image,* but instead *schéma corporel.* Body image, as Murray suggests, may be a misleading translation, because *image* is far too visual: "What Merleau-Ponty has in mind with *schéma corporel* is a kinesthetic body, a body actively 'polarized by its tasks.' Through the *body schema,* Merleau-Ponty posits that the body does not end at its skin, but rather extends into the world."[144]

With Merleau-Ponty's theory of perception and the lived body's extension into the world, the ground is laid for new discussions to evolve surrounding questions of concrete embodiment. These questions concern the gendered body and the racialized body in new ways. Nevertheless, concreteness also is realized by another dimension, namely language and how the body is embedded in it. In linguistic terms we can say that from Husserlian phenomenology's focus on the systemic side of language, the *langue* or the *parole parlante,* Merleau-Ponty puts the emphasis on the pragmatic speech-act side of the *parole parlée.* In this realm Merleau-Ponty slowly distantiates himself from the Husserlian distinction between *Körper* and *Leib,* substituting it with a broadened *Leib*-notion, in which language becomes the body of thought.

His emphasis on the interdependency of body and world, and the resulting notion of embodiment as inseparable from the original kinship with the world, turned Merleau-Ponty into arguably the greatest influence for body theorists of the twentieth century. Whether maintaining a constructivist, a performative, a volatile, or even an essentialist account of the body, all of these ways of thinking of *the body* presume that the body is *access to the world* (given, construed, performed, or even all at once). Merleau-Ponty's philosophy thus has not diminished in its influence and importance, especially as it has been reinterpreted in recent times, for instance in the work of the contemporary French philosopher Renaud Barbaras.[145]

Barbaras reminds us of a crucial quote in the *Phénoménologie de la perception* in which Merleau-Ponty declares that the body "'*has* its world or understands its world without having to pass through representations'; it '*is* the potentiality of the world.'"[146] The importance of the Merleau-Pontian account of the body for the theoretical framework of *Getting Under the Skin* lies in the fact that, in such a conception of the body, the medium that signifies the body, its *representation,* no longer is any different from the "raw material" of the body itself. Without mediation the body is nothing. However, mediation already is what the body always was, in its various historical and cultural strata.

In that sense the body *constitutes* mediation and vice versa. It is by following this very conception, namely of the *body as constitutive mediation,* that *Getting Under the Skin* aims to trace back a body concept that oscillates between holism and fragmentation. Since Merleau-Ponty's phenomenology theories were posited at the latest, this universe no longer is conceived in a Cartesian manner that takes the thinking subject as a secure point of departure against the objects in the world; the body—"the fabric into which all objects are woven"[147]—is thus not a mere *intermediary,* in-between the subject and the world, but rather a unifier of a holistic subjectivity and a fragmented objectivity that effectively undermines the existence of these very categories. As Murray puts it: "There never is an 'objective world out there' or a 'subjective world in me.' Subject and world, in Merleau-Ponty, are linked through the flesh."[148]

Many different authors—among them Barbaras—have pointed out that Merleau-Ponty's phenomenological account of the body cannot be understood without its uninterrupted dialogue with both Husserl, the father figure, and Heidegger, who was himself a student of Husserl's. There are many converging moments in both Merleau-Ponty's and Heidegger's phenomenologies; one of them, however, is clearly their interest in language. For Merleau-Ponty, "meaning is something intended by the sign, that is, something still veiled or concealed within it."[149] In this pragmatist approach to semiosis, the sign is constituted as such only at the moment of signification. At any moment prior to signification the sign remains a pure potentiality, in fact a materiality, not separable into what structuralism has coined the levels of form and expression. It is with this very notion of language, the "soil" of all genesis,[150] that Merleau-Ponty encounters Heidegger.

In his "Letter on Humanism," Heidegger states: "Language is the house of being. In its home human beings dwell. Those who think and those who create with words are the guardians of this home."[151] As the "house of being," language has been "freed" from grammar, the absoluteness of its use in science and research, and the "dictatorship of the public realm."[152] It is thanks to thought and poetry that language has found its essential origin and the truth of being. Language comes from that place where humanity means "standing in the clearing of being," a position that Heidegger calls "human ek-sistence."[153] *Ek-sistance* means the ability of standing outside of oneself, which is also what, for Heidegger, distinguishes humanity from nonhuman animals' being-in-the-world. Language is what Heidegger further calls the "clearing-concealing advent of being itself."[154]

What saves language for Heidegger is thought, neither a practical nor a theoretical process, since it happens before this decision is made. Thought is *thought of being* and nothing else. Thought is a "building" of the *house of being.* Heidegger points out many times that these are not mere images and metaphoric uses of language, building, or dwelling. On the contrary, the house of being is the essence of being itself, not its image.

But what does Heidegger mean by this language that for him constitutes being's house? If we are attentive to Heidegger's use of language in his first great work, *Being and Time,* we see that what Heidegger means by language is nothing other than primordial mediation:

The fact that the explicitness of a statement can be lacking in simple looking, does not justify us in denying every articulate interpretation, and thus the as-structure, to this simple seeing. The simple seeing of things near to us in our having to do with . . . contains the structure of interpretation so primordially that a grasping of something which is, so to speak, *free of the as* requires a kind of reorientation. When we just stare at something, our just-having-it-before-us lies before us *as a failure to understand it* any more. This grasping which is free of the as is a privation of *simple* seeing, which understands; it is not more primordial than the latter, but derived from it. The ontic explicitness of the "as" must not mislead us into overlooking it as the a priori existential constitution of understanding.[155]

For Heidegger, in other words, there can be no perceiving subject who then enters into relations of mediation with objects and other people. On the contrary, the very act of perception is at its basis always already an act of perception *as something,* that is, always already the referring of some thing, place, or time to some other thing, place, or time. This constant referral is why, at its heart, Dasein is ek-stasis, and why the house of this ek-static identity is none other than language.

Heidegger's basic move, then, is to represent the relation between the knowing subject and objective world—which he argues had been the basic assumption of the history of Western metaphysics—as a secondary, derivative splitting of a previously holistic unit he calls being-in-the-world. This splitting—which, in at least some cases, Heidegger traces to modernity ("World Picture")—can for our purposes be associated with a shift from the late Middle Ages to early modernity, when with the founding of anatomy the body was literally cut into pieces, opened up, and explored as an object of knowledge. The event of anatomy, in other words, may be seen as a historical correlate to the objectified, extended entity that Descartes distinguished from the thinking thing that is our mind.

In his lectures on Nietzsche—no coincidence[156]—Heidegger formulates his famous statement that one does not *have* a body but rather *is* a body: "We do not 'have' a body in the way we carry a knife in a sheath. Neither is the body a natural body that merely accompanies us and which we can establish, expressly or not, as being also at hand. We do not 'have' a body; rather, we 'are' bodily. Feeling, as feeling oneself to be, belongs to the essence of such Being. Feeling achieves from the outset the inherent internalizing tendency of the body in our Dasein."[157]

Having traced psychoanalysis, phenomenology, and other philosophical theories that have made room for a holistic body concept that one does not have, but inhabits like a *world,* I am suggesting that we understand the history of the body as such as a gradual "unconcealment"—to speak Heideggerese—or revealing of the *body as mediation.* This is indeed what *Getting Under the Skin* traces: the history of the body as a struggle between holism and fragmentation. That this dilemma is in some deep sense irresolvable is shown by the fact that the same period during which such discourses as psychoanalysis and phenomenology have developed a conception of the body as a whole depending on the experience of mediation has also seen the intensification—through technological and medical progress—of domains of expertise dedicated to removing layers from the body's "skin," to unraveling its "inner truth" (to make it last longer, to cure it, or to replace it). This dilemma is also shown by the "striking coincidence"[158] that the medical discipline of dermatology had its peak in the very cultural and even geographical climate (that is, Vienna) in which Freud developed his theory of psychoanalysis.

The postpsychoanalysts Deleuze and Guattari, whose concept of the body-without-organs I address more completely in the third chapter, have reconfigured the process of fragmentation as a relation of "organ-ized" strata to a state of radical and virtual disorganization they call the plane of immanence. The body in this view no longer is mediation, but rather the potentiality underlying all mediation. In recent body installations under analysis in this book, this struggle between holism and fragmentation has been widely staged and emphasized, from feminist performance art to cyber-performances to recent examples of architecture. All these examples share a dialogue between the body as a whole and as a multiplicity of fragments; what the history of their time demonstrates—and what I am ultimately arguing—is that the apparently contrary vectors of fragmentation and holism are in fact part and parcel of the same historical development. In other words, the discovery of the body as mediation has converged with an age of mediative proliferation, such that what we are witnessing in the apparent continuing fragmentation of the body is the work of mediation itself *as* the body. It is for this reason that there can be no history of the body that is not at the same time a study of the various media that constitute embodiment as such.

The advent of new media has facilitated enormously the move of the reunion between holism and fragmentation. One must acknowledge that it is thanks to posthuman technology such as nanotechnology and robotics, and more generally thanks to new media, that the body has survived not as a whole, but rather in a dispersed and scattered way—or better: because of this technology, the body was able to adapt to a new form of wholeness that manifests itself as a multiplicity and plurality of mediative forms. The result of this discussion is a new body concept that could have emerged only from the grounds of early-twentieth-century phenomenology and psychoanalysis. But that concept would be inconceivable outside of the achievements of artificial intelligence and cognitive science on the one hand, and the feminist criticism of the resulting notion of disembodiment on the other hand, as well as outside of the digital revolutions of the latter twentieth century.

The following chapters trace the history of the body neither via a strictly psychoanalytic nor a phenomenological reading of bodies configured in popular culture, performance art, new media, and architecture. Rather, these body practices are there to reveal mediality as corporeality in the various languages that they employ. Chapter 2 begins by historically tracing body performances in the realm of art production and connecting these definitions of the body with the philosophers and theorists already discussed.

Body Performances from 1960s Wounds to 1990s Extensions

How would you define your particular priorities as an artist?

Well, I think it's giving other people the possibility to experience things that I have experienced—revelations—in one way or the other. . . . And I found that this thing called the camera—the video camera—and the screen, the monitor, are tools that can do that by their nature, because they give you the world back, but in the process of doing that—because it's not your own experience, but yet it's not mediated to another person, it's this kind of mechanical art—it can give you new points of view and new insights in a very simple way, a very direct way.[1]

—BILL VIOLA IN AN INTERVIEW WITH NICHOLAS ZURBRUGG, *ART PERFORMANCE MEDIA: 31 INTERVIEWS*

What we today know as the pastiche or collage style, a structure inherent to the logic of postmodernity and the new media,[2] is—as I explore in this chapter[3]—ultimately an effect of a mediatized environment that reached the peak of its development in the second half of the twentieth century. This chapter analyzes the implications of an increasingly mediatized environment, as well as the effects of new media in the realm of body performances from the beginning of the twentieth century (avant-garde) to current times.

After the undeniable influence of the early twentieth-century avant-garde, especially futurism and Dadaism, the "happenings" of the 1960s were primarily the product of an increasingly intensified media-environment inspiring actionists and happening artists of the time to stage mass media related concepts such as *simultaneity* in their performances. Fifty years earlier, for instance, the futurist Filippo Tommaso Marinetti, had idealized and dreamed of simultaneity as a result of the new technologies of representation (such as photography and film) that started to allow for such practices as morphing and superimposition, practices that we often think of as typical only of our current digital era. This chapter considers performance art from 1960s Wounds to 1990s Extensions with a focus on the history of this genre and on the possibilities of future development. Along the way, I ask such questions as: Which concepts have been inherited from the avant-garde? Which body configurations are in fact new and path-breaking at the turn of the millennium? And, most important, what can a new era of digital performance offer to this kind of discourse? The "wounded" versus the "extended" body here is a metaphor for what actually happened to the body throughout the last decades in this discourse universe of performance, and how the body—ultimately—has become a disembodied frame, or a mere instance of mediation. We will see, in other words, how performance could evolve from the theme of the emphasized materiality of the body, for example, in such performances that stage self-mutilation, to the merging of human flesh with digitality to dispense of the body as an entity, and to "flatten it out" onto the screen.

To put my hypothesis in the media-theoretical terms of Jay David Bolter and Richard Grusin, the actionism movement of the 1960s followed a *double logic of remediation,* consisting of the following paradox: "Our culture wants both to multiply its media and to erase all traces of mediation: ideally, it wants to erase its media in the very act of multiplying them."[4] Indeed, these two seemingly contradictory logics are characteristic of the current era of new media, which expresses itself through a visual style of *hypermediation,* a style that "privileges fragmentation, indeterminacy, and heterogeneity and . . . emphasizes process or performance rather than the finished art object."[5]

That the logic of hypermediation was a present force in the art scene of the 1960s and 1970s, and not just a consequence of postmodernism, is proven by the existence of actionism and happenings. These new artistic expressions were performed by artists embodying their own artwork while at the same time trying to erase the trace of the action itself by eliminating the traditional frame of the spectacle. The new environment of the spectacle was no longer a traditional performing space; instead, anything could be turned into the artistic environment. The Viennese actionist Günter Brus, for instance, chose to perform at

Vienna University by randomly entering lecture rooms. These brief events, or happenings, eliminate the traditional position of the spectator by transforming him or her from one who is harmlessly and passively pursuing daily activities into an active spectator of performance art. It is evident that from its inception, happening art aligned itself with the Dadaist *disturbances* of public spaces. And it is precisely in this sense that performance art follows the double logic of re-mediation, namely, the desire to appropriate and stage all possible facets of the artistic form, and to pretend that there is no mediation involved by integrating artistic scenarios into natural environments (for example, streets, cafes, universities) and the accidental spectator from the street.

The artistic practice of happenings has never ceased to inspire performance artists, as many examples from contemporary performances and actions illustrate. In *Flash Mob,* for example, performed on the streets of the world's major cities, participants meet in chat rooms and determine when they will meet in real time on a street, at the subway, or in another urban setting to act in a *spontaneity play.* A play, that is, which in 2003 in Berlin consisted of participants turning on their cell phones and shouting "Ja, Ja" into them for exactly one minute, then leaving as if nothing had happened.[6] Similarly, *The Angel Project* by British director Deborah Warner positioned forty "angels" at nine different habitats in New York City during July 2003. The performers took on different identities, for example, by wearing nun's clothes, naturalizing the city's environment into part of this action, and testing people's reactions to unusual or provocative activities like open bible readings.[7]

One aspect of remediation is that the very notion of the body, as an entity distinguished from the artifact, tends toward erasure, a novelty that would inhabit performance art to the heights of embodiment not attained since the 1970s. There could not be a better way to describe this process of a collapse of body, materiality of expression, and environment than as expressed by Brus in his manifesto for the action *Painting—Self-Painting—Self-Mutilation* (1965): "Günter Brus is the name of the man who is no longer content to paint on canvas and thus lays hands on himself. So he besmears himself, simultaneously hinting at self-mutilation, and he and Vienna's five happening specialists state that this is art."[8]

There is a direct connection between the tendencies of self-mutilation[9] in question and the mediatized frame of observation. It is almost as if the medium could hold together the body, so that it can fall into pieces and be "dispersed" into the environment. Thus, Brus continues:

I sever my left hand. Lying somewhere or other is a foot. A suture on my wrist bone. I press a drawing pin into my spinal cord. I nail my big toe to my index finger. Lying on a white plate is hair from my head, armpits, and pubic area. I slit open my aorta lengthways with a razor blade (Gillette). I drive a tintack into my ear. I split my head open lengthways into halves. I insert barbed wire into my urethra and gently attempt to twist it and slice the nerve (autocystoscopy). I bite open my pimples and suck them dry. I have everything photographed and observed.[10]

The tendency of decorporealization by damaging oneself is an expression of a *body dysmorphic disorder* typical of the spirit of the avant-garde, and it establishes a connection between hysteria, ecstasy, and technology.[11] But the process of "getting rid of oneself" has to be seen as a broader cultural phenomenon—ultimately an effect of postmodernity typical of the 1970s—hence, of a body falling into pieces as a symbolization of a disembodied era, in which, as Virilio has put it, "that which happens is much more important than that which lasts (*ce qui dure*)—and also than that which is solid (*ce qui est dur*). There is a dematerialization that goes parallel to deterritorialization and decorporation."[12]

There is, of course, also the psychoanalytical reading of self-mutilation in art, as proposed by Kathy O'Dell in her analysis of the "masochistic performances" of the 1970s.[13] O'Dell's Lacanian argument holds that "masochism is generally used by artists as a metaphor representing key moments in one's psychic development, particularly the stages leading up to the Oedipal phase."[14] The artistic expressions of these psychic stages, namely the oral stage (separation from the mother), the mirror stage (recognition of the *split self*), and the Oedipal stage (world of the law and establishment of the symbolic order), according to O'Dell, point to troubles in the social institutions of the law and the home in the 1970s.[15]

The interpretation I propose of the history of performance art in this chapter, however, is not of a psychoanalytical nature (although there are several psychoanalytical readings), but rather the approach is of a media-theoretical one. The body is studied in relation to its medialization and the increasing use of *mediative extensions,* a process marked by an eventual complete substitution of immediate and intimate bodies facilitated by the logic of new media. In cyberspace, objects are no longer distinct from their environment; they merge and push into the environment or context, becoming part of *one* world. In other words, what holds the body parts together is no longer the entirety of the physical body, but the frame through which one experiences it. In fact, it is the remediated frame that hosts the "pure real action" by trying to convince the interlocutor that there never was any frame nor window involved. In this regard, the performances of the 1960s and 1970s can be seen as precursors, or, better still, "trapped" in the same logic of "reality-bleeds,"[16] which is present in such recent cyberpunk narratives as *The Matrix* series (1999–2003) or *eXistenZ* (1999). The preoccupation of such narratives is a world that at first seems to be a fantasy world, a virtuality, but at last turns out to be reality itself.

As these examples make clear, our Western cultural imagination is today increasingly under the influence of the fusion of new media with old media (for example, the medicine industry or the film industry), or as Lev Manovich suggests, the real "revolution" of new media lies simply in the fact that all media now can be transcoded into numerical digital data. With that, the "old" media may not have lost their original semiotic power, but rather they have "gained" something, a machinic level that may be invisible on the level of representation. On the level of the materiality of the medium, however, this new dimension is most meaningful:

The structure of a computer image is a case in point. On the level of representation, it belongs on the side of human culture, automatically entering in dialog with other images, other cultural "semes" and "mythemes." But on another level, it is a computer file that consists of a machine-readable header, followed by numbers representing color values of its pixels. On this level it enters into a dialogue with other computer files.[17]

The double-sidedness of new media, in that they "appear" in the realm of the old image but are driven and empowered by a machinic logic, is precisely what moves new media art. I discuss this issue further in chapter 4. I want to allude to this problem, however, with an example from the photographer and painter Chuck Close (figure 2.1). Standing closely in front of his pixel-paintings, we cannot recognize any traits of faciality, but by distancing ourselves from the paintings, the pixels slowly start to make sense and "create" close-ups.[18]

Close's digital realism is remediated in a perverted sense in that it simulates the logic of new media through the real (by using real paint), erasing the traces of the digital pixels by the distanced gaze. What it reveals in a playful sense is a deep concern with the double facets of new media. The Austrian artist Gabi Trinkaus steps beyond a digital realism with her fashion model glamor-shot collages made of cut-up beauty magazines, such as *J'adore* (2005) on the cover of this book. Unlike digital blowups, as in Chuck Close's portraits, these fashion

Figure 2.1. Chuck Close, *Kiki,* 1993. Oil on canvas. Courtesy of the collection of Walker Art Center, Minneapolis (gift of Judy and Kenneth Dayton, 1994).

portraits are comprised not of mechanized units, but of clippings from our image world.

Recent tendencies on the World Wide Web further show how we can substitute actual bodies, and experiences of physical closeness, with hypermediated *reality-web-theater-environments,* such as webcams installed in people's private homes where we can experience the intimacy of the stranger (for example, http://www.anacam.com), or reality computer games such as *The Sims.* These examples show how the desire for the real has become more and more eminent in the immersively present media environment of the late twentieth century, and how at the same time a strong fantasy has arisen—the fantasy for the medium to disappear, and for reality to *push through the fourth wall.*

The following is an attempt to reconstruct this process of remediation through the history of performance—from the avant-garde to the 1960s happenings to our current era of disembodied performances—with special regard to the status and use of mediative frames represented in these artistic expressions.

The Avant-Garde as Precursor of 1960s Wounds

The format of the happening has been said to be a result or an effect of the modernist collage style, a pastiche of painting and sculpture.[19] The early happenings took place in painting and sculpture galleries. The first artist to have transgressed the borders of painting and sculpture to *action art* by moving the picture out into the real space of the room was Allan Kaprow, whose *18 Happenings in 6 parts* (Reuben Gallery, N.Y., 1959) baptized this new style of art. Through the title of this happening—a title that is highly reminiscent of Marinetti's explosive novel *8 Anime in una Bomba* (1919)—it becomes quite clear that the happening is strongly under the influence of avant-garde movements from earlier in the century, on the one hand, and of the artistic genre of the "tableaux vivants"[20] on the other. One of the main concerns about the presentation of artistic content during the avant-garde and in the culture of happenings was—as previously noted—the notion of *simultaneity.* This notion today is known as a marker of postmodernity, in that a modernist logic of subsequent historic moments has been replaced with a "presence of simultaneity"[21] in which any historic feeling of the past can be *imported into the present* by means of simulation (for example, Las Vegas).

In his manifesto *Vita simultanea futurista* (1927) the futurist Fedele Azaro theorized *ex ante* the posthuman in quite an astonishing way: "When mechanical surgery and biological chemistry will have produced a standard for an incorruptible, resistant, and almost eternal man-machine, the problems of velocity will be less bothersome than today."[22] Velocity and rapidity are Azaro's answers to the desired prolongation of life.

Kaprow's *18 Happenings* were a sort of simultaneous action collage, all "happening" at the very same time, and could be experienced only through a compartmental logic of simultaneity (one next to the other). Through the trope of simultaneity it becomes clear that here performance no longer is based on unity, as in traditional theater, but rather on fragmentation, separation, and difference.[23] One of Kaprow's teachers, the composer John Cage,[24] highly inspired by the Dadaist-futurist tradition himself, used the term *simultaneity* for one of his early works from 1952: "Simultaneous presentation of unrelated events."[25]

The Dadaist *soirées* and the futurist theater events could not be described better than in Cage's title, for it emphasizes the important notion of simultaneity by which the performance itself is relativized (one happening is no longer in a subordinated sense less important than the other), and stresses the nonsensical, self-ironical structure of *events-words in freedom,* or *unrelated events and words.* The traditional syntax of performance had been abandoned since Marinetti—among many other members of the avant-garde—had started to redefine the traditional syntax of poetics in his early manifestos *Technical Manifesto of Futurist Literature* (1912), and *Destruction of Syntax-Imagination without Threads-Words in Freedom* (1913).[26] The new literary models proclaimed in these manifestos were no longer the traditional, old-fashioned style of literature,[27] but, by introducing the synaesthetic dimension of sounds, odors, and images, the new model emphasized the overlapping of codes. However, Marinetti also wanted to enrich this technical style with an "intuitive element" reflecting the molecular life of the universe. Later, the surrealists transformed this intuition into the attempt to represent the psychic dimension of the unconscious and the dream, turning this fragmented speech of the psyche into an *écriture automatique,* an automated writing of the soul, and exploring especially the medium of film to let the soul speak. In *Le sang d'un poète* (*Blood of a Poet,* 1930), for instance, Jean Cocteau presented four distinct compartmental filmic parts, just like Kaprow's *18 Happenings in 6 parts*—a true piece of simultaneity.

The concept of simultaneity, in itself inspired by the revolutionizing late-nineteenth-century technologies of representation, that is, photography and cinema, contributed strongly to such a fragmented, dispersed collage style, which has been claimed to be one of the central techniques of twentieth-century visual art.[28] What is crucial in this style is the fusion of the product with its creation process and—most important—with its environment: "As an Environment the painting took over the room itself, and finally, as sort of an Environment-with-action, became a Happening."[29] The practice of the (photo)collage became a common style of modern art, for instance, in the collage paintings of the Dadaist Kurt Schwitters (figure 2.2) in the 1920s and 1930s. In regard to the merging of the canvas and its *ingredients,* it is important to mention that from an image-anthropological perspective, such a distinction is entirely mind-internal, as German art historian Hans Belting points out: "When we distinguish a canvas from the image it represents, we pay attention to either the one or the other, as if they were distinct, which they are not; they separate only when we are willing to separate them in our looking."[30]

According to Michael Kirby, the futurist Umberto Boccioni had given birth to the photocollage in 1911, when he first used parts of a wooden frame in a piece of sculpture.[31] Later, it became a usual practice to integrate the material content and environment into the painting: Picasso and Braque pasted scraps of newspaper and wallpaper on their canvases. Marcel Duchamp went so far as to use any utensil, from an old wheel to a hammer, and reintegrate these pieces in what he called a "ready-made." His first ready-made, *Bicycle Wheel* from 1913, inaugurated the revolutionary introduction of commonplace, mass-produced objects as artworks, with which the idea of the uniqueness of the work of art was deconstructed.

The awareness of the process (as in processing mass-produced objects) rather than the product has changed the figurative arts not only since surrealism and cubism and the rise of the ready-made, but even since impressionism. The Russian abstract painter Woks said in an interview in *Art News* in 1959: "Since Cézanne, it has become evident that, for the painter, what counts is no longer the painting but the process of painting . . . . Whether you regard painting as a means of penetrating the self or the world, it is creation."[32]

Materiality and process, and the juxtaposition of pieces are of course key concepts for postmodern art. Many postmodern artists have experimented with materials on canvas. Jackson Pollock most famously produced drip-action paintings, which inspired the performances of Kaprow. Willem de Kooning slashed his brushstrokes onto the canvas. Yves Klein used the bodies of female models as "living brushes" in his *Anthropometrie-Performance* on March 9, 1960. The entire movement of pop art—in its auto-reflexivity—can be seen as an emphasis on the materialities and medium involved. It is the concept of the ready-made,

Body Performances from 1960s Wounds to 1990s Extensions

45

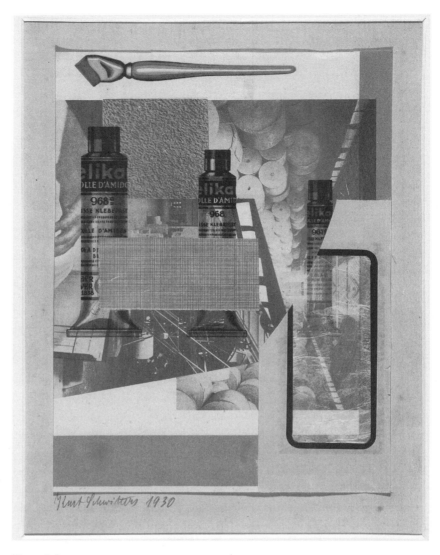

Figure 2.2. Kurt Schwitters, *Untitled* (*elika*) *Collage,* 1930. Paper on paper. Courtesy of the Sprengel Museum Hannover with permission by the Artists Right Society, New York.

Figure 2.3. Chris Burden, *The Big Wheel,* 1979. Courtesy of the artist.

though, that brought the focus on materiality (not only of the body, but of objects, too) into performance art.

In 1979, Chris Burden presented *The Big Wheel* (figure 2.3), in which artifacts were completely decontextualized and served as experimental materialities in process. The emphasis in *The Big Wheel* lies on the process and materials involved rather than on the product. He explains: *"The Big Wheel* consisted of a 3-ton cast iron fly wheel mounted in a vertical position and set in motion by the rear tire of a motorcycle. The iron wheel was accelerated to a speed of 220 revolutions per minute. *The Big Wheel* would spin freely for two and a half hours before it would need to be recharged."[33]

Simultaneity, fragmentation, and collage bring still another important dimension into play, that is, the redefinition of the theatrical space, such as the theater, the gallery, the museum, etc., in order to break right into *reality.*[34] By 1915, Marinetti and his colleagues Emilio Settimelli and Bruno Corrà formulated the new guidelines for the Synthetic Futurist Theater *(Il teatro futurista sintetico).* In the homonymous manifesto they claimed that the "scenic action will invade parterre and audience." It is not surprising that one of the titles of these theater plays was *Simultaneity,* a "Theatrical Synthesis," as Marinetti put it.[35] Surprise, provocation, and shock were the mechanisms of these very short and not very famous futurist attempts to revolutionize theater. Dadaism, on the other hand, was more successful in these regards. Hugo Ball, Tristan Tzara, Hans Arp, and later André Breton met during the difficult times of World War I in the Cabaret Voltaire in Zurich to perform Dada-*soirées,* in which they criticized the traditional laws of beauty,[36] and expressed their disagreement with bourgeois values.

In 1921, the German Dadaist Kurt Schwitters formulated the guidelines of his *Merz*[37] *{commerce} performance theatre* in the *Merz composite work of art:* "Materials for the stage-set are all solid, liquid, and gaseous bodies, such as white wall, man, barbed wire entanglement, blue distance. . . . Even people can be used.— People can even be tied to backdrops.—People can even appear actively, even in their everyday position."[38] Three years later, in 1924, Schwitters went one step further in his search for the *Gesamtkunstwerk,* transforming his own house at Waldhausenstrasse 5b in Hanover into a *Merzbau.*[39] This series of environments no longer is a house, but rather the collapse of the idea of a house.

With a similar drive for the totality of space, Walter Gropius—the main representative of the Bauhaus architectural movement in Germany—built a *total theater,* in which projection screens completely surrounded the audience.[40] Gropius' attempt can be interpreted as a remediated way of creating a reality experience, claiming that reality itself can be achieved "directly" only by means of simulation. Such a notion of an intensified, simulated reality, or "hyperreality"[41]—that is, a simulated reality that no longer can be labeled as real for lack of the reality principle itself (for example, Disneyland)—has become a zeitgeist at the turn of the millennium, a zeitgeist that emphasizes more and more remediated spaces in which original cultural references have been forgotten and can be revitalized in a nostalgic simulation.

But nobody could have revolutionized the new idea of theatricality resulting from an intensifying media-culture, in which the outer world collapses into the inner world and vice versa, more thoroughly than the "actor-director-playwright-poet"[42] Antonin Artaud, with his theory of the *Théâtre de la Cruauté.* In this theater of cruelty, art is no longer mimetic of life, but rather life is the simulation of a transcendent communication principle. The signified collapses into the signifier, form into content, and life into representation.[43] For Derrida, Artaud's simulation of life anticipates the end or *closure* of representation, for it is no longer a recitation of something already written, thought, or lived—hence, no longer "representing" another semiotic system (such as literature)—but rather representation here becomes self-presentation of the visible and the purely sensitive. *Cruelty* therefore means necessity and rigor, which meant that the performances in Artaud's theater of cruelty were not intended to be improvised, but on the contrary were structured and well planned. Unlike the surrealists, who were looking for ways of acting out the unconscious and the language of dreams, Artaud wanted to express consciousness and awareness, which for him meant the color of blood and cruelty. In one of his letters on cruelty from 1932 he declares: "I have therefore said 'cruelty' as I might have said 'life' or 'necessity,' because I want to indicate especially that for me the theater is act and perpetual emanation, that there is nothing congealed about it, that I turn it into a true act, hence living, hence magical."[44] For Jacques Derrida, therefore, "the theater of cruelty is not a *representation*. It is life itself, and therefore it is irrepresentable. Life is the non-representable origin of representation."[45] Theater, then, becomes a sacred or magical feast, an act of pure presence and active forgetting; no book, no work of art, but energy, and in that sense the only art of life.[46]

The breaking down of the walls between life and representation in these explicit terms was of direct inspiration for Kaprow who proclaimed that "the line between art and life should be kept as fluid, and perhaps indistinct, as possible."[47] The dissolution of difference between life and art was most relevant also for the Viennese actionists Günter Brus and Otto Muehl, who used the space of the streets, or the University of Vienna—in brief, any public space—for their actions, turning these spaces into happenings. In this type of happening there remains no space between the product, its process of creation, and the artist; they all become one. This process of total collapse, or fusion of the self with the artwork, already was present in Schwitter's *Merz* projects. One of the posters for the election of the Reichstag in 1920, which Schwitters disseminated to campaign for his poetic invention "Anna Blume" as a representative of the Dadaist Merz party (*M. P. D.* = *Merz-Partei Deutschland/Mehrheits-Partei DADA*), coined the tautological structure "Merz = Kurt Schwitters."[48] Schwitters had become what he had created. He *was* the Merz movement just like he was the artist Kurt Schwitters.

While Schwitters merged into Merz, the Viennese actionist Rudolf Schwarzkogler merged into his paintings. Schwarzkogler defined the blurring of life and representation with the substitution of the construction of the image with the construction of the *conditions* necessary for the paint-action producing the image (*Manifesto Panorama I/The Total Act*).[49] For this move from painting to the body itself, as Kristine Stiles points out, photography was a necessary intermediary through which "the hegemony of the stable aesthetical medium of painting was deferred to the instable medium of the body."[50] Schwarzkogler's actions have to be understood as continuations of paintings, or as he himself called them *paintings in motion:* "the pictorial construction on a surface is replaced by the construction of the pre-conditions for the act of painting as the determinant of the action field, of the space around the actor = the real objects present in his surroundings."[51]

In his sixth action, performed in his flat in Werdertorgasse, Vienna, the bandaged Schwarzkogler performed a light bulb–black mirror–dead chicken piece, in which he stages a connection between his body and the body of a dead chicken through electric cables, as shown in figure 2.4.

The fusion of the product with the process of its creation and the environment, and consequently, the reconstitution of the theatrical space into "life" and the "outer world" results in what the Viennese group called *Direkte Kunst*[52] (direct art): "A total action is a direct occurrence (direct art), not the repetition of an occurrence, a direct encounter between elements and reality (material)."[53] Just like Artaud, who refused the representational character of traditional theater because it stands for, or represents, the written text, Brus wanted to break through the fourth wall by directly encountering a truth that he called "reality."

The total action—to *look* and to *become* what one *does*—is expressed in different actions by the Viennese actionists: Brus's action of besmearing himself with paint, integrating his head into his painting (*ohne Titel* [untitled], 1964), has been mentioned already; Schwarzkogler's selection of foods according to aesthetic criteria—for he saw them as manifestations of his environment, an environment that had "invaded" the artist himself. Direct art thus, means nothing else than the necessity and rigor that Artaud claimed for this theater of cruelty. It means that there remains no trace, no indirectness, no quotation, no referentiality, but mere imminence and immediacy.

The happening as an effect of the hypermediated environment is central to the investigation of today's digital performances. What happens if this fusion of the artistic process with the product, the medium of representation with the artist, and the artist with the work of art, collapses into an internalized space— the body? What happens if the engine, the prosthetic vehicle, becomes the human body itself? These questions are discussed in the section Hypermediated

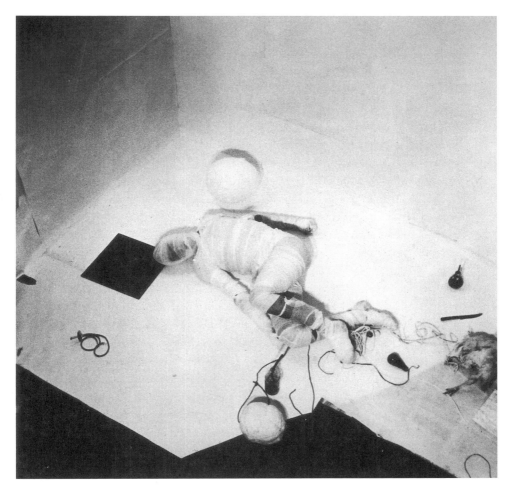

Figure 2.4. Rudolf Schwarzkogler, *Action 6,* spring 1966. Photo © MUMOK, Museum Moderner Kunst Stiftung Ludwig Wien.

Performances or 1990s Extensions. Beforehand, though, we need to look more closely at the logic of the happening, or brief event, in order to be able to decide whether digital performances even can be called performances in the sense of happenings any longer.

The Syntax of Performance

In linguistics, *performance* is defined in contrast with *competence*.[54] The American linguist Noam Chomsky introduced both terms in the 1960s (*Aspects of the Theory of Syntax,* 1965). Performance is the realization or use of a speaker's competence to apply a grammatical system (syntax, semantics, phonetics, etc.) of a given language. In speech act theory, "a communicative activity is defined with reference to the intentions of a speaker while speaking and the effects achieved on a listener."[55] J. L. Austin calls this very intentionality the "illocutionary act," and the impact on the listener the "perlocutionary act."[56] An illocutionary act is realized *in loqui* (in or through speaking). One of Austin's famous examples is the question "is the window open?" with which a speaker expresses a warning, or a wish that the window be closed, or just wants to communicate that he or she feels cold; and the listener, instead of answering "yes," or "no," might just get up and close the window. These utterances involve actions and therefore can also be called performative. Common examples for performative acts are religious acts such as baptism, or legal acts such as marriage and sentencing. These are acts that come into force by the uttering of certain phrases or sentences by one person, invoking a change of status in another person. Usually these phrases are accompanied by a symbolic act as well, such as pouring water on the head of the baptized. It has been pointed out that such performative utterances (normally expressed by performative verbs such as *to warn* or *to promise*) cannot be expressed in negative terms. In other words, there is no negation of a performative utterance. It is always affirmative.

Performance art of the twentieth century has worked with the materiality of embodiment—for instance, in queer performances staging the other sex or stereotypically gendered roles such as female film divas, Barbies, nuns, and the like.[57] What seems primary to these performances is the incorporation of the messages into the artists' own bodies. Thus, it is not surprising that gender and transgender performances often are staged by women and by homosexual men, both social groups representing bodies that have been victims of oppression and essentialism, as discussed in chapter 1. Male Japanese artist Yasumasa Morimura, for instance, is famous for his female personifications of stereotypical gender roles (figure 2.5) shown below.

Although the body discourse in these performances can be seen in the framework of a politically liberating activism, what matters is that artists' bodies have become more and more their primary artistic material. As Brus puts it: "The actor performs and himself becomes material: stuttering, stammering, burbling, groaning, choking, shouting, screeching, laughing, spitting, biting, creeping, rolling about in the material."[58] Characteristically, the genre of written texts involved in performances is the manifesto. From the futurists, Dadaists, and surrealists to Stelarc's recent cyber-manifestos, this genre gives the performance its performative force. What is more, the performance as such can be recognized and fully understood only in consideration of its grounding manifesto, its directions, its text of invitation, etc. Paradoxically, immanence and presence are reached only through the frame of the performative setting. In this very aspect, we cannot help thinking that the syntax of performance resembles the logic of the mediated screen, as in television or film. We are confronted with a performative frame, such as "news" through which we consume "real happenings." We would not take them for "real" were it not for the setting (such as a news program) in which we decode them.

Performance, however, must be understood not as a *movement* but as a form of expression that is most typical for the twentieth century, as Frazer Ward explains it relating performance art to artistic movements such as conceptual art:

Performance art was not a "movement," in the way that Minimalism or Conceptualism were, whatever attempts have been made to situate it as one. Rather, performance has surfaced and disappeared throughout the twentieth century as a kind of undercurrent, periodically bubbling up within—or in some relation to—various avant-garde movements: the Soviet avant-gardes, Futurism, Dada, the Bauhaus, neo-Dada, Fluxus, Pop, Minimalism, perhaps even Abstract Expressionism if we consider the arena-like quality of Jackson Pollock's painting on canvases rolled out on the studio floor. In works not only by Acconci, but by Chris Burden, Jan Dibbets, Dan Graham, Douglas Huebler, Bruce Nauman, Dennis Oppenheim, Hannah Wilke, and even Daniel Buren (e.g., his Sandwichmen [1986]), and others, it certainly surfaced in a close relation to Conceptual art—as much as it might have surfaced in the work of other artists, against Conceptualism.[59]

In the following, however, I am not just trying to distinguish the genre of performance art in opposition, say, to conceptual art and other respective artistic

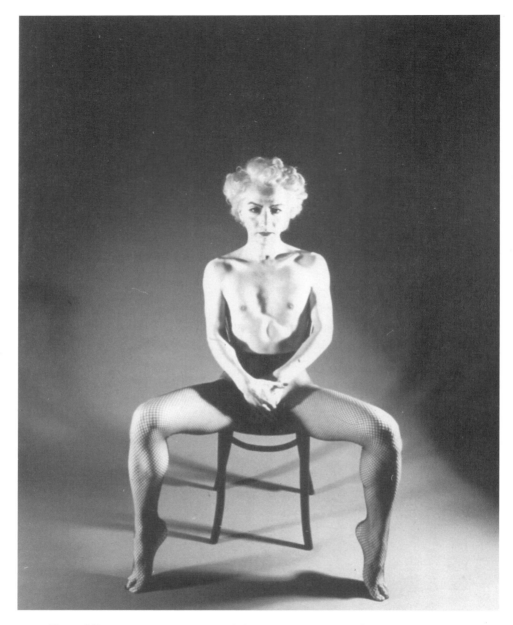

Figure 2.5. Yasumasa Morimura, *Psychoborg17,* 1996. Courtesy of the artist and Luhring Augustine, New York.

mainstreams. I point to the inspirations of performance art at the beginning of this chapter, in which it becomes clear that this artistic expression can be understood only in the spirit of the avant-garde earlier in the twentieth century. What interests me—in order to situate the possibilities of performance art within cyberspace in the next step—is not so much the historic constitution of performances, but the very syntagmatic system that it is based on. In other words: How are performances structured? Do they even follow a certain paradigm? If so, what does it look like? And if not, what does its nonstructure look like?

In his essay "The Happenings Are Dead: Long Live the Happenings,"[60] Kaprow expresses the paradoxical syntax of the happening in his contradictory title. By "dead," Kaprow means the following: "The Happenings are the only art activity that can escape the inevitable death-by-publicity to which all other art is condemned, because, designed for a brief life, they can never be overexposed; they are dead, quite literally, every time they happen."[61]

In this quote it becomes quite clear that it is the age of "mediatized reproduction" that Kaprow criticizes in his art form, an age that wants to record, to simulate. He wants to confront it with the truth and authenticity of the brief event of the happening. Just as for Artaud, for Kaprow there is an inseparability of process, product, and environment. In Kaprow's work, though, this inseparability takes place in the subculture. The happening should be "as artless as possible," and the desire is to place it at the intersection of urbanity and high technology, just as the futurist's dream of accelerated accidents: "a tour of a laboratory where polyethylene kidneys are made, a traffic jam on the Long Island Expressway are more useful than Beethoven, Racine, or Michelangelo."[62] The life-representations that interest Kaprow take place in "non-places" such as drugstores and airports, for the sense of life in question is a "life above ground," which—and here is another paradox—is "underground."[63]

Kaprow's happening-syntax is a collage of events, fragmented in certain spans of time and in certain spaces. Sometimes the events may overlap in time so that it becomes literally impossible to follow them all. Besides, they are performed only once, which emphasizes their authenticity, and creates the reality effect. The following happening of a car accident reminds of current reality television shows like *Cops:* "Two cars collide on a highway. Violet liquid pours out of the broken radiator of one of them, and in the back seat of the other there is a huge load of dead chickens. The cops check into the incident, plausible answers are given, two truck drivers remove the wrecks, costs are paid, the drivers go home to dinner. . . ."[64]

But unlike the Dadaist–*soirée*–happenings, which were put on in limited spaces for limited audiences, Kaprow does not care that one cannot follow his events, because he is not interested in the audience at all—and here is what is decisively different in respect to the actions of the early-twentieth-century avant-garde—rather, he wants to eliminate the audience entirely. There is no proscenium stage, no time-place matrices; absence of the observer is the syntactic core-rule of the happening. The audience consists of randomly involved spectators on the one hand, and the *after-audience* on the other hand who will experience or witness the action via photographic stills, or sometimes even via video recordings. Since there is no audience that can watch the entirety of a happening in real time, it is the knowledge of what is going to happen that turns the audience into an after-audience. For instance, "twenty rented cars are driven away in different directions until they run out of gas. . . ."[65] Not only would it be impossible to follow all rental cars at the same time, but the audience of this happening consists of people who—as they speak or read—become witnesses of this event, be it true or false, for the mere fact that it is reported to them. Besides, as Kaprow points out, there is another realism factor involved. The happenings are performed by nonprofessionals in order to increase the unpredictability and reality-effect of the event.[66]

What results from these choreographic directions is that the performances, as designed by Kaprow, are highly influenced by a mediatized logic, such as is inherent to the medium of film, which is recorded or shot once and viewed or experienced—not live, but in retrospect and in absence of the actors or performers. There is even another pertinent medium involved in the way Kaprow designs his happening, namely photography. As we know from Roland Barthes's *La Chambre Claire* (1981),[67] photography is an anticipation of death, in that it represents and eternalizes a scenario that will never come back. Kaprow says that "happenings are dead," by which he stresses the stillness, unrepeatability, and thus uniqueness of the event. This brings a desire into play, a sentimentality, or melancholic mourning for the past or lost object.[68] For a happening in Kaprow's sense, we have heard of it, or were told about it. Presence or witnessing would be felt as something unusual, or almost something exceptional—like surviving a catastrophe.[69]

In that spirit, Chris Burden plays with the absence forced upon the viewer and the impossibility of being seen while performing his action *You'll never see my face in Kansas City,* on November 6, 1971, in Kansas City (figure 2.6): "For three hours I sat without moving behind a panel which concealed my neck and

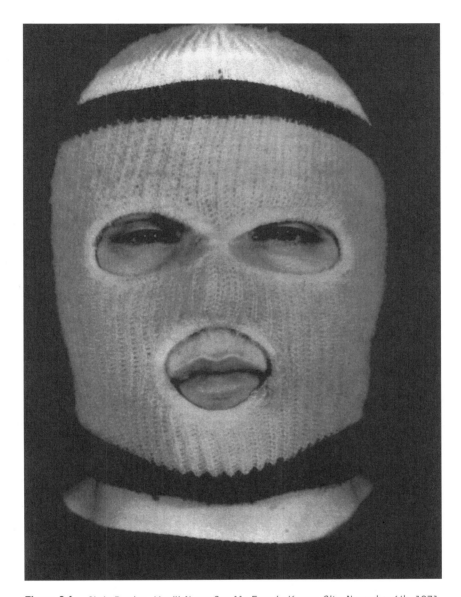

Figure 2.6. Chris Burden, *You'll Never See My Face in Kansas City,* November 6th, 1971. Courtesy of the artist.

head. No one could see behind the panel; a piece of board sealed the underside of the space. In conjunction with the performance, I wore a ski mask at all times during my stay at Kansas City."[70]

In Kaprow's *Self-Service: A Happening* (1967), another important factor that comes into play besides the absence of the audience, namely the chance factor:

Self-Service, a piece without spectators, was performed in the summer of 1967 in Boston, New York, and Los Angeles. It spanned four months, June through September. Thirty-one activities were selected from a much larger number. Their time and locality distribution were determined by chance methods. Participants selected events from those offered for their city; each had to pick at least one, although doing many or all was preferable. Details of time and place were flexible within each month; choices made from month to month overlapped, some actions recurring.[71]

The syntax of this action is reminiscent or anticipates a chance-generated computer game, similar to digital installations, which is discussed in Chapter 4 in more detail (see The Corporealization of the Image in New Media Art).[72] Some possibilities are given; others are randomly constructed during the action or game. It is precisely this logic of chance that anticipates a digitized environment for performance art that will culminate in the hypermediated 1990s extensions. For the rest, the directions read like a screenplay for a short film involving many people and cars: "People stand on bridges, on street corners, watch cars pass. After 200 red ones, they leave."[73]

What is more, the logic of the viewer's absence at the event approximates a televisual format (for example, a news program), in which a notion of truth and presence is created merely through the performative discourse of authenticity and witnessing ("This is Wolf Blitzer for CNN, Washington"). What becomes clear in *Self-Service* is that Kaprow no longer shocks the audience in a Dadaist manner; rather, we witness the anticipation of an intersecting logic of film and computer culture within this kind of happening art. No longer centered is the individual happening; instead we focus on the remediated knowledge of the happening.[74]

Along with Kaprow and Burden, many other happening artists of the 1960s either withdrew themselves from their audiences or turned the one-time viewers of the action into witnesses of crimes and violence (for example, Burden's *Shoot,* November 19, 1971, 7:45 p.m., F Space, in which the artist had himself shot in his upper arm by a friend with a bullet from a copper jacket .22 Long

Rifle), or into voyeurists of extreme actionism (for example, Burden's *Five Day Locker Piece,* April 26–30, 1971, University of California, Irvine, in which he had himself locked into a 60 × 60 × 90 cm. locker). The Fluxus artist Yoko Ono, for instance, not only turned the audience into voyeurs, but also made them active participants in her self-damaging by offering the viewers of her performance *Cut Piece* (Kyoto, 1964) scissors to cut the clothing from her body.

In these actions the performers become *survivors* of their bodily challenges. *Survival in Alien Circumstances* is also the title of Stuart Brisley's action in 1977, when he spent two entire weeks in a dirty, muddy pit—a physical challenge similar to his *Hungerstrike* in 1979. Violence as a signifier for truth and depth (often taken very literally by cutting into the performer's skin), and the audience's presence at or even involvement in the artist's violent experience, is at the center of these *reality-happenings.* What is crucial from the viewer's perspective is the dimension of the first person's experience: "How do you know what it feels like to be shot if you don't get shot?" is the question that Burden asked when explaining his motivation for his performance *Shoot.* Gina Pane seriously harmed herself with a razor blade in *Psyche* (1974), when she kneeled in front of a mirror, put on some makeup, and cut herself under the eye. The Austrian performance artist and filmmaker, Valie Export, who was not a member of the Viennese actionists (not least because she is female), wounded her body in several actions. In *Eros/ion* (1971), for instance, "the naked performer rolls first through an area strewn with broken glass, then over a plate of glass, and finally onto a paper screen."[75]

The sacrificed body is also a key element in the Austrian Hermann Nitsch's early paintings of the 1960s, in which he used dead animals, their blood and organs, to paint his canvas. Moreover, in his early paintings, Nitsch introduces the themes of memory, history, and biography (figure 2.7)[76]—along with an everlasting obsession with religious iconography that still determines his work today.

Just as in Pollock's action paintings, this ritualistic form of painting emphasizes the *moment* that the artist uses the material in the presence of a particular, very selected audience (similar to religious practices). The metaphysical motivation for action art becomes very clear in Nitsch's later *Orgien Mysterien Theater* (Theater of Orgies and Mysteries), in which he accompanies action painting with symbolic actions, such as the sacrifice of animals (figure 2.8). During these feasts, for instance, a bull is immolated (following the Greek myth of the god Dionysus, who was born as a bull in Hera's elbow), the organs pulled out of his body, and—together with the animal's blood—smeared on a human body.

Figure 2.7. Hermann Nitsch, *o.T.* (untitled), 1961. Courtesy of the artist with permission of the Artists Rights Society, New York.

By addressing the orgiastic instinct in his art, Nitsch wants to free himself and the participants, as well as the audience, of the controlling intellect that predominates real lives. The Viennese actionists, though, were not the only ones to celebrate shocking and religiously charged action art in the 1960s. In his *Messe pour un corps* (1969), the French Michel Journiac made a black pudding with his own blood, offering it as a "holy communion" to the viewers at the performance.

Figure 2.8. Hermann Nitsch, *Das Orgien Mysterien Theater* (Theater of Orgies and Mysteries), Salzburg, 1990. Courtesy of the artist with permission of the Artists Rights Society, New York.

Body Performances from 1960s Wounds to 1990s Extensions

Actionism, however, has also violated the law *for real:* Muehl had to spend seven years in prison (1991–1998) for having engaged in sexual intercourse with minors, illicit sexual acts, rape, and drug offenses. He was not the only member of the Viennese actionist group to encounter legal problems or prosecution for his transgressive actions. One of the transgressions that was never officially problematized, however, consisted of the Viennese actionist's insistent misogyny in their actions, as pointed out by Roswitha Mueller in her study of Export, the female counterpart of the Viennese art scene: "In accordance with the sexual politics of the day, women's bodies were primarily passive objects to be acted upon rather than actors in their own right. The packaged, smeared, used, and abused bodies of women were central to some Actionist fantasies of destruction."[77]

Performances of the Female Body

Returning to the definitions of performances and performativity, I would like to pay additional attention to female performances, or performances staging the female body. The implications of the powerful male gaze have been staged by many different female artists since the 1960s. As Amelia Jones points out in her influential book *Body Art: Performing the Subject,* late-twentieth-century body art performances are one of the primordial expressions of their time to understand the questions and dilemmas of postmodern subjectivity. For Jones, body art is then the instantiation of this decentered questioning subject, a dislocation she believes to be "the most profound transformation constitutive of what we have come to call postmodern."[78]

It is not surprising, then, that at the peak of postmodernism in the art scene of the Western hemisphere, the 1980s, body performance should become one of the most significant forms of artistic expression. Since the 1980s we could already speak of a canon of female, and often feminist, performance art with the performances of such well-known and well-exhibited artists as the American Cindy Sherman, the Japanese Mariko Mori, the Korean Lee Bul, the Austrian Elke Krystufek, and the French Orlan, to name just a few.

In an *expressis verbis* feminist performance, Orlan—considering her body as raw material for her art—had herself cut in several plastic surgical operations that she staged in video-taped actions (for example, *Successful Operation Nr. X,* 1991) and in classic one-time event happenings (for example, *New York Omnipresence,* November 21, 1993). In her "theater of operation," in which the artist

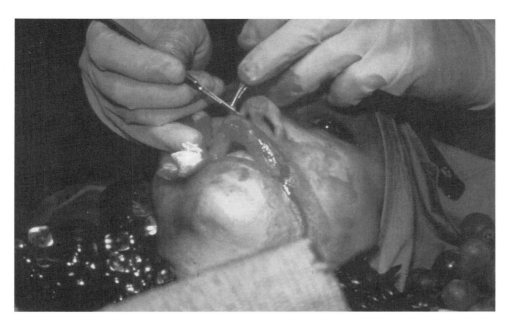

Figure 2.9. Orlan, *Hommage à toutes les bouches qui onte quelque chose à dire, 5° opération-chirurgicale-performance. (Homage to all mouths that have something to say, fifth surgical-operation-performance.)* Still from video-performance, *Successful Operation, December 8, 1991.* Cibachrome dans diasec vacuum: 1.10m × 1.65m. Alain Dohmé for Sipa-press. Courtesy of the artist with permission of the Artists Rights Society, New York/ADAGP, Paris.

had implants sewn into her chin and other facial parts, Orlan reflects on issues concerning the construction of the "female body under the male knife."[79] The hybridization and reconfiguration of herself in these surgical interventions are an expression of Orlan's critique of the mediatized (female) body, onto which beauty ideals have been violently inscribed throughout history. *Successful Operation Nr. X* (figure 2.9) is about the change of image, the deceptiveness of the skin, or the "I as another," as Orlan states during her performance.

Orlan is not the only female artist to critique the image of womanhood in a mediatized society and thus propose a more complex image of femininity. Valie Export, Cindy Sherman, and Mary Kelly analyze womanhood through the images of female markers that have been "inscribed onto the female body," from the Venus of Milo to Marilyn Monroe. But this is more than a feminist critique of the male gaze and the female object (as for instance proposed by Laura Mulvey[80]), rather it is a rebellious battle waged against the image of womanhood as such.

For Export, for example, it is through only the complete detachment from the female body and the images of womanhood that emancipation can take place. *Touch* is the core issue of her legendary performance *Tapp und Tastkino* (1968), in which the question of voyeurism is at stake. The viewer becomes a groper, and his or her anonymity in the dark movie theater is given up to the theatrical moment of being seen while touching Export's breast, hidden in the "mini-movie theater" of a plastic box with curtains strapped over her bare chest.[81]

Almost thirty years after Valie Export's *Tapp und Tastkino,* another Austrian performance artist staged similar questions around the female body and its identity. In *Suture* (1994),[82] Elke Krystufek touches upon the delicate question of the female body's boundaries, its fractal construction in the mirror, and its dependency on the outside perspective (figure 2.10). What is remarkable about this photocollage is the split frame. On one side we see the artist looking at herself through her own legs (construction of self), and on the second side we see an image of the "sutured vagina" in the other's—namely her own—gaze.

Like Orlan, Krystufek has incorporated questions of vision and visibility into her body art performances, and therefore has united this art form with the question of mediality itself. What is most relevant for my argument is that throughout the history of performance art—which evolved from the dreams of simultaneity and acceleration of the early avant-garde into one of the most prominent forms of postmodern expression—it becomes evident how corporeality and mediality have not only been staged together, but have revealed themselves as indistinguishable. It is through this medium that the body became prominent in the twentieth century, and it is through various modes and tropes—among them performance art, but also new media—that the medium will show itself as intrinsically corporeal.

In these feminist performances and actions—whether they included or excluded the audience, whether they were more or less harmful for the performer—what became clear is that the human body had become the new canvas of twentieth-century art. There remained literally no room for a representational medium to step "in-between" the artist and her work. No paintings or sculptures are being ready-made anymore, but—as Orlan puts it in her "Art Charnel" project—the body itself becomes a "modified ready-made." The performer thus embodies the idea, breaking down the wall between reality and representation. Not only does life become a theater of cruelty, as in Artaud's earlier tautology—a theater in which the viewer automatically becomes a witness of

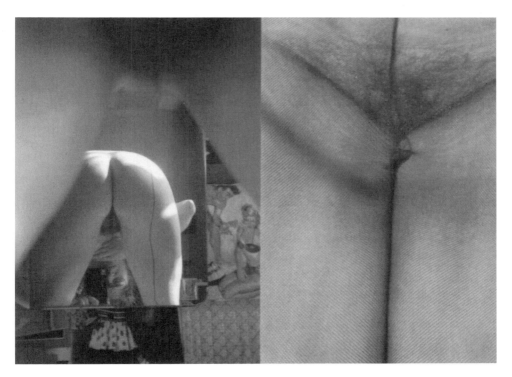

Figure 2.10. Elke Krystufek, *Suture,* 1994. Courtesy of Elke Krystufek and Galerie Georg Kargl, Vienna.

something that actually *happens* to the performer—but it is the human body it-self that is turned into the theatrical *Gesamtkunstwerk* ("complete work of art").

Nevertheless, the bodies we are looking at in the era of 1990s extensions are no longer aestheticized like the beautiful Yves Klein models of the early 1960s. Rather, as best shown in Orlan's and Krystufek's cases, these are bodies in pain, full of blood and other markers of violent inscriptions. Thus, the body in end-of-twentieth-century performance art shows itself as a suffering body-in-pieces—what we see as detached, and often severed, entities in these feminist performances are loci of an essentialist femininity, such as the female genitalia,[83] the breast, and the "beautiful face."

As Amelia Jones points out, Orlan literally enacts the reversibility of self and other, as theorized by psychoanalysis and phenomenology: "Enacting herself (and literally rearranging her body/self) through technologies of representation as well as medical technology, Orlan produces herself as posthuman: her body/self is experienced (both by herself and by her audience) in and through technology."[84]

What matters to the analysis of these examples of body art is that we can detect a clear shift from an emphasis on the *body* as raw material in 1960s wounds to an emphasis on the *media and the media technologies* and their discourses,[85] as well as the wide range of its interpretations in 1990s extensions. This new emphasis is of major importance for a theoretical development from corporeality to mediality throughout the rest of the book.

Finally, I stress the fragility and volatility inherent to the act of "interpretating" these body performances, as pointed out by Amelia Jones and Andrew Stephenson in their book *Performing the Body/Performing the Text,* in which they depart from the assumption that interpretation itself is an "*invested* kind of performance."[86] In that sense, it is of utmost importance not "just" to read these body performances as cultural productions, but to read the writings on and around them as well. Hence, performance and text can never be addressed as separate sets of data, but rather are tied together such that any performance is text, and any text is always performative. What is more, many of these performances consist of, or have, textual components (manifesto) to begin with.

Hypermediated Performances or 1990s Extensions

I want to return to some of the departing questions of this chapter: What happened to the body? And what are the differences between body art in the era of 1960s wounds and 1990s extensions? The answer to this question can be given on the basis of Amelia Jones' historical analysis of body performances of the twentieth century. Jones points out that the body had undergone two moments of particular reevaluation in twentieth-century art. As we have seen, throughout the 1960s and 1970s the body was featured as *raw material,* a site of the inscription of cultural meaning. In these body installations, the body had just come out from the realm of painting, having replaced the materiality of the paint brush and color with the materiality of the actual body. Additionally, the body was often harmed physically, as featured in the examples of "1960s Wounds." The body as raw material, according to Jones, features the transition from a modernist body subjectivity that was struggling with the Cartesian body and mind split, to a dispersed postmodern subjectivity of a bodily self that is construed into a variety of forms and shapes with the help, and through the eyes, of the audience or witnesses. During the 1980s, however, Jones detects a "turn away from the body,"[87] which she interprets as a reaction to the politics in the Western hemisphere: "This turn away from the body was also in some ways unfortunately coincident with the disembodied politics of the Reagan-Thatcher era, characterized by political retrenchment and reactionary, exclusionary economic and social policies and by the scrupulous avoidance of addressing the effects of such policies on the increasingly large number of bodies/selves living below the poverty line."[88]

Since the 1990s we have witnessed a dramatic return to the body and body art practices. These works, as Jones states, "acknowledge the deep implications of the politics of representation in relation to the embodied subject."[89] In these hypermediated extensions of the body the self is explored no longer mainly in relation to culture and context (constructivism). Now, through new possibilities of the technologies of the body, particularly those enhanced by new media, the body is under "technophenomenological" examination. To quote Jones once more: "The body/self is technophenomenological: fully mediated through the vicissitudes of bio- and communications technologies, and fully engaged with the social (what Merleau-Ponty called 'enworlded'). The body/self is hymenal, reversible, simultaneously both subject and object."[90]

From a phenomenological standpoint, this body-in-pieces is subject and object at the same time as it is trying to "see" itself as objectified. However, this objectification no longer is the result of a social constructivist critique, but stems from the mere observation that "seeing" is "creating a distance," to borrow one of Merleau-Ponty's famous statements. Thus, the 1990s body performances question the very attempt to learn anything about the body via the particularized knowledge we may have accumulated about its bits and pieces. These 1990s bodies often do not feature any original bodily identity at all; they do not reveal a graspable subjectivity. One almost could say that they are returning to more primordial questions regarding the materialities of the body, such as questions of the body's appearance through its skin, the ego envelope, or the border zone between inside and outside. Technology is the body's crucial counterpart in these performances that break down the distinction between a body's interiority and exteriority, between a being in the body and a distance to the body. Technology serves as a partner in these often eerie and alienating body performances, as becomes clear in the analysis of Stelarc's techno-body performances.

But to return to the Lacanian notion that the body image is always, and by nature, deceptive (framed by the other's gaze), these performances also express a deep skepticism and an almost nihilistic irony in their use of media and technology to promote such a confused and unstable body. Derrida describes media artist Gary Hill's work as revealing "that there is not and never has been a direct, live presentation."[91] It is in this sense that the 1960s wounds differ drastically from the 1990s extensions: these latter installations are no longer mainly concerned with the reality of the gaze, of politics, of the injustice done to the body. The body is no mediator. Rather, these performances use the body to experiment with media. As a result, our current media environment offers innumerable varieties of such immersive media environments, from computer games to virtual reality environments, from chatrooms to media art installations.

As pointed out, Bolter and Grusin describe our visual culture as an era of *remediation,* characterized through the inseparability of reality and mediation. Remediation in this view is always mediation of mediation, just as—according to Derrida—interpretation is always reinterpretation. In this highly mediatized world, "representation is conceived of not as a window on to the world, but rather as 'windowed' itself—with windows that open on to other representations or other media."[92] Reality itself becomes a window, as shown in an interview with a MUD user: "I split my mind. I'm getting better at it. I can see myself as being two or three more. And I just turn on one part of my mind and the another when I go from window to window . . . . And then I get a real-time message (which flashes on the screen as soon as it is sent from another system user), and I guess that's RL [real life]. It's just one more window."[93]

Philip Auslander connects Bolter and Grusin's concept of remediation with performance theory in a mediatized culture. However, Auslander does not see any ontological difference between mediatized and live performances: "within our mediatized culture, whatever distinction we may have supposed there to be between live and mediatized events is collapsing because live events are becoming more and more identical with mediatized ones."[94] Sports events and pop concerts are some examples that support this ontological collapse in which viewers do not only *watch* the players or performers in their live actions, but at the same time *engage* with the supermega screens and, thus, the mediatized presentation of what is happening right in front of the viewers. Auslander also sees the remediation effect in pop concerts, in which what is performed is already known to the viewer through the mediatic frame of the music video. For instance, Madonna performs the exact image of her own recording (to be seen on screen at the same time as in concert) in her 2001 HBO show "Drowned World Tour," including the "ass-kicking-cyber-queen-performance (figure 2.11)."

Liveness, here, is no longer a *non-matrixed* experience, but rather follows the *remediated liveness* of television. Since its onset, television has absolved the dis-

Figure 2.11. Madonna. Still of concert, "Drowned World Tour," 2001.

tinction between liveness and representation. Stanley Cavel observes: "There is no sensuous distinction between live and repeat or replay in television."[95] What have remained from this televisual logic in mediatized performances, however, are the main markers of television: intimacy, immediacy, and proximity. What has become of them in cyberspace is now addressed.

I have defined hypermediation as a fragmented, heterogeneous style emphasizing the process rather than the result or the finished (art) object. This kind of a style reminds of the logic of new media and vice versa. Bolter and Grusin give many different examples of fragmented interfaces and screens that may be seen as effects of remediation and hypermediation. The newspaper *USA Today,* for instance, has a layout that resembles a multimedia computer application, and television stations like CNN "show the influence of the graphical user interface when they divide the screen into two or more frames and place text and numbers around the framed video images."[96] CNN is also a good example of hypermediation for the structure of its website, which borrows its "sense of immediacy from the televised CNN newscasts."[97] The televised newscasts, on the other hand, resemble the very website that resembles the newscast, a classical loop effect of hypermediation in which reality and virtuality feed each other with interchangeable input.

The desire for the real and for the "authentic first person's experience" results from these latest tendencies in our culture of representation and simulation, a desire that—paradoxically—grows stronger as more ways of representation are invented. In other words, the more we are trying to mediate, the stronger the wish to "go back," "to unmediate," or "get past the limits of representation and to achieve the real," as Bolter and Grusin suggest.[98]

The quest for the ultimate proof of the "real" and for the authenticity of the first person's experience is of course not new, but has to be seen as, and in the context of, one of the leitmotifs of modern art. Ever since the avant-gardes, this desire has been pursued and widely represented. Hal Foster points out how the strategies of the real can be traced to several art movements of the 1960s—among which the "minimalist genealogy of the neo-avant-garde," pop art, super-realism (photorealism), appropriation art and others—and since then it has become one of postmodernity's trademarks.[99]

To get beyond representation can also mean, in its extreme sense, to make the medium disappear entirely. The best example for this desire is virtual reality, a surfaceless entity that has no outside or inside, but where "inside is always outside, and outside is always inside."[100] Virtual reality is direct and immersive, which means that it is a medium whose paradoxical purpose is to disappear. In his historical approach to the concept of virtual art, Oliver Grau points out that virtual reality is not a new phenomenon:

the idea of installing an observer in a hermetically closed-off image space of illusion did not make its first appearance with the technical invention of computer-aided virtual realities. On the contrary, virtual reality forms part of the core of the relationship of humans to images. It is grounded in art traditions, which have received scant attention up to now, that, in the course of history, suffered ruptures and discontinuities, were subject to the specific media of their epoch, and used to transport content of a highly disparate nature. Yet the idea goes back at least as far as the classical world, and it now reappears in the immersion strategies of present-day virtual art.[101]

The current trend for a "transparent immediacy" can be found even outside of the new media logic *strictu sensu* (unless we want to consider the influence of new media logic always to be an *inside logic*). High fashion designers, architects, and interior designers all want to create *interfaceless interfaces* with smooth, morphing, or even nonvisible transitions between materials, contents, and appearances—in other words, there is a tendency to break down any kind of border between an inside and an outside.[102] This strategy, however, is certainly not to convince the interlocutor (if there still is such an individual) that the representation *is* the thing itself, but to install a realistic looking fantasy screen. The difference from the postmodern experience, as pointed out by Slavoj Žižek, is that everybody is aware of this process, consciously or unconsciously, but still wants to play the game.

In order to discard the interface one can apply different techniques. One of these techniques is complete *erasure* through *replacement.* The best example for replacement is the hypertext of the World Wide Web, a set of windows laid over each other. But even outside of the Internet, such software programs as Microsoft Word constantly suggest the logic of replacement with such possibilities as *cut* or *paste,* opening new windows that are layered behind the main document, and—as in Macintosh's operating system since OS X—may be "swallowed up" by the desktop while not in use. Replacement, however, leaves behind a trace, and the question that remains open is what is done with what is being replaced? Where does the previous "window" go? A very radical answer to this question was given by Muehl, in 1963: "I can imagine nothing significant where nothing is sacrificed, destroyed, dismembered, burnt, pierced, tormented, harassed, tortured, massacred, . . . stabbed, destroyed, or annihilated."[103]

In other words, replacement seems to be a creative strategy, or—as for Muehl—a destructive necessity to create or produce anything new. The difference from the collage style discussed earlier, however, is that replacement is no longer a superposition, like Schwitters's collages, in which the different layers were shimmering through. Replacement here is an erasure in the sense of a substitution of what was there before. It never comes to a "stop," like the layered collages by Schwitters, but rather has to be—by definition—"activated" (for example, by clicking on the document hiding underneath the one in use) for the layers to show.[104]

One common mode of replacement is what contemporary entertainment industry calls "repurposing"—a logic certainly best represented in the World Wide Web—taking property from one medium and reusing it in another.[105] The logic of repurposing was acknowledged by Marshall McLuhan, who linked this process to its original essence in the transmission of pure information through electric light: "The instance of the electric light may prove illuminating in this connection. The electric light is pure information. It is a medium without a message, as it were, unless it is used to spell out some verbal ad or name. This fact, characteristic of all media, means that the 'content' of any medium is always another medium. The content of writing is speech, just as the written word is the content of print, and print is the content of the telegraph."[106] It should not be surprising that in a society of simulation and hypermediacy repurposing should become one of the major tropes of communication. As the American theorist of postmodernism Fredric Jameson pointed out, postmodern art is a form of imitation that is cynical of the original.[107] This kind of cynicism can indeed be found in today's hypermediated performances, for example, those of the Wooster Group:

In hyperkinetic performing environments, where video monitors, movable scenery, microphones, and frantically gesticulating performers compete for the viewer's attention, the Wooster Group takes texts, often from playwrights like Eugene O'Neill . . . and Gertrude Stein, . . . and "deconstructs or fragments them, eliminating recognizable timelines, as live performers compete for viewers" attention with videotaped versions of themselves. In capitalizing on the uniqueness of O'Neill or Stein, they offer graphic representation of what social theorist and critic Frederic Jameson cites as the postmodern artists "seizing on their idiosyncrasies and eccentricities to produce an imitation which mocks the original."[108]

There are endless examples of repurposing, which becomes clear once we make ourselves aware of the many possibilities inherent to McLuhan's thesis that the content of a medium lies in another medium. Therefore, a society obsessed with media and mediatic frames would eventually produce copies of copies of copies, and imitations of imitations of imitations. What remains to be analyzed, and what is of most interest regarding repurposing, is what content is being staged or borrowed for what purpose.

Another—and recently most popular—way to get beyond the screen is to (make) believe that there is no screen, or that the medium is not a medium but in fact part of the real, of which it is "just another window." Such a replacement of reality with virtuality leads to the so-called media equation: "Media equals real life," as suggested by Byron Reeves and Clifford Nass in their study about how people interact with computers.[109]

The most recent and apparently most successful way of achieving a getting-beyond-the-screen effect is the incorporation of the mediatic frame into the utterance itself. *Make the spectators aware of being spectators, make them enjoy the medium!* goes the underlying instruction for use: "In the logic of hypermediacy, the artist (or multimedia programmer or web designer) strives to make the viewer acknowledge the medium as a medium and to delight in that acknowledgment."[110] It is in this sense that we have to read such blockbusters as the *Blair Witch Project* (1999), or reality television shows like *Survivor* and its endless imitations, as acknowledgments of the medium, and euphoric—or (pseudo) dysphoric—explorations of the interface.

At this point I return to this chapter's inaugural inquiry, namely, the question of what new media performances have to offer, and whether performances like those from the avant-garde to the 1960s can, or are continuing to, exist, or whether new media and their double logic of remediation have changed the workplace for performances. To phrase it differently, have new media redefined or disbanded the genre of the happening, as previously described in its evolution? Does the disappearance of the real material body in cyberspace mean that wounds can no longer have the reality-action effect that Kaprow and Burden would hope to provoke? Are Steve Mann's wearable computer[111] and Kevin Warwick's computer-arm[112] even bodies in the old sense, or have they assumed the status of posthumanity?

Performances in the Era of New Media, or the End of Performance?

The transition from the body as raw material in the 1960s and 1970s wounds performances and the return to the body as extension in the 1990s cannot be better instantiated than in the work of the Australian performance artist Stelarc (Stelios Arcadiou), who has performed a fusion of new media with the real on his own body for more than thirty years. Stelarc is probably *the* example of how body discourse in performance art has changed during the last thirty to forty years. In the 1970s and 1980s, he suspended himself with hooks in his skin in such actions as *Stretched Skin* (1976) in Japan, and *Street Suspension* (1984) in New York. In the 1970s, Stelarc experimented with body levitation, trying to transcend pain. Since the 1980s and up to his current new-millennium installations, he is trying to change his body by redesigning its interface. Stelarc ironically proclaims the body's obsolescence: "It is time to question whether a bipedal, breathing body with binocular vision and a 1,400cc brain is an adequate biological form. It cannot cope with the quantity, complexity, and quality of information it has accumulated."[113]

However, by obsolescence Stelarc does not mean that the human body should or could be replaced by a machine, or that intelligence is becoming disembodied. Rather, he provokes us to think that our bodies are constantly being outperformed by machines in speed, strength, endurance, and so on.[114] Stelarc's cyber-body installations need to be seen as philosophical investigations into the very experience of embodiment. His philosophy is based on technological transcendence combined with a teleology of the spatial era.[115] Stelarc's phenomenological approach in his body art has been emphasized by him and by his many critics. As Mark Poster puts it: "Stelarc puts into motion Heidegger's pronouncement that technology brings into question the human essence."[116]

In response to the cyberculture of the turn of the millennium, Stelarc is developing what he terms an "evolving URL body." This body is an object rather than a subject. It is constructed at the hands of multiple user-hackers. Similarly, the "ping body" is a barometer for Internet activity. In *Movatar,* the body itself is turned into a prosthesis performing "involuntary movements." In this "inverse capture system" muscle signals are recorded and transmitted onto a prosthetic device (for example, an arm).[117] These random signals now determine the motor control, finally taking over a person's body. The body, here, has become a contingency—a system out of control and in the hands of others, symbolizing the complexity of agency, self, and identity.[118] As Edward Scheer points out in his critique of Stelarc's e-motions, *Movatar* "literalizes our condition of being trapped, as Wittgenstein says, 'inside a picture.'"[119]

In his installation *Prosthetic Head* (2003) Stelarc investigates the limitations and possibilities of artificial intelligence (figure 2.12). The automated, animated *Prosthetic Head,* designed after the artist's head, speaks when a person interrogates it through a keyboard. To the question "Will you marry me?," the head answers "Why don't you download me instead?"[120]

In this piece, Stelarc plays ironically with notions of agency and the responsibility of the socially embedded intelligent agent. The *Prosthetic Head* serves as an avatar, assisting the artist in handling the many questions that people have asked him about his work:

In recent years there have been an increasing amount of PhD students requesting interviews to assist in writing their thesis. Now the artist will be able to reply that although he is too busy to answer, it would be possible for them to interview his head instead. And as a web avatar it would be possible to download the transcript of the conversations people have with it. A problem would arise though when the *Prosthetic Head* increases

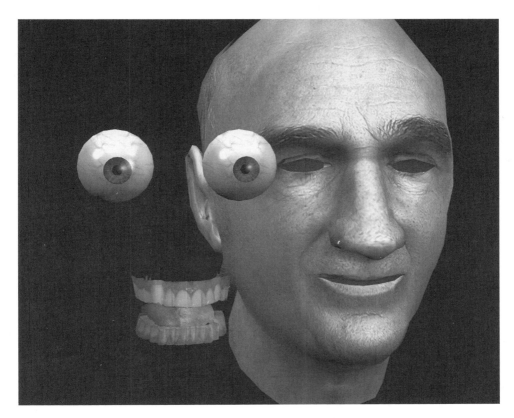

Figure 2.12.   Stelarc, *Prosthetic Head,* 2003. Courtesy of the artist.

its data base, becoming more autonomous in its responses. The artist would then no longer be able to take full responsibility for what his head says.[121]

In Stelarc's performances and installations it becomes very clear that the position of the uttering subject has complicated itself through a multiplication of positions. In his desire to merge with technology he expresses the collectivity of agents and subjectivities involved in hypermediated environments. Following the double logic of remediation, a multiplication of mediatized environments, especially *cyberspace*—as famously coined by William Gibson in *Neuromancer* (1984)—has turned individual or unique experience (symbolized through the importance of the chance factor), or the first-person view, into the utmost object of desire.[122] This is why in today's culture we are witnessing the excess of emphasized authorship and, at the same time, its very loss, with the stress on the notion of collective consciousness—from classic cyberpunk thrillers like *Strange Days* (1995), in which we are confronted with a memory-CD market of snuff films that can be viewed through a *head-wire* linked directly to the brain; to excess in use of the subjective camera from such *mocumentaries* as *The Blair Witch Project* (1999) and art films such as *Elephant* (2003); to the Super Bowl televised transmission, in which the technique of digitizing a scene and reproducing it seconds after from the players' (various and variously impossible) perspectives is used to increase the viewers' engagement in the logic of the game.

To return to the difference in 1960s wounds versus 1990s extensions performances, while Schwarzkogler staged the vulnerability of embodiment, Stelarc reflects on the vulnerability of disembodiment. The idea of the body, and the possibilities of collective-versus-displaced-versus-external agency is staged in these disembodied cyber-environments. These virtual environments can be seen as *spatializations* of the former wounds, signifiers of a time in which authorship and personal experience were performed to problematize agency, for example the problematization of male agency over the female body. The hypothesis that real bodies and their proof of authenticity in 1960s wounds have been replaced by a cyber-logic that is inspired by (while at the same time producing) a paradigm of space is also supported in Valie Export's view: "some video installations and techno-body performances of the seventies are the precursors of the cyperspace of the eighties and nineties."[123]

Export, in fact, compares the concept of agency in the era of 1960s wounds versus 1990s extensions with "images from the outside" versus "images from the inside."[124] The first ones come from the outside into the apparatus reproducing an external reality. Film and photography were the analog media that were typically used to represent this external reality. Similarly, in 1970 Vito Acconci talked about "showing himself outside" in the text accompanying his action *Trademarks* (1970), in which he repeatedly twisted his body and craned his neck to bite into his arms, legs, and shoulders. The "trademarks" of his teeth were then covered with printer's ink and used to stamp various surfaces, "producing signs of the body's attack on itself."[125] The rage against this externally mediated and fragmented image of oneself through the mirror could not have been expressed better than by Pane in her performance *Discours mou et mat* (1975), an action consisting of smashing mirrors and culminating with her making a small incision in her lower lip (similar to the above mentioned performance *Psyche*).

"Images from the inside" that are created in the performances of the 1990s extensions offer a different logic of agency. This is an agency that—as Amelia Jones pointed out—is loose and unstable; or in the words of Mark Poster, when the body is no longer the subject's limit "I cannot consider myself centered in my rational, autonomous subjectivity or bordered by a defined ego, but I am disrupted, subverted, and dispersed across social space."[126]

This new concept of subjectivity is intrinsically related to the logic of new media. Elizabeth Grosz posited in her analogy with the Möbius strip that subjectivity is not the combination of a psychical depth and a corporeal superficiality but a surface whose inscriptions and rotations in three-dimensional space produce all the effects of depth.[127] This description fits the realm of 1990s extensions in that the external twists itself toward the internal where it merges the two regimes together. As a result, the body starts to matter differently, as a whole and in its fragmentation as mediatic strata. The body, to put it in a different metaphorical context, becomes a "frame" or a "filter" to bring the fluctuating images from the inside to a halt, to give them support, or stop them from floating. Or as Mark Hansen has it: "Beneath any concrete 'technical' image or frame lies what I shall call *the framing function* of the human body qua center of indetermination."[128] The body, becomes the "frame" of the bodiless, unstable, decentered digital information. This is precisely where new media reveal themselves as facilitators of the reunion between holism and fragmentation, as discussed in chapter 1.

Throughout this chapter we see how the avant-garde of the early twentieth century made room for profound investigations of the body by means of such media-related tropes as simultaneity, multiplication, and acceleration. The avant-garde set the rhetorical stage for the body to claim in performance art, an art form that started with a male and overtly patriarchal discourse regime, but was soon displaced by the concerns around the female body, now staged in feminist performances. The history of performance art is unthinkable outside of the body's need for visuality and, hence, for representational media and their discourses. To return to the Bill Viola epigraph that started this chapter, the media, employed around questions of subjectivity, identity, and the body, function to support the artists' investigations and to provide both artists and the viewers with new insights.

However, something else helped immensely to reshape the body during twentieth-century body performances: the body started to collapse, to become part of the frame together with its environment. This collapse was symbolized in the bodily wounds of the 1960s, in which the body had become a modified ready-made. But the dissolution of materialities and environments and the collapsing into the inner world has produced (and was also produced by) something else: the digital image, or better, the logic of new media. The modules of new media have literally opened up the body, dematerializing its corporeal layers into fragments of information. A body-in-pieces that appears to be fully autonomous, having left behind its holistic body notion, has been born out of this new configuration, which is the content of study in the following chapter.

How Faces Have Become Obsolete

Man has, as it were, become a kind of prosthetic God. When he puts
on all his auxiliary organs he is truly magnificent; but those organs
have not grown on to him and they still give him much trouble at
times.[1]

—SIGMUND FREUD, *CIVILIZATION AND ITS DISCONTENTS*

Over the last two decades, the discourse around and about the body, as represented in popular science, in the arts, in theory and cultural studies, and even in
the realm of advertisement and fashion has gotten increasingly *under the skin.*[2]
The importance of outer appearances to the representation of the body has
receded as the inner body has come to be discovered, relevant, and ever more
present. Once the denizens of a dark continent of highly specialized medical
knowledge, organs, tissue, cells, and blood have recently come into circulation
as markers of individual and group identity. Moreover, since the 1990s the inner body has been recorded and "eternalized" through new technologies—such
as the Visible Human Project, the Human Genome Project, and the Anatomy
Art of Gunther von Hagens—that have indeed changed the knowledge of and
approaches toward the human body.

One of the important moves in this process of getting under the skin has been
the fragmentation of the body: the presentation of a body-in-pieces—as discussed in chapter 1's, "Historical Fragments of the Modern Body-in-Pieces." This
process, however, is not new, but has been burgeoning since early modernity
(that is, the sixteenth century), in other words, since the emergence of the new

insights and technologies concerned with viewing the body anatomically. In this chapter, I show how the discourse of a body-in-pieces has recently been overcome, or how the fragmented body—a result of a 1990s extended concept of (digital) corporealization—has become obsolete. Beyond even Gilles Deleuze and Félix Guattari's call for bodies without organs,[3] the body at the turn of the millennium has turned into an organ without a body, or into an organ instead of a body. In this synecdochic move the first, and probably most important, body part that has to be overcome is the face. The face, which has always "overcoded" other body parts, has now ceased to be the most representative signifier of human appearance; under the skin every organ has an (inter)face. Potentially, each organ may stand in for the whole body.

In recent examples of popular culture, from high fashion to cinema to even cosmetics advertisements, we can trace a movement that leaves behind the fragmentated body, which moves beyond the notion of a body-in-pieces. In this posthuman body, every part—interior and exterior—is autonomous, that is, separate from the body in its entirety. It is therefore no longer a body-in-pieces, but a "defaced" body: one that has lost the quality of faciality, hence, of over-coding, or standing in for the whole. The fragmented body already was eulo-gized by what Deleuze and Guattari called a "body without organ(ization)s," a plane of consistencies, a surface of inscription in which any body part pushes toward the surface, and becomes able to overcode the rest of the body.[4] But in the current discourse universe, even the body itself would no longer seem nec-essary; rather, what must be recognized is the insistence on "organs instead of bodies (OiB)," namely, organs that are configured as inside out, having lost their quality of being "in" the body. Of foremost concern for this chapter's analysis is that OiB is a "flattened" body[5] that has attained the value of a screen, a surface of reflection—in other words, a medium in itself.

Techniques of Fragmentation

As we see in chapter 1, bodily fragmentation in the cultural imagination is not new, but ever since the era of postmodernity it has been newly emphasized and has become emblematic of the order of new media, an order that follows the logic of pastiche and collage (for example, a "windowed" organization of knowl-edge). In the following, I look at specific techniques of fragmentation that are characteristic of our current imagination, and that open up a particular vision of the inner body and its control.

For my purposes, both the Visible Human Project and the Human Genome Project, commissioned by the U.S. National Institutes of Health, constitute such revolutionary fragmentation techniques. In addition, the new technique of plastination developed by the German anatomist Gunther von Hagens has produced the exhibit Body Worlds ("*Körperwelten*") touring the world as Anatomy Art since 1995.[6]

The Visible Human Project was inaugurated in 1993 when researchers successfully scanned—digitally recorded—the dead body (interior and exterior) of Joseph Paul Jernigan, a Texan on death row since 1981. In 1995, Jernigan was given a female counterpart, the digitized anatomical data of a 59-year-old unnamed housewife from Maryland, who was—as several commentators have pointed out—past her reproductive years: "The Visible Man consists of 24-bit digitized computer tomography, magnetic resonance, and photographic images of over 1,800 one-millimeter cross-sectional slices of a male corpse, and the Visible Woman is composed of 5,000 images of .3-millimeter slices of a female corpse."[7] As Lisa Cartwright suggests, the "Visible Couple" serves a familiarizing normative function by juxtaposing the Visible Man and Woman as a "digital Adam and Eve."[8] The data from the sliced digital couple was made available to the medical public throughout the 1990s. In 2003, Insight Toolkit was developed as open-source software for individual segmentation and registration of the Visible Human data.[9]

The Human Genome Project, in contrast, does not give us such a visualized insight into the human body by collecting information and data; it rewrites the human body by mapping the genetic code in what was called the "Book of Man."[10] This human database contains a sequence map of three billion base pairs and between fifty and one hundred thousand genes.[11] The two human projects both understand the body as a network of informational systems made of codes producing signals, which are themselves transcribed into certain body functions. There can be interferences or noise causing miscommunication and, as a result, imperfections. Posthuman medicine in the postbiological era of computation seeks precisely to study such noise and imperfections for the purpose of retracing the "perfect and infallible human." This model of humanity resembles the communication model of the 1940s in which information is evaluated as unrelated to its context and is therefore *bodyless.*[12] Similarly, in these posthuman visions of humankind, the human is not a socially embedded subject but driven organic matter. The body is understood as an archive, an organic form of storage and replication, a "data ghost," as criticized by Catherine Waldby:

While the HGP tries to map the microstructure of the human species, the genetic instructions that are generally understood to tutor the unfolding of the body's morphology, the VHP maps the morphology itself, the gross anatomy of the male and female human body rendered as a database. Hence in both these Human Projects, the limits of the human as species is set out as a large yet finite information database, a spatial graphic ordering which acts as a digital archive, retrievable through computer networks and readable workstations.[13]

What is more, the real problematic novelty inherent to the Visible Human Project, for Waldby, is that it no longer produces an "image of a body," but instead "a workable relationship between human body and computer."[14] The digitally visualized data from the Visible Human Project create a homogenous interior bodily space—a utopian space that ignores the heterotopias of the anatomical body by simplifying the restricted point of view that its precursor the endoscope could provide.[15] Through such new procedures as virtual endoscopy,[16] the Visible Human Project constructs a bodily interior from utopian viewpoints, views that do not correspond to any human reality precisely because they can be obtained only through a computerized vision of the body.

Von Hagens developed a procedure of plastination at the University of Heidelberg in 1977. Just as in the Visible Human Project, it has been claimed that the drive for realism has taken precedence over the treatment of real corpses; so too has Body Worlds been said to exhibit an increasing "realness" and "authenticity" of body images.[17] The real corpses, which have been deep frozen in acetone, are sliced and impregnated with silicon rubber to be preserved eternally for public display. As a result, we can see nerves precisely delineated, organs in athletic postures, or bodies posed as thinking chess players. In von Hagens's body processing, each body part, each organ, deserves special attention and can be looked at as a fragment. The exhibit catalogue and flyers feature a plastinated body with a *skin-coat*. The triumphant flayed man serves as a logo for von Hagens's "Anatomy Art," (figure 3.1) the official English title of the show, and seems to be saying: *Look what I have under my skin!*

In the exhibition video, von Hagens and one of his colleagues explain that they want to explore and make accessible the internal configuration of the body, the motor system, the nervous system, and the organs in order for a vast public to "better understand the human body;" this knowledge should not be reserved just for anatomy students, but for whoever is interested in the human body "as our very own nature."[18]

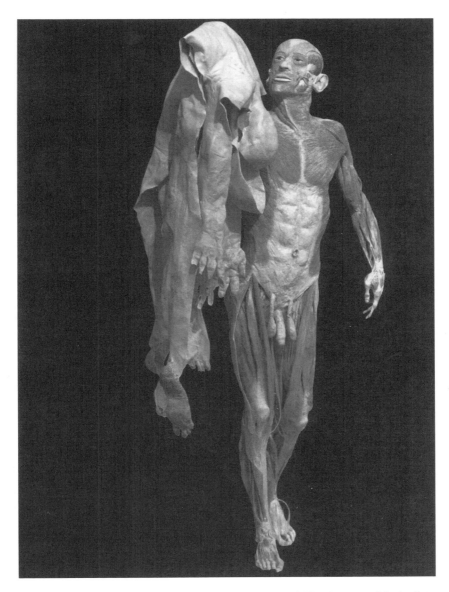

Figure 3.1. Gunther von Hagens, *Whole Body Plastinate with Skin*. Courtesy of the Institute for Plastination, Heidelberg, Germany; www.bodyworlds.com.

How Faces Have Become Obsolete

As with the Visible Human Project, the body is presented in the exhibit as a natural miracle, a technology made by nature. Anatomy Art places stress on the fascination of the mysterious inner body: "What is concealed beneath the skin which protects and covers our body?" asks one of its guiding questions.[19] Von Hagens wants to see his own work and the Body Worlds exhibit in the tradition of the "art of anatomy," that is, of craftsmanship such as that introduced by Vesalius and Leonardo da Vinci. Similarly, the Visible Human Project has been presented in different exhibits around the world, much along the lines of a continuous tradition of Anatomy Art. In an art gallery in Japan, for instance, the images were juxtaposed with da Vinci's anatomy drawings—just as von Hagens himself had suggested.[20]

However, an aesthetic interest in the body's interior universe has been revealed in recent popular culture not only by von Hagens's controversial exhibition, but in a number of popular publications on medical imaging technology. Writer Dan Nadel and artist Jonathon Rosen, for instance, praise the beauty of scanning, MRI, and CT technology in a 2004 issue of *I.D.* magazine. Their description, however, goes beyond a simple depiction of the technical scanning procedure. The conceptual illustration *Through a scanner, darkly* created by Rosen (figure 3.2) combines his drawings, paintings, sculptures, found objects, digital-compositing, and photography. The image reveals an attractive woman's exterior, her back, but what strikes us most is the aestheticized interior—construed by a gaze that literally has gone under the model's skin; what is more, the model actually is wearing her skeleton as a prosthesis that has not only merged with her flesh, but that she also wears like a fashion statement. In this image we see how current medical imaging technology has influenced and constructed a split gaze, one that on one hand is still directed at appearance, remaining on the surface of medical representation (to which of course belongs the beauty of the woman in question); on the other hand, however, this is a techno-gaze capable of screening the body's interior and revealing its skeletal structure. The skin is no longer represented as an outside border to this body; if anything, the skin belongs to the body's interior sphere, and it is the skeleton, the whitened bone-structure, that faces the outside world.[21]

What becomes clear in these examples of recent imaging technologies of the human body, and especially its interior, is not only the aestheticization and sexualization of the exposed body (be it a sickly or a healthy body), but the immense control factor inherent to such a screening of the body. Control also is deployed by medical technology via the dissecting gaze—a gaze that no longer differentiates between inside or outside, organ or nerve cell.

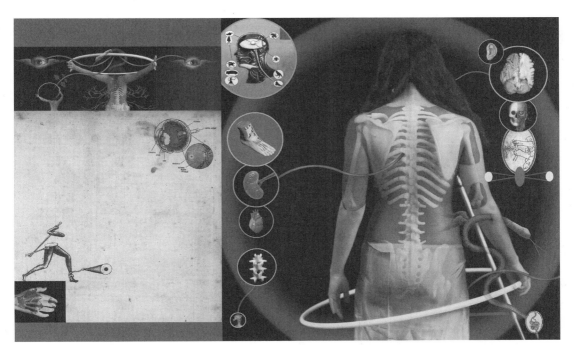

Figure 3.2. Jonathon Rosen, *Through a scanner, darkly: imaging the body.* Courtesy of the artist.

Indeed, in the discourse regime of getting under the skin, *any* body part, big or small, interior or exterior, can attain dominance over the rest of the body with fluidity characteristic of the synecdoche. How this stylistic trope is currently flourishing more than ever is best shown in advertisements featuring body parts that have replaced the body. But unlike the rhetoric of synecdoche typical of early modernity, in which the part stood in for the entirety of the unified body, current body language has rid itself of the unified-body concept, presenting body *parts* as independent, self-sufficient biotopes.

The Austrian health insurance company Merkur, for instance, advertises the high value of insurance with the image of a single female breast (figure 3.3). In the image, a child's hand is holding the breast's nipple as if it were a button of an extremely sensitive machine. The association here is that the nipple is the first object with which the child develops its motor skills. The text reads: "We insure highly active minirobots with well developed fine motor activity in all deliverable sizes." Another example of a biologistic discourse stressing nature's perfect *design* of the body, the advertisement draws a direct analogy between a

Wir versichern neugierige
Miniroboter, die mit
hochentwickelten Sensoren
die Welt begreifen.

WIR VERSICHERN DAS
WUNDER MENSCH

MERKUR
DIE GESUNDHEITS-VERSICHERUNG

Figure 3.3. Merkur advertisement, 2001.

child and a minirobot. This breast and, in the reference to the fine motor development of the child's hand, even the nipple have taken over the body as a signifier for fertility, nurturing, reliability, and, only in the very end, sexuality. I do
not have to emphasize the political incorrectness of this Austrian advertisement.
What is important is that this is a body devolving into parts—not just the lost
parts of a once perfect or ideal whole body in the Galenic sense, but, on the contrary, parts that are autonomous in themselves. These body parts have never
been thought of as a whole.

Sexual organs, such as the breast in the Merkur advertisement, are not surprisingly one of the most visible examples of this rhetorical coup. In a cover
story in the popular Italian magazine *Focus,* female sexuality is explained as a
function of the "change of inner organs at the moments of pleasure," namely at
the "orgasmic point G," the much discussed "G-spot."[22] Beneath the headline
we see a scheme showing how the female and male genitals are anatomically of
common origin. What this and many other stories of the kind indicate is how

the rise of body parts is above all a sociopolitical phenomenon: (sexual) organs are depicted as responsible for certain feelings, and, as a consequence, femininity and masculinity are explained in purely anatomical terms. This is one of many examples of how popular science recently found its way into a biologistic-discourse universe. This revolution, as we know, has to do with the remarkable changes in biomedical technology that we have been witnessing since the latter half of the twentieth century—changes that have opened up new possibilities of penetrating, viewing, and controlling bodies, and have, as a result, exponentially intensified debates about what it means to be human and, especially, what it means to have a (gendered) body. The accumulation of knowledge around and about the body and progress in biomedical technologies have led, however, to the paradox that this accumulation has not made things easier and clearer, but rather the opposite: it has differentiated views and produced an almost inconceivable number of standpoints.

De-facement

I take the face to be the figure of appearance, the appearance of appearance, the figure of figuration, the ur-appearance, if you will, of secrecy itself as the primordial act of presencing. For the face itself is a contingency, at the magical crossroads of mask and window to the soul, one of the better-kept public secrets essential to everyday life. How could this be, this contradiction to end contradiction, crisscrossing itself in endless crossings of the face? And could de-facement itself escape this endless back-and-forth of revelation and concealment?[23]
—MICHAEL TAUSSIG, *DEFACEMENT: PUBLIC SECRECY AND THE LABOR OF THE NEGATIVE*

That the human face is the "screen" of the body, the place of encounter between individuals, has been theorized and poeticized in many ways. The philosopher Emmanuel Lévinas, for example, theorized the encounter between human beings as taking place with the acceptance of the face and the gaze of the other. The human face is to be understood here as the absolute breakthrough between individuals, and it is at this point, too, that ethics is installed: "It is my responsibility before a face looking at me as absolutely foreign (and the epiphany of the face coincides with these two moments) that constitutes the original fact of fraternity."[24] The very opacity of the face constitutes for Lévinas a window onto the other. Everything else can lie, but the face cannot. Individuals, when they encounter each other, cannot but react to that. The face in this phenomenology is the only "naked truth" situated not on a referential metalevel, but on the very ground of existence: "The face has turned to me—and this is its very nudity. It is by itself and not by reference to a system."[25]

To give another example of how the face matters in critical theory, film theory, particularly screen or apparatus theory, takes the instance of the facial close-up as the moment of utmost identification for the viewer, that is, the moment when the film protagonist "convinces" the viewer of his or her presence within the medium. The 1920s French film theorist Jean Epstein theorized the filmic power upon the spectator of what he called *photogénie,* a force present in the relationship between the apparatus, the spectator, and the external world.[26] In this phenomenological approach to the new medium of film, Epstein also reflected on the impact of proximity via the rhetorical trope of the (facial) close-up, especially in slow motion:

I know of nothing more utterly moving than a face giving birth to an expression in slow motion. A whole preparation comes first, a slow fever, which it is difficult to know whether to compare to the incubation of a disease, a gradual ripening, or more coarsely, a pregnancy. Finally all this effort boils over, shattering the rigidity of a muscle. A contagion of movements animates the face. The eyelash wing, the jaw a spur, begin to stir too. And when the lips finally part to herald the cry, we have attended the whole of its long and magnificent dawning.[27]

Similarly to Lévinas's phenomenology of the face, what counts here is that with the appearance of the face on the screen an authenticity is reached, a point at which one almost can feel pain. Later in the twentieth century, psychoanalytical aspects of the spectator-to-screen relationship become more relevant for apparatus theory. Freud's theory of the scopic drive (scopophilia) and Lacan's mirror stage (see chapter 1) become the psychoanalytical background for apparatus theory throughout the 1960s and 1970s.[28] Two moments are relevant here. First, the establishment of the spectator as a subject and beholder of the gaze, as in the mirror stage, and second, the desire or pleasure of looking, as in the scopic drive.

If it is through (the recognition of) faces that human beings encounter each other, then we can say that the skin surfacing the face plays a very special role in this interaction. We "see" the people behind faces. We address people by *facing* them. This is also why the facial skin has been interpreted all along as a mirror to the soul. It reflects the state of the mind, the degree of a person's well-being behind a face. Yet, in a time of such cosmetic drugs as Botox, which has been in use since 1991 (originally only to treat spasmic disorders), faces smoothed of wrinkles are losing their ability to express worry lines: the surface of the face is made into a mask, behind which we no longer can decipher the person.

This idea of faces is nothing new; what is new is how *perfect skin* and *perfect faces* have been defined differently over time. In her *Body Project* Joan Jacobs Brumberg analyzes how American girls have lived (with) their skins over the last hundred years. In the nineteenth century, girls may have thought of their faces as "windows to the soul."[29] But by analyzing yearbook pictures from the early sixties to the present, Brumberg shows how the focus on faciality has gradually diminished. The face as the window to the soul, (as in classical portraits) has been increasingly replaced with the image of the whole body, and especially with bodies involved in some kind of activity, such as sports. Today, the focus in yearbook pictures is no longer on faces, but on healthy and strong looking body parts such as arms and legs. Once again, any body part can now gain the status once exclusively enjoyed by a face as a window to the soul. It is not necessarily behind faces that we expect the person to be revealed. Faces are becoming obsolete.

"Words usually reserved for your face are now possible all over your body," reads an advertisement for the body wash Oil of Olay (figure 3.4). What we see in the advertisement is not a beautiful woman with a beautiful face, but an "even-toned" body with a "smooth texture" that is supposed to look "radiant and resilient." These new characteristics are shown in a healthy looking body (mostly legs and arms), indicating a fit body. Similarly, although applying a different rhetorical trope, Lancôme uses a close-up image of a detached part of skin, shaped as an organic leaf, in the recent "Re-Surface" anti-wrinkle campaign. Nevertheless, not all beauty product advertisements have left out the face in their recent campaigns. For its latest product, "Draine'Up Lifteur," Biotherm uses a female face in profile (figure 3.5). What we can see behind her, as if there is some sort of integral link between inside and outside appearances, is a microscopic representation of what the product does when it gets under the skin.

Interior and exterior merge into each other through a red line that comes out of the microscopic image and spreads over the "real" face. This line symbolizes how cosmetic companies have started to compete with cosmetic surgery: the red line in the picture corresponds exactly with the line along which the first surgical cut would take place for a face-lift operation.[30] Beauty discourse has

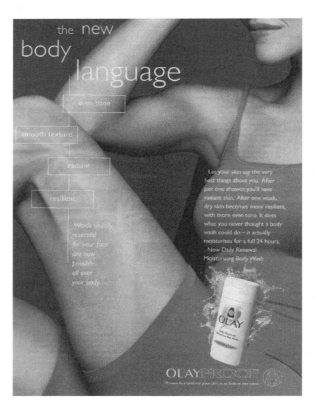

Figure 3.4. Oil of Olay advertisement, 2002.

penetrated the inner body, where our real capital is hidden: our organs, our blood, our DNA.

A more recent example of the competitive discourse between dermatological cosmetic products and cosmetic surgery is the line of night treatment products by Lancôme, "Absolue Night" (figure 3.6). The advertisement for this product has literally gotten under the skin of a blue rose, which is visually split in half. The image on the left side clearly is intended to evoke a computer graphic morphing program using fractals, like the finite-element model used in a surgical reconstruction program.[31] It shows us the highly complex, but yet penetrable (by computer technology) and imitable structure of the archetypal symbol of beauty: a rose. The part of the image on the right side represents the outer skin of the rose. By proximity to the discourse universe of the (aging) skin,

Figure 3.5. Biotherm "Draine'Up Lifteur" advertisement, 2001.

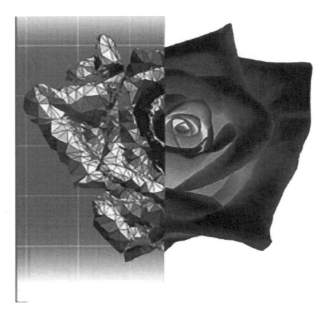

Figure 3.6. Lancôme "Absolue Night" advertisement, 2004.

the rose stands for the "miracle made by nature," one of the key rhetorical figures of this discourse regime. The color blue is an association with the night treatment, while resonating with the implied word "absolute." The entire image with the visualizations of both the inner and outer aspects of a rose evokes technological progress, control over beauty, and, at the same time, sublime beauty "made by nature."

But what does it mean that in the era of posthumanity the face has been "lost," that it has ceased to be a sur-face? To reformulate, what my study shows is not only the loss of the face over the rest of the body, but how the priority of the face—in other words, faciality—has moved *into* the body to organs, DNA, and other important hidden information concerning the "Book of Man." In short, any body part has the potential to become this special window to the soul. That is why in current advertisements for beauty products we see legs, arms, or whole bodies in action, and almost no classic portraits of faces. The face can now "hide" inside the body, as in the Anatomy Art by von Hagens, where the spectator finds no shortage of "smiling" organs, nerves, and tissue.

According to Deleuze and Guattari, the rhetoric of faciality is that of a "decoded body." In order to become a "face," one body part has to overcode the rest of the body: "[for] the face is produced only when the head ceases to be a part of the body, when it ceases to be coded by the body, when it ceases to have a multi-dimensional, polyvocal corporeal code—when the body, head included, has been decoded and has to be overcoded by something we shall call Face."[32] Faciality, therefore, may no longer be seen as the a priori of the human encounter, as in Lévinas's philosophy; indeed, it is precisely this impulse to attribute primordial communication to faciality that Deleuze and Guattari are criticizing. Through their ironic notion of the "year zero," in which faciality is established, they insist on the "coded nature of the face." In other words, the body fragment of the face is produced because all other body parts have been (violently) overcoded.[33]

In this postfacial era, the face proves to be a code precisely by the fact that its role can be taken over by any other body part. To this end, the head and the face have lost their position of prominence. For example, note the software advertisement for Vignette (figure 3.7) in which we are witness to a head with a switch on it: the head or brain becomes merely an accessory body part that can be switched on and off like a computer. In a way that corresponds exactly to this image, the body is described as the "brain's best interface to the outside world," and the whole organism as a "brain-body-machine."[34]

Similarly, the German clothing line Oui makes the head of a woman into a "favorite fashion accessory," as the model's words—the ad's text—informs us (figure 3.8).

These are postfacial expressions because they represent heads with faces as body parts to be turned on, or chosen as, an accessory, something extra added to one's body.

What has become clear in these recent images of the body is that faciality is a code, hence a construct or convention reflecting how we are accustomed to seeing and interpreting human bodies. This way of seeing determines how we think about faciality; equally, how we think about faciality is expressed through these ways of seeing. It would appear, then, that the code of faciality has started to migrate into the spheres of the bodily interior. As a result, the "miraculous universe of the body," as von Hagens puts it, must indeed be redefined. This circumstance could not have been foreseen any better than by Foucault who—in the 1960s—predicted the "end of man" through the trope of the loss of the face:

As the archeology of thought easily shows, man is an invention of recent date. And one perhaps nearing its end. If those arrangements were to disappear as they appeared, if some event of which we can at the moment do no more than sense the possibility—without

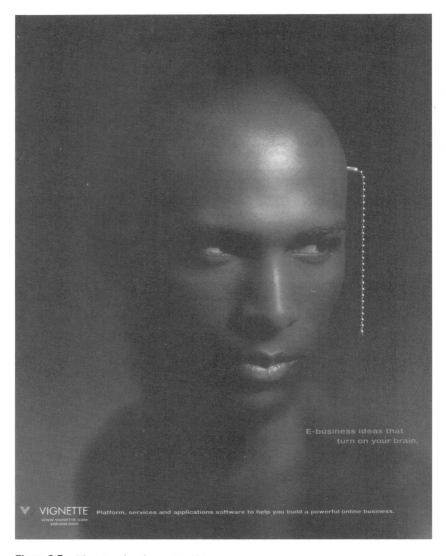

Figure 3.7. Vignette advertisement, 2001.

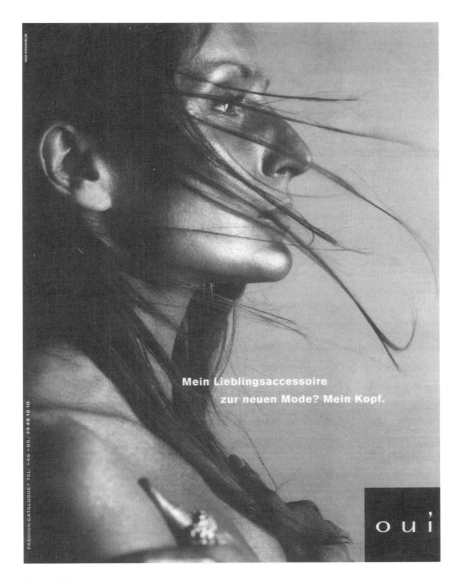

Figure 3.8. Oui advertisement, 2001.

knowing either what its form will be or what it promises—were to cause them to crumble, as the ground of Classical thought did, at the end of the eighteenth century, then one can certainly wager that man would be erased, like a face drawn in the sand at the edge of the sea.[35]

The erasure of the epistemic configuration of humans, then, the various possibilities of their replacement (by cyborgs, animals, cells, women, nothing) is compared with the picture of a face drawn in the sand. It is only fitting that this disappearance be portrayed as due to the irresistible force of the sea—a sea change in the way the body is coded—washing away the contours of the face. We might be able to hypothesize, then, that the erasure of the face could be seen as a precursor of an erasure that affects human corporeality as such. Indeed, by navigating interior corporeal spaces, similarities between humans, animals, and machines become much clearer and no longer are "disturbed" by the codes of visibility. For that matter, we are becoming more and more aware of being akin with animals in terms of our genetic coding. This kind of a redefinition of similarities, and as a result, of categories that define humanness from animalness, or humans from machines, can be understood culturally through a rhetoric of *getting under the skin* that is getting rid of faces and other such overcoded markers of humanness.

In regard to the notion of de-facement it is important to include Donna Haraway's recent work on the "companion species," which she describes as a continuation and enhancement of her "Cyborg Manifesto" from the 1980s: "Telling a story of co-habitation, co-evolution, and embodied cross-species sociality, the present manifesto asks which of two cobbled together figures—cyborgs and companion species—might more fruitfully inform livable politics and ontologies in current life worlds."[36] In her usual breakdown of species and other ontological borders, Haraway makes another kinship claim—this time one that approaches dog and man in their evolutionary history.[37] What is of relevance to my argument is the fact that it is not only through technology, that is, questions around the posthuman and postvital living[38] that the boundaries of the human body have been broken open, but that we are already well under the experience of these consequences from a crossover between the machinic and the human. What is more, these boundaries are being questioned in recent evolutionary studies, such as Haraway's, in which the multidirectional gene flow between animals and machines are being reevaluated.[39]

Sur-face

Surface is no longer superficial; nor is it profound. In simcult [the culture of simulation] the very opposition between depth and surface must be refigured. The approach of the surface, which has been a long time coming, has not yet fully reached arrival. The erasure of depths is the inverse image of the disappearance of transcendence.[40]
—MARC C. TAYLOR AND ESA SAARINEN, *IMAGOLOGIES: MEDIA PHILOSOPHY*

If any body part can become a face, any such part must be able to create its own (textual) sur-face. But this is not a surface that is spatially organized so as to cover a deep content; rather, it represents the implosion between inside and outside, a relation between outside and inside that exists intensely, to return to Dagognet.[41] To make this point even clearer, the interior bodily universe is extending and urging toward the outside, creating its own inter- or sur-face in the form of a skin.[42] This skin can now cover anything of importance, any significant content that is hidden under the sur-face. As a result, we can see how the representation of the skin has increasingly gained presence in recent advertisements, such as the 2002 Swatch campaign, the "Skin Swatch" (figure 3.9).

According to the ad, the Skin Swatch's model is paved in gold, and the Swatch features the same surface texture as the woman's golden face, particularly the area around the eye, which is close to the Swatch itself. The Swatch's flesh has merged with the woman's; they are sharing a similar sur-face. On the Skin Swatch website[43] we can see other watch and women models, all showing a parallelism between some facial traits, or specific facial parts such as eyes and hair, with the form or color of the watch.

The skin, or epidermis, is the organ that first needs to be penetrated to get into the body; it is the organ that sur-faces the body and, just as in a synecdochic trope, it constitutes the entrance to the inner body universe. But, as discussed in the psychoanalytical reading of the skin, the skin no longer is a border between the outer and the inner body. Rather, according to Grosz's figure of the Möbius strip, the surface of the skin is both endogenous and exogenous.

At this point, it is worth returning to the history of the skin detailed in chapter 1. Benthien shows in her analysis of the skin in various cultural domains, from language and literature to visualizations of the skin, that we are reviving the "perceptual aesthetic theory of the eighteenth-century sensualists—what is

Figure 3.9. "Skin Swatch" advertisement, 2002.

seen or heard can be an illusion, while things explored by touch prove to be compellingly real."[44] In other words, the proprioceptive perception of touch that historically precluded a collective experience has been rediscovered at the turn of the millennium through such *teletactile* new media practices as virtual reality. Thus, while the twentieth century can be called a visual century, the new millennium reveals itself as favoring the haptic over the visual.[45]

Due to the revival of the notion of touch at the end of the twentieth century, the entire world appears as an extension of the skin and no longer an extension of the image.[46] We are surrounded by images of skin in different close-ups— from popular scientific investigations of the usefulness of certain chromosomes (for example, Area 22 chromosome in *Wired Magazine,* August 2000), to Nokia convertible cellular phone skins, to high fashion images as in the Gucci watch ad featuring an almost alienatingly extreme skin close-up of a white wrist against the backdrop of black skin (figure 3.10). This is not only a United-Colors-of-Benetton message; it is a message about the fusion of skins of different colors.

We can see the theme of the skin being increasingly addressed in the figurative arts. Female sur-faces and skins have been especially represented in artistic projects, critiquing the way that the female skin is penetrated not only by the (male) gaze, but also through cosmetic surgery, beauty products, clothing, and the like. Many U.S.-based artists could be mentioned in this regard. Kiki Smith, for instance, focuses on the human body and its internal configurations in her various body sculptures and installations. In the following, I discuss two European body artists: Maya Rikli and Alba d'Urbano.

In her earlier work, the Swiss artist Maya Rikli presents a skin-bust or body in her collage *O.T. {untitled}, 1992* (figure 3.11). This collage represents a fragmented body: its surface has been "cut out" in the shape of a bust, but the bodily interior shimmers through, revealing body features such as the curvature of the belly and the size of the breasts. This is a body fragment presented as a detached surface texture, a skin-bust that looks like it could be worn.

In other pieces, Rikli has been working with various skin(like) objects (for example, fragments of baby bodies), creating images of femininity with bodies that are assembled by cuts.[47]

The Italian artist Alba d'Urbano works on the theme of the skin within the digital realm. She experiments with images of her own skin (figure 3.12), which she digitizes, processes, reshapes, and cuts into the pattern of a "skin-suit." In her project *Hautnah* (1995), d'Urbano "takes off her own skin" in order to offer

How Faces Have Become Obsolete

Figure 3.10. Gucci advertisement, 2001.

Figure 3.11. Maya Rikli, *O. T. [untitled],* 1992. Soap on nettle and painters' filling, 140 × 90 × 14 cm. Courtesy of the artist.

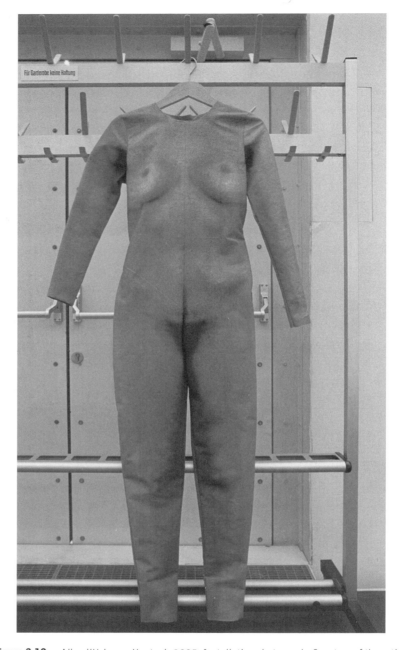

Figure 3.12. Alba d'Urbano, *Hautnah,* 1995. Installation photograph. Courtesy of the artist.

others the possibility of "walking through the world hidden 'under the skin' of the artist."[48] *Hautnah* makes concrete the examination of the body as naked other, as confrontation between inner consciousness and outer reality, bound with the idea of abandoning one's own skin or of entering somebody else's skin. As Benthien points out in her history of the skin, the concept of nakedness is relatively young, as it could only arise with the idea of the skin as a (natural) border between individuals. In *Hautnah* (German for "close as skin," but also idiomatic for "immediate" or "very close"), d'Urbano criticizes this notion of the autonomous modern "self that leads to the discovery of the tragedy of isolation and disconnectedness from the world."[49]

In this critique of the skin as sur-face, and as bodily exterior versus interior, the artist ironically hangs her skin-suit on a coat hanger.[50] Significantly, the skin-suit—made of material printed with images of the naked skin of the artist's body—has neither hands, feet, nor face. These "interactive body parts," as the artist calls them, have been cut off. Of special interest in this context of the fragmented-body concept is that the artist has us look at a faceless, handless, and footless entity, which is nevertheless clearly a body. In other words, the body no longer needs the connecting parts that stand in as sur-faces for the entire body to be featured as whole. We may thus read the absent interactivity represented here not only as a feminist critique of a male-dominated gaze that has literally torn a female body into pieces, but also precisely as the wish to dissociate from the body, as well as from the search for a subjectivity or originality of the body tout court. The sentence "Für Garderobe keine Haftung" (not responsible for items left in coat check) can, hence, be read as *This skin-suit really belongs to nobody. We are not responsible for it. You may hang it here, but you may not find it again upon your return.* *Hautnah* makes clear what Amelia Jones states for 1990s body practice in general: "a return to a notion of embodied subject as necessarily particularized . . . (in its) relation to other subjects in the social arena."[51]

In her study of body images, Weiss reminded us that *inscription* does not occur without the subject's intercorporeal relationship with other human or nonhuman bodies. In *Hautnah* d'Urbano challenges this notion, presenting a body-in-pieces that is beyond inscription as such. It hangs all alone in a wardrobe that no one even wants to take responsibility for. It has been left alone, with no claim of a subject's "belonging" other than the artist's, whose nonsignature stands underneath it. The only inscriptions the skin-suit *Hautnah* features are the sexual body parts of a woman, her breasts and her vaginal hair. We may now read this as we wish: are these the material parts that cannot be gotten rid of? Maybe.

What matters for my own concern is, however, that the genitals are part of the skin-suit. They belong to the realm of appearance.

In our cultural imagination the representation of a skin that is not part of a specific body has become normal. A generation that has seen killers sewing female body suits out of their victims' skin (for example, *Silence of the Lambs,* 1991) is no longer alienated by skins that can be worn like pieces of clothes. In other words, we have started to adopt a new notion of the skin, one that is separated from its natural body-environment, that is, from its function of *surfacing* a body.

The fragmented skin as a metaphor for an organic exterior, capable of adapting itself to its natural (or even computerized) context, also has become an important issue in architecture; more about this will appear in chapter 4's special focus on new media art and architecture. The New York–based architects Elizabeth Diller and Ricardo Scofidio have, since the early 1990s, proposed a Flesh-Architecture.[52] Their interest lies exactly in the border zone of the flesh, "the outermost surface of the 'body' bordering all relations in 'space.'"[53] Diller + Scofidio express a zeitgeist that corresponds not only to the architectural climate of deconstructivist architecture (for example, Peter Eisenman and Frank Gehry), but to a general artistic movement of surpassing the antonymic relation between interiority and exteriority.[54] Philosophically, this collapse between inside and outside results from a rethinking of the exterior not as "eternally counterposed to an interiority," but rather as the "transmutability of the inside," as suggested by Grosz in the spirit of Deleuze's poststructuralist thought.[55]

In introducing Diller + Scofidio's architecture, Georges Teyssot connects architects and artists who have emphasized the flesh, or its exteriority, since the seventies: "Art and architecture no longer refer to underlying principles like harmony, balance, proportion (classicism), or cohesion, order, tension (modernism). Art activity now addresses the pure exteriority of meaning. Such exteriorizing tactics are at work in a whole series of experiments by artists such as Gordon Matta-Clark (*Split House,* 1973), Vito Acconci (*The Board Room,* also titled *Where We Are Now {Who Are We Anyway},* 1976), Dan Graham (Mirror Window Corner Piece, 1974–76), . . . and D and S (the *withDrawing Room,* 1986)."[56] Diller + Scofidio's *withDrawing Room* (figure 3.13) was an installation in San Francisco in collaboration with the sculptor David Ireland. The theme of the installation was the transformation of a century-old San Francisco frame house into a studio and gallery. A chair, which is attached to the dining table by hinges, hangs rotating from the ceiling at the distance diners should be seated from each other, as dictated by the famous etiquette guide author, Emily Post.[57]

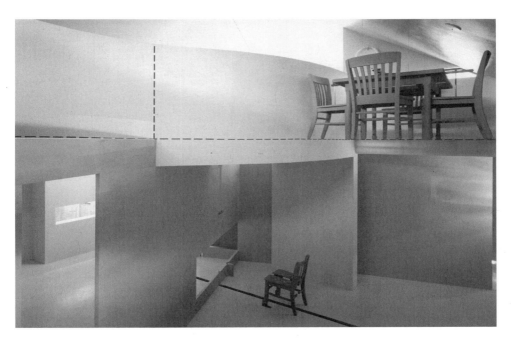

Figure 3.13. Diller + Scofidio, *withDrawing Room,* 1986. Courtesy of the architects.

In this ironic installation, Diller + Scofidio are questioning the architectural concepts of interiority and exteriority, proposing open folds and hanging furniture in a logic that deconstructs several of the home's organizational strategies: rules of etiquette, seating arrangements, vulnerable surfaces, and inside and outside boundaries or protections. The *withDrawing Room* thus becomes an experimental space of reflection on the conventions of sociability within interior spaces by adding to it through the proposition of sociability, and at the same time referring to its original meaning. Diller + Scofidio play with the essential undecidability of the internal space of public representation in the familial sphere, the private place to which visitors—although outsiders—are nevertheless permitted to adjourn; by constantly withdrawing to the drawing room, the outside ceaselessly contaminates any stable sense of privacy or intimacy, and subsequently there is no point at which one is entirely, or permanently, withdrawn.[58]

In a similar vein, the media artists Aziz + Cucher question the meaning of interiority. Aziz + Cucher have presented computerized environments called *Interiors* (1999–2002), in which they reconstruct the texture and general appearance of the skin (figure 3.14).

How Faces Have Become Obsolete

Figure 3.14. Aziz + Cucher, *Interior Study #3,* 2000. Color photograph. Courtesy of the artists.

In these digital environments, the organic is merged with the inorganic, as Frazer Ward explains:

The seamlessness with which the skin becomes wall becomes representation may be new, so that the technology may be said to enable a different-than-before form of visual metaphor. Aziz + Cucher's photographs, however, are metaphors for the abandon and terror of the collapse of distinctions between human and non-human, the attraction and repulsion of the dissolution of limits.[59]

In Aziz + Cucher's "images from the inside" it becomes clear that the desire for the organic, the natural, and the perfect skin "made by nature" is on one hand reconstructed artificially, but on the other hand the digital technology involved tries to convince us of the *naturality* of the environment, attempting to erase its very traces. This "new interior tactility" follows Bolter and Grusin's "double logic of remediation" as discussed earlier in chapter 2. Aziz + Cucher show us digital interiors that actually are represented by external material, the human skin. Here the journey into the body is not about the discovery of the organs, the hidden capital, as in von Hagens's attempts. What Aziz + Cucher aim at is an exterior that achieves the value of the interior, as stated by Teyssot. The skin—despite its exteriority—has thus become an interior, or, its exteriority has merged into its interiority.

This move has been described by Mark Hansen as a part of a "larger shift currently underway in our incipient digital culture: from the preformed technical image to the embodied process of framing information that *produces* images."[60] If we follow Hansen's argument, this shift has major consequences: the very purpose or function of the digital image no longer can be regarded in terms of its represented content. Rather, this is a shift that has produced a new artifact, the "digital-facial-image," as Hansen calls it,[61] which, in turn, through the new aesthetic of images getting under the skin, has produced a new epistemology. As discussed in chapter 1, this is an epistemology that is in desperate need of the body, and the consideration of processing information through and with the body. The body in other words, adopts the function of the mirror: since there is no exterior to the digital environment—because it is always an "inside" within a set frame—it is only through the body that the digital image can function and fully adopt its purpose of affection.[62]

Synthetic Flesh

The play with reality and virtuality, the deconstruction of the concepts of interiority and exteriority, as presented in the works of Diller + Scofidio and Aziz + Cucher, exhumes the old question concerning the possibilities of the fusion of human and artificial flesh. This desire to blur the realms of the virtual with the real has led some to get involved with their own skin.

In 1998, Kevin Warwick, a British professor of cybernetics, had a silicon chip transponder surgically implanted in his left arm. Warwick has a computer-controlled transponder in his body to pick up signals from his nervous system and transmit them to a computer. In his book *I, Cyborg* (2002), Warwick asks the question of whether we can use technology to "upgrade" humans.[63] Similarly, the Canadian Steve Mann has been building wearable computers since the late 1970s. In his *Cyborg* (2002), Mann reflects that he has literally "become computer, camera, telephone, videophone, and, of course, myself—all in a single entity."[64] In addition to demonstrating a technologically enhanced or synthetic body, Mann's cyber-performances carry a political message. "Sousveillance" is what Mann coins his constant recordings of his environment, a reaction against surveillance practices: "We [cyborgs] try to bring the camera down to eye level, away from a God's-eye view."[65]

Orlan, whose performances are a subject of the feminist art critique in chapter 2, has a political agenda in her body installations, too. Surveillances of the female body are under investigation and critique in Orlan's psychoanalytic interpretation of the skin as a platform between the visual (image) of the self and the experience of the body. In *Successful Operation Nr. X,* Orlan talks about the deceptiveness of the skin while she underwent cosmetic surgery, quoting the Lacanian psychoanalytical theory of Eugénie Lemoine-Luccioni: "The skin is deceptive. Breaking the skin's surface does not necessarily assure something good. One doesn't get anything more. All the same, the skin does tell something about the individual. It is after all the skin which is torn, separated, cut to create life."[66]

Orlan summarizes this representational dilemma in the sentence, "I am never what I have."[67] But she also invokes another important issue here, namely, the impossibility of becoming one with one's proper image in the mirror or on the screen. Therefore, for Orlan it becomes necessary to masquerade herself, putting on the skin of different icons throughout the centuries, just as Alba d'Urbano hung her own skin-suit on a coat hanger. What Orlan is pointing to in her performance art is that behind the masquerade there is nothing, a *no-space.*

Figure 3.15. Valie Export, *Syntagma,* 1983. Still. Courtesy of the artist with permission of the Artists Rights Society, New York.

This dilemma of what-lies-behind-it has also been thematized by Valie Export in her film *Syntagma* (1983). In this film we follow a woman in her self-reflexive, self-questioning manner on the streets of Vienna. We can follow her through various reflections, through the glass of a telephone booth, the window of the subway, and of course we see her on the screen. Similar to Orlan, the woman (who is the artist herself) quotes passages on femininity inspired by La-can's theories. The impossibility of ever seeing the entirety of one's own image is symbolized through a series of film cuts (figure 3.15) in which we see the woman climbing stairs in high heels. Every cut corresponds to one step that the woman takes, but these are not just recorded in one long shot. The abrupt cuts are all taken from slightly different perspectives; however they seem to be *almost* the same. As a result, the woman's steps never appear to overlap, but she always seems to step on the same step. This never stepping onto the next stair leaves open a space in-between the stairs, which cannot be seen on the screen as such, but is suggested through the not quite overlapping cuts.

What is alluded to here is precisely a cinematic space that, by definition, remains empty. This space resembles the "empty image" that Marie-Luise Angerer speaks of in her book *body options;* an image that remains empty because it is *behind* the body image, it is a surplus to the image, and reveals itself only through its absence—the absence of the signified.[68] This emptiness or "no-space" is also characterized by the fact that it creates an unreal subject position, for it cannot be looked at from any possible position in real space. As Angerer puts it in her analysis of Orlan's performance art, this is a representation that never takes effect in an unbroken way.[69] Orlan emphasizes precisely the empty position created by these "breaks" in the symbolic order. These breaks have to be masqueraded constantly—and most prominently—by the event of gender formation. This empty position is what Angerer calls an "intimate exteriority,"[70] suggesting an instability of the skin as a border between the inner and the outer body. The term *extimité* was coined by Lacan,[71] by which he meant that the most intimate aspect of the human psyche is simultaneously the most external. Joan Copjec explains *extimité* by taking the female breast as an example for an extimate object, in that it is "an object, an appendage of the body, from which we separate ourselves in order to constitute ourselves as subjects."[72] In other words, the breast is extimate in that it "is in us that which is not us."[73]

However, synthetic flesh cannot only be found in the realm of media and installation art, but in many instances of a culture that increasingly merges the virtual with the real. For example, high fashion designers are not just busy covering bodies with clothes and accessories anymore, but are also interested in the process of merging human and techno-flesh. Jean-Paul Gaultier already had started to use techno-skin outfits in the early 1990s, for example, the costumes in the Spanish film *Kika* (1993) by Pedro Almodóvar. The Austrian fashion designer Helmut Lang, on the other hand, has started a cosmetic line with a new perfume, aiming his advertising discourse at the skin-surface, as formulated by the artist Jenny Holzer[74] (see figure 3.16).

Since 2001, Lang's new perfume line has been presented in a store in New York's SoHo district that looks like an apothecary, replete with old-fashioned distillation equipment. Holzer reinforces the techno-critique by using her well-known sculptures of scrolling messages in electric light, hence a hypermediated technique of expression with contents connoting an antitechnological encounter between real individuals and real skins, in which no technology other than real bodies are involved. Holzer's written "messages from the unconscious" have gained iconic value in today's art. We encounter her messages covering the

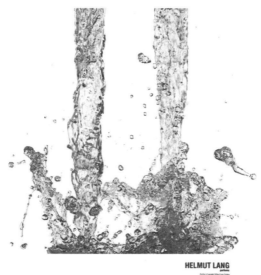

Figure 3.16. Jenny Holzer, advertisement for Helmut Lang. Courtesy of the artist with permission of the Artists Rights Society, New York.

surfaces of urban environments or engraved into sarcophagus-like benches.[75] What matters for my current concerns in this particular skin-related poetic message from the unconscious is that here the skin's surface does not only refer to a physical experience; rather, the skin is the metonymical platform for any human contact, be it within the realm of the five senses or beyond. Moreover, the skin adopts a temporal dimension (as in the ad's text: "On my skin . . . I wait for you"), as well as narrative scenarios as expressed by the verb "teasing," with which we connote many configurations from children's games to amorous play. Finally, the skin becomes a signifier for performativity, expressed through the collocation "walking in." The skin opens up various spheres, physical and beyond, for human encounters.

In cosmetics, just as in the figurative arts, the skin has become a detached commodity. Marketers think about it in absolute, abstract, and detached terms. Successful cosmetic marketing focuses first on the physical contact between the sales agent and the customer, and second on the contact between the customer and the product:

Essentially, you put the product on the back of the customer's hand, . . . and you place the bottle in their other hand. You ask, "Please, would you hold this for me?" This allows them to see the product, and get comfortable with the bottle. We touch them first, and then they touch our products. We are an interactive company. We touch our customers. And they come back.[76]

Touching the skin and interactivity also are common themes in the 2002 perfume by Christian Dior (figure 3.17). "J'adore" features a blond and golden mermaid, quite similar to the golden Swatch model, who is in tune with the golden liquid from which she rises. In the video that once was on the Dior website, we could hear her voice saying: "I can't resist. I can't resist temptation. I can touch it. J'adore." Adoration and touch are here part of the same utterance.

Peter Allen and Carla Ross Allen from the design collaborative KnoWear[77]— founded in 2000—have created some futuristic examples of synthetic flesh. *Skinthetic* is a procedure in which labels and bodies will become one: "Where in 2002 we as consumers put labels on our bodies through the act of clothing, by 2022 we will be implanting designed body parts that are not only genetically coded but also will bear the signs and identities of the couture and product house that have created them."[78] Among KnoWear's case studies for the new

Figure 3.17. Christian Dior, "J'adore" advertisement, 2002.

Skinthetic label-flesh is a quilt implant by Chanel (figure 3.18) allowing the user to adopt Chanel's "flesh."

The body as synthetic and the global implications of the body's embeddedness in today's brand culture resonates even more clearly in KnoWear's latest project, *The Façade of the Synthetic* (2004), in which they sample current branding and advertising campaigns in a series of Body Billboards (figure 3.19). KnoWear does not propose a particularly critical reading for their Body Billboards, which include such brands as Nike and MasterCard: "The onslaught of advertisements presented in the Body Billboards are purposefully left open to the viewer's interpretation, inviting the audience to decide whether the body is the next venue of public media manipulation (synthetic), or whether the body should remain sacred and untouched (natural)."[79]

What these projects prove so skillfully, however, is that the brands and products circulating in between bodies do not participate only in the body's appearance, or phenotype, but actually penetrate its genotype by implanting the brands into the skin. It is in this way that KnoWear point out how today's global brands are getting under the skin.

How Faces Have Become Obsolete

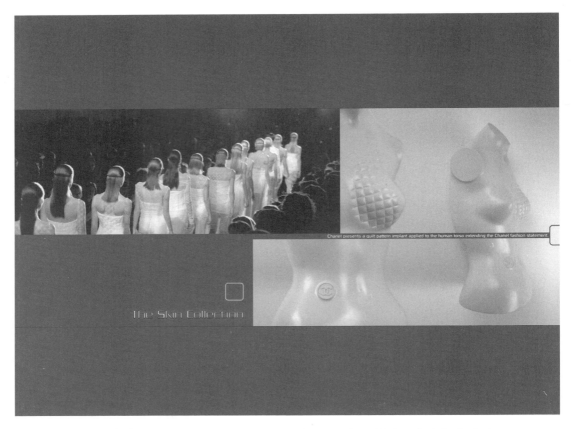

Figure 3.18. Kno Wear, *Skinthetic* 2002. Photo by Peter Allen. Digital manipulation by Carla Ross Allen and Peter Allen. Courtesy of Peter Allen and Carla Ross Allen.

Under the Skin

> Under the skin the body is an over-heated factory, and outside, the invalid shines, glows, from every burst pore; such is a Van Gogh landscape at noon.[80]
>
> —ANTONIN ARTAUD, "VAN GOGH, THE MAN SUICIDED BY SOCIETY"

Long before Artaud wrote about the body as an "over-heated factory" (1947), Nietzsche, in his *Genealogy of Morals* (1887), described the body as "our underworld of utility organs working with and against one another."[81] For Nietzsche, organs are both such abstract notions as consciousness ("consciousness is an or-

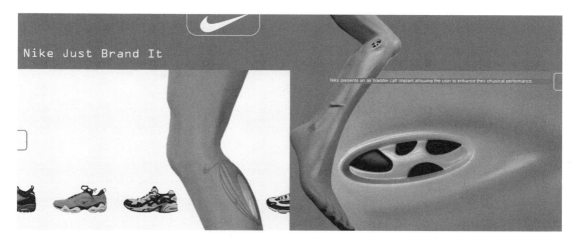

Figure 3.19. Kno Wear, *The Façade of the Synthetic* 2004. Photo by Will Taylor. Digital manipulation by Carla Ross Allen and Peter Allen. Courtesy of Peter Allen and Carla Ross Allen.

gan like the stomach"[82]), as well as concrete body parts like the stomach and particularly its digestive functions, one of Nietzsche's favorite metaphors for the interpretation of culture. Nietzsche draws connections between body parts and the mind because for him the body is not a dualistic system, but rather "the body, as a *relation of forces* of the *assimilated* signs, is an *interpretive* space."[83] As discussed in chapter 1, for Nietzsche, asking what the body is can be equated with asking what interpretation is: "The will to power *interprets* (—the formation of an organ is the result of an interpretation): it limits and fixes degrees of power, and the differences between them."[84]

Inspired by Nietzsche's body metaphors, Artaud talks about the inner body on the occasion of the death of Vincent van Gogh, to whom he dedicates this homage. Van Gogh, Artaud claims, was "suicided" by a "sick society" that "invented psychiatry to defend itself against the investigations of certain visionaries whose faculties of divination disturbed it."[85] The "lunatic" van Gogh was a man who was able to utter certain unbearable truths, as Artaud interprets his work—truths "that society does not wish to hear but wants to prevent from uttering."[86] Artaud dedicates his revolutionary analysis to medicine, particularly psychiatry:

Medicine is born of evil, if it is not born of disease, and it has even, on the contrary, provoked sickness out of whole cloth in order to give itself reason for being; but psychiatry is born of vulgar black earth of people who have thus rooted out of their own nothingness a kind of Swiss Guard, to sap the rebellious drive which is the origin of all geniuses.[87]

For Artaud, this is a way of organ-izing, of domesticating the body, which has not brought mankind any good; or, to borrow Nietzsche's terms, when the process of interpretation comes to an end, the body dies. According to Artaud, the domestication of the body "killed" geniuses like van Gogh, for "one does not commit suicide alone. No one was ever born alone. Nor has anyone died alone."[88]

What Artaud brings into the picture here is that the "over-heated factory" of the interior body is a universe made of liquid borders—borders that are not in between spaces, but are inside and outside at the same time. What counts for the dematerialized, fragmented body is that, through such porous borders, it is easy to get under the skin in order to screen or map the human flesh, as in the case of the Visible Human Project. Nevertheless, we must recall that for the performance artist Orlan, for example, "nothing" is revealed under the skin, and nothing is hidden underneath its surface;[89] the skin is rather a border that deceives us constantly.

The skin as "no border," or as a signifier for the empty space behind the screen or mirror cannot be entirely understood without referring to the redefinition of the (gendered) body throughout the last decades. Recall Grosz's notion from chapter 1: the body is

a pliable entity whose determinate form is provided not simply by biology but through the interaction of modes of psychical and physical inscription and the provision of a set of limiting biological codes. The body is constrained by its biological limits—limits, incidentally, whose framework or "stretchability" we cannot yet know, we cannot presume, even if we presume some limits.[90]

In the previously discussed video installation, Jenny Holzer poetically describes various modes of psychical and physical bodily inscription, referring to the "pliable entity" of the skin. The instability of the skin as border has also been pointed out by Haraway in her "Cyborg Manifesto,"[91] according to which the cyborg is the instantiation of the breakdown of the skin as border, merging human flesh with that of the machine. "Why should our bodies end at the skin, or include at best other beings encapsulated by skin?"[92]

It is through these new definitions of the body and the surface or border of the skin—which themselves are provoked by the emergence of new technologies for getting under the skin—that popular culture and art have been inspired to produce innumerable examples of what has been labeled *flesh-art*.

Let us put the discussed examples from popular culture for modes of getting under the skin into a broader philosophical frame. In this context, the examples of flesh-art can be understood as an intensification and transformation of what Deleuze and Guattari had criticized and foreseen in the late 1970s and early 1980s in their notion of the body without organs (BwO):

It is not at all a question of a fragmented, splintered body, of organs without the body (OwB). The BwO is exactly the opposite. There are not organs in the sense of fragments in relation to a lost unity, nor is there a return to the undifferentiated in relation to a differentiable totality. There is a distribution of intensive principles of organs, with their positive indefinite articles, within a collectivity or multiplicity, inside an assemblage, and according to machinic connections operating on a BwO.[93]

The idea of the body without organs is not directed against the specific organs of our bodies, such as the skin, but against organ-ization, especially the organization of organs in a medical way just as with Artaud's opposition to the dominance over the body by psychiatry. The organism, they claim, is the Judgment of God—hence the conforming to a preordered and premoral system. Organizations are always hierarchical. Consequently, one does not *own* a body without organs, but the "*moi* is on it, or what remains of me, unalterable and changing form crossing thresholds."[94]

Deleuze and Guattari's essay, "How Do You Make Yourself a Body Without Organs" takes as its starting point November 28, 1947. This is the day Artaud "declares war on organs,"[95] the day he wrote the (never-broadcasted) radio play "To Have Done with the Judgment of God," in which he coined the phrase "body without organs," a formulation that will be rediscovered and revitalized throughout the entire poststructuralist revolution: "For you can tie me up if you wish, but there is nothing more useless than an organ. When you will have made him a body without organs, then you will have delivered him from all his automatic reactions and restored him to his true freedom."[96] Whereas for Freud the body consisted of different strata of which the skin constituted a "sack," Lacan defined the ego not as a surface but as a fictional substantiality within the symbolic order. As a consequence, gender is a necessary substance, a strategy of masquerade, or "the most important lie."[97] For Deleuze and Guattari, on the other hand, the universe of the body is made of zones and matrices of intensities; the body is a "plane of consistency."[98] It is a field of immanence (like Tao), a plateau, on which nomadism is the decisive movement. "It is not space, nor is it in space."[99] Deleuze and Guattari emphasize the flatness of this body notion, and not the depth of it as in Freud's notion. The BwO consists of vectors such as desire: "The BwO is desire."[100]

In this notion of flatness driven by vectors of desire, one thing becomes clear: the body without organs is a body seen from the viewpoint of its possibilities.[101] Deleuze and Guattari had foreseen the obsolescence of a hierarchized bodily overcoding, in which only certain body parts, such as the face, have privilege over other body parts. In this latest body discourse at the turn of the millennium, all organs have the possibility of overcoding and being overcoded. The BwO has gone beyond fragmentation and synecdoche. New medical and representational technologies allow for the synechdochic potential of organs to code the way the face did before. But precisely because of this potential, the posthuman BwO no longer needs the holism of the body; it has become an OiB, an organ instead of a body. In an intriguing inversion of Deleuze and Guattari's notion, the wish no longer is to think of the skin, for example, as an ego-envelope in the way Anzieu describes it, but as an organ instead of a body—a detached universe in itself. OiBs, such as the skin, have become faces, and it is no coincidence that the skin gets such attention in this discourse universe. For the skin is "flat," and in its digitized representation it has a "slippery surface,"[102] exactly like Deleuze and Guattari's BwO. The body and all of its organs, in other words, not only serve as media of expression through appearance to the outer world, but have adopted the characteristics of media. The discourse of getting under the skin was necessary to "free" the strata of a given hierarchy. The skin and the other organs, thus freed, have taken on the role of pure mediation, of a flat screen, of the sur-face on which the body as such is produced. The following final chapter traces this movement in detail, analyzing examples from architecture and new media art.

The Medium Is the Body

Changing our way of thinking about the world is a necessary first step, but it is by no means sufficient: we will need to *destratify reality itself,* and we must do so without the guarantee of a golden age ahead, knowing full well the dangers and possible restratifications we may face.[1]

— MANUEL DE LANDA, *A THOUSAND YEARS OF NONLINEAR HISTORY*

While for Nietzsche images were metaphors of the body, for Bergson the body was an image that acts like other images.[2] For the contemporary anthropologist of images Hans Belting, these analogies between body and image are no coincidence: "internal and external representations, or mental and physical images, may be considered two sides of the same coin."[3] This is why, for Belting, images cannot be described by an "exclusively medialogical approach."[4] Rather, he reminds us that images always imply life—indeed, that they live in need of our bodies even to show up. Bodies, in fact, serve as living media that make us perceive, project, or remember images. In this image critique, images are thought of as *happenings* or *interventions* performed by bodies, which have been exposed to images from the outside.[5] In that sense, the media are transmitters rather than producers of images, and it is the active participation of the body in the reproduction of the images that is relevant to Belting's anthropology of images.

It is via an approach to image theory that I pool the notions of body and medium in this chapter, with special regard to the context of new media. I argue that the notions of body and image have come together in what can be called an epistemological shift from a *body* emphasis to a *medium* emphasis. Through examples from new media art and architecture, I argue that what has previously been known as *medium* has adopted the characteristics of *body* within the techno- and new media sphere of the new millennium. The notion of the *body as constitutive mediation* developed in the previous chapters serves as the backbone to this argument.

In chapter 3 I show how, in the realm of corporeal configurations at the turn of the millennium, the skin and other organs were "freed" of a given hierarchy and have taken on the role of pure mediation. Chapter 3 traced the synecdochic move in which the face has ceased to overcode the rest of the body and has become a body stratum like any other body part. In this move, contemporaneity, rather than linearity, becomes the underlying trope. Regarding this process of corporeal dematerialization and destratification, the issue was not only to find the operating metaphors at work in popular culture—to promote this newly destratified body image—but also to think of the millennial body as a conglomerate of "nonlinear strata," and "interacting accumulations."[6] To understand this body image, we need to emphasize the accumulation, rather than the resulting substitution of, bodily bits and pieces. What interests me, in other words, is not so much which part has replaced which other part, but how and in what configuration have the body parts been accumulated.

Just as de Landa—inspired by Deleuze and Guattari's "plane of consistency" of the body without organs—sees history as a "mixture of coexisting 'ages'" in which synchrony is what counts, we might think of the millennial body as a body whose entire inscriptions over the last thirty (or even the last hundred thousand) years matter in one way or another.[7] But how do they matter? What does it mean to say that we have created an extended, flattened body of simultaneities, coexisting possibilities, that is, a body of pure potentialities?

Before this crucial question can be answered, I confront the question of how the flattened body in cyberspace has found its restratification in recent millennial bodily installations. The underlying hypothesis of the previous chapters is that the current wave of body discourses could be seen as the reflection of an intensifying medialization that has gripped Western culture since the onset of the new media era. Digital media have produced a collective (and at the same time dispersed) consciousness of multiple subjectivities that have fragmented the body, redistributing and extending it or its traces and substitutions in cyberspace. Chapter 1's feminist body critique discussed why it was especially necessary to free the female body (image) from hierarchies by replacing it with a multiplicity of bodies and subjectivities, thus resulting in such body concepts as the "nomadic body" (Braidotti), the "volatile body" (Grosz), or the "imaginary body" (Gatens).[8]

In this final chapter, I investigate the mutual dependence upon and influence of body and mediation, which is attested to by the gradual collapse (throughout the rise of a mediatized environment in the twentieth century, and especially under the influence of the early avant-garde as demonstrated in chapter 2) of the genre of performance art, from a fixation on the body's wounds (1960s) to the exploration of its technophenomenological extensions (1990s). On the basis of this history, I propose to reconfigure the discipline of body criticism into one of new media criticism. I argue that the medium and questions around mediation have literally taken over the space and place of the individual body, as featured in former body performance art or beauty advertisement. The body in the installations under analysis in this chapter has emerged in place of something else, namely, in place of the very mediation that once represented it for us. The medium, in other words, has become the body. This final chapter argues this movement via the analysis of new media art and architecture—the most concrete embodiments of the current epistemological pillars upon which the status quo of body criticism is built.

Flatness and Architecture

> As soon as we speak . . . we are caught in what traditionally are called spatial metaphors, architectural metaphors. Philosophy is full of them: foundations, systems, architectonics, which in philosophy means the art of the system, but even in more everyday language the spatial metaphors are irreducible, unavoidable, and anything but accidental. So the problem of space and of being inscribed through language space, without any possibility of dominating this situation, compels you to deal with architecture without being aware that you are.[9]
> —JACQUES DERRIDA, "JACQUES DERRIDA: INVITATION TO A DISCUSSION"

This prophetic quote by Jacques Derrida makes clear it is no coincidence that current discussions on and around the body have extended into the realm of architecture, whether through the proliferating Deleuzian discourse of the body without organs—in which bodies are conceived as animated matter similar to

3-D models—or within a philosophy that deals with architecture "from the outside,"[10] or within cyber-spheres themselves, where new concepts and configurations of spatialities are being explored by new media technologies. These new media technologies have put a renewed emphasis on the issues of flatness and surface, and consequently on the notion of skin and borders. The architecture theorist Alicia Imperiale coined the term *new flatness*[11] for this kind of surface-driven architecture, or skin architecture. Flatness stands here in opposition to a *deep-architecture,* an opposition that goes back to the modernist "pure" forms and shapes that were identified in a binary logic such as inside versus outside.

Architectural metaphors of the early twentieth century were often borrowed from the semantic field of the human body (for example, façade). In the early twenty-first century, on the other hand, the semantic field of the screen, that is, of technology, is preferred. Bodies are not flat. Screens are. Flatness, in architecture, is a result of the implosion of inside and outside. This state was predicted by Jean Baudrillard some time ago when he analyzed the postmodern media society and its categorical imperative of communication: "In any case, we will have to suffer this new state of things, this forced extroversion of all interiority, this forced injection of all exteriority that the categorical imperative of communication literally signifies; . . . we are now in a new form of schizophrenia. No more hysteria, no more projective paranoia, properly speaking, but this state of terror proper to the schizophrenic: too great a proximity of everything, the unclean promiscuity of everything which touches, invests and penetrates without resistance."[12] We now explore this "implosion of inside and outside" even further. In the philosophy of Deleuze, for example, *intensive* thought is dedicated to the notion of surface and the implosion of inside and outside. Grosz examines Deleuze's notion of surface as it emerges in his *Foucault* and *Cinema 2: The Time Image* in her book *Architecture from the Outside,* and comes to the following trenchant insight: "So it is not as if the outside or the exterior must remain eternally counterposed to an interiority that it contains: rather, the outside is the transmutability of the inside. Presumably for this reason Deleuze wants to link the outside not with the inside but with the real. This is no way to align the inside with the unreal, the possible, or the imaginary; it is to see that the outside is a virtual condition of the inside, as equally real, as time is the virtual of space. The virtual is immanent in the real."[13] The outside as a virtual condition of the inside could not have been better envisioned than in such computer-animated architectural projects as those proposed by the architect team Kolatan/Mac Donald Studio. In 1999, Sulan Kolatan and William J. Mac Donald developed a serial housings project, *Housings: six maisons non-standard,* which takes the notion of composite identity into serial production.[14] The initial design parameters are set as a kind of gene pool with information from a range of existing morphologies. This allows for a sliding scale of variance that can be tuned relative to different criteria of viability with the intent to produce conditions of *useful schizophrenia* in the form of hybridized housing. *Housings* is realized with the 3-D graphics software Maya, a program that animates contemporarily in time and space. The two models of *Housings* as represented in figures 4.1 and 4.2 are extrapolated from the entirety of a *Housings* potential, which is situated within the Maya continuum. The continuum is defined by a random beginning and ending point. At any point on this continuum, a model can be built by the interpolation of data such that the context for the model remains self-referential and hence independent of the "real world."[15] *Housings* focuses on the experimental designs for mass-customized prefabricated housing.

Raybould House, another project by Kolatan and Mac Donald, is a house-addition project for a property in Fairfield, Connecticut (1997–2000). This chimera of organic and serial hybridization takes its cues from the logics of the traditional house and the landscape, respectively. The framing of *Raybould House,* which defines its unique profile, is paradoxically the element that is prefabricated by CNC (computer numerically controlled) machines. Kolatan and Mac Donald have created such mutated architectural entities by blending *Raybould House* with a series of target objects.

Raybould House stands on a partly wooded plot of land on which there are several existing structures: a barn, a swimming pool, and a traditional saltbox house, to which this project will be connected. The new house is the outcome of the twofold procedure of cocitation mapping and the chimera developed by Kolatan and Mac Donald. *Raybould House* is seen as a chimera-like hybrid between the logic of the existing architecture and that of the surrounding landscape. The lines and contours of the site and the irregular outlines of the section inform one another. The features of the land, cocited in the form of the house, however, are transformed by the addition of parts of molds used to build it. The architects have opted for a system of concrete panels onto which a flexible mixture of aluminumized polyurethane will be cast. Concrete offers the advantage of taking on the role of structure and surface alike. It is malleable, and makes it possible to meet the architectural conditions both technically and formally.[16]

Similarly, the architect and theorist Greg Lynn created *Embryologic Houses*©™ that represent the new flatness in the realm of today's (in)organic architecture

Figure 4.1. Kolatan/Mac Donald Studio, *Housings: six maisons non-standard,* 1999. Courtesy of the architects.

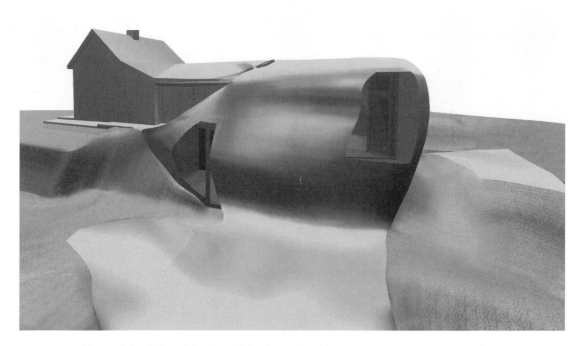

Figure 4.2. Kolatan/Mac Donald Studio, *Raybould House,* 1997–2000. Courtesy of the architects.

Figure 4.3.   Gregg Lynn, *Embryologic Houses©™*, 2000. Courtesy of the architect.

(figure 4.3). In this project, Lynn proposes a series of "surface envelopes" or "shading skins" composed of 2048 panels, 9 steel frames, and 72 aluminum struts that are networked together to form a monocoque shell, and which are connected to the ground.[17] *Embryologic Houses©™* are designed as soft flexible surfaces of curves rather than as a fixed set of rigid points. As Lynn points out: "This makes a shift from a Modernist mechanical hit-of-parts design and construction technique to a more vital, evolving, biological model of embryological design and construction."[18]

Lynn has theorized the merging of organicity with inorganicity since the early 1990s: "There is a two-fold deterritorialization in becoming a multiplicity: the loss of internal boundaries allows both the influence of external events within the organism and the expansion of the interior outward. This generates a body that is essentially inorganic."[19] The expansion of the interior outward is the dominant trope of the architectural language of new flatness, in that this literal superficiality reduces everything to a flatness exhibiting a new "depth-lessness."[20] Fredric Jameson has pronounced *surface* to be one of the determining features of postmodernism, as opposed to *depth* as a feature of modernism.[21] One of the classic postmodernist operations at stake in these examples of new media–driven architecture is to replace modern depth by (multiple) surfaces.

Other examples of how imaging technologies erase depth stem from current medicine. Virtual endoscopy, for example, is a method of diagnosis using computer processing of 3-D image datasets, such as CT or MRI scans, to provide simulated visualizations of patient-specific organs. By using algorithms and high performance computing, these cross sections may be rendered as direct 3-D representations of human anatomy from the visible human datasets of the Visible Human Project.[22] Through such new procedures as virtual endoscopy, a bodily interior is constructed from utopian viewpoints that do not correspond to any human reality precisely because they can be obtained only through a computerized vision of the body. What is more, the real problematic novelty inherent in these new technologies is that they no longer produce an "image of a body," but rather "a workable relationship between human body and computer."[23] The digitally visualized data from the VHP create a homogenous interior bodily space—a utopian space that ignores the heterotopias of the anatomical body by simplifying the restricted point of view that its precursor the endoscope provided.[24] I would reformulate and say that the disappearance of depths has given rise to a new language that does not mediate transcendence, but rather speaks it. We can see this language configured in examples of architecture in which the surface has gained depth, or better, in which the surface has become the building itself. One such example is the extension of the Palais des Beaux-Arts in Lille, France, by Jean-Marc Ibos and Myrto Vitart (1992–1997). This "blade-like extension"[25] of the Palais des Beaux-Arts in Lilles (figure 4.4) turns the viewers into voyeurs, allowing us to get under the skin of the building, or in the words of Imperiale: "[it] alternately pushes you to its surface, where a web-like grid of small reflective surfaces reflect the auspicious rear façade of the neo-classical museum in a pixilated fashion."[26]

This surface-driven building is also an example of the trope of remediation, in that the original neo-classical building is "pixilated" retroactively—as a result of which its mediation seems multiplied.

Similarly, the Swiss architects Jacques Herzog and Pierre de Meuron proposed an architectural skin (figure 4.5) for the Technical School Library in Eberswalde, Germany (1997–1999), as a "serilith process whereby symbolically

Figure 4.4. Jean-Marc Ibos and Myrto Vitart, Palais des Beaux-Arts in Lille, France, 1992–1997. Courtesy of the architects and photographer Georges Fessy.

Figure 4.5. Jacques Herzog and Pierre de Meuron, Technical School Library in Eberswalde, Germany, 1997–1999. Courtesy Margherita Spiluttini photography.

The Medium Is the Body

charged images are transferred to the building's concrete surface and directly silk-screened onto the glass. . . . What remains is a 'tattooed concrete skin.'"[27]

Slippery, evanescent surfaces can be found in the Cartier Foundation in Paris by French architect Jean Nouvel and, since the second half of the twentieth century, in innumerable examples of surfaces that serve as media screens. The theme of video projections onto slippery evanescent surfaces and the adjacent theme of mirror reflection have been explored widely, for example, by Dan Graham in his various viewing environments.[28] Graham's *Two Adjacent Pavilions* (figure 4.6), his first outdoor two-way mirror pavilion, was realized at the Documenta 7, in 1981. Graham says about his own work: "In *Two Adjacent Pavilions* and other pavilions, the inside and the outside views are both quasi-reflective and quasi-

Figure 4.6. Dan Graham, *Two Adjacent Pavilions,* 1981. Courtesy of the Kröller-Müller Museum, Otterlo, The Netherlands.

transparent, and they superimpose intersubjective images of inside and outside viewers' bodies and gazes along the landscape."[29]

In this quote it becomes clear that architecture has to be seen, if not as a forerunner of, then at least as intrinsically related to new media art and the new media regime. The material superimposition of *intersubjective gazes* provided in Graham's pavilions is precisely what so many new media art installations aim at—the deconstruction of the single viewpoint, and with that the introduction of randomness or the chance factor triggered by the viewer-participant's interaction with the installation. These installations also introduce the visualization of the process of getting under the skin, and with that the aestheticism of a new interior universe, or "deep surface."[30]

I should add here that I completely agree with Pierre Lévy and Lev Manovich on the problem of describing new media as *interactive.* As Manovich points out, *interactive* is too broad a term, and even in some sense tautological,[31] as an information receiver is always active unless dead.[32] Media started to become interactive much before the advent of new media (that is, at the end of the nineteenth century), and ultimately have to do with the "modern desire to externalize the mind."[33] In interactive computer media we are constantly asked to follow preprogrammed, objectively existing associations, reminiscent of Louis Althusser's concept of *interpellation,* in which "we are asked to mistake the structure of somebody else's mind for our own."[34]

Mistaking the other's mind enough to follow its patterns, of course, also means a deemphasis of subjectivity, agency, and originality. It is this very aspect of new media art and architecture that is of importance to the analysis of corporeality and mediality in the examples below.

Deep Surfaces

Deep surface refers to the ambiguity between inside and outside as proposed, theorized, visualized, and materialized by architects, artists, and theorists. In this new notion of virtual space, "the architecture is no longer a geometric, vertical volume that rises from the passive, horizontal, tamed natural ground plane. Rather, the ground becomes an active constructed plane where the architecture emerges as an improbable, fluctuating figure."[35] The deep surface–driven architecture expands into verticality rather than horizontality, and yet can be thought of as an antiarborescent rhizome. Depth is replaced by (deep) surfaces. The question remains if this is a mere rhetorical shift, or also an ontological one.

Let us look at current reformulations of some of the pillars of modern architecture by representatives of this new postorganic architecture. While the international modernist style of Le Corbusier (for example, Villa Savoye) and Frank Lloyd Wright (for example, Unity Temple) used extension as the incorporation of the environment or landscape into the building's anima, and the outside as a reflection of the inside, Jameson described as a typical feature of postmodern architecture "the strange new feeling of an absence of inside and outside, the bewilderment and loss of spatial orientation in Portman's hotels."[36]

But the current examples of new flatness and deep surface architecture propose something even beyond the collapse of inside and outside. Now it is the building as *body* itself that is extending, urging toward, and making the outside. As Grosz put it, the outside is no longer a reflection of the inside but a virtual condition of it, a condition that is realized in such architectural examples as *Housings* and *Embryologic Houses©™*. This symbiotic concept of outside and inside is often symbolized through the Deleuzian notion of the fold, on which Deleuze elaborated in his analysis of Leibnizian philosophy and the Baroque: "In the Baroque the soul entertains a complex relation with the body. Forever indissociable from the body, it discovers a vertiginous animality that gets it tangled in the pleats of matter, but also an organic or cerebral humanity (the degree of development) that allows it to rise up, and that will make it ascend over all other folds."[37] On the first page of his analysis, Deleuze states that "the Baroque fold unfurls all the way to infinity,"[38] hence, "a fold is always folded within a fold, like a cavern in a cavern."[39] What matters for architecture is that—through the notion of the fold—a new relationship between vertical and horizontal, figure and ground, inside and outside can be established. Furthermore, through the notion of the fold, buildings no longer are subordinate to or separate from their environmental fabric, but continue within it, merge with it, or even better, they *become* their environment. That there no longer is a difference between the environment and the inside of a building can be seen in the examples by the architects Kolatan and Mac Donald, *Golf Course House* (figure 4.7a) and *Hot Tub House* (figure 4.7b).

In order to generate deep surfaces and deconstruct inside and outside in architectonic terms, one preliminary move had to be made: the move toward a digital architecture and the computer-generated virtual environments. The architect Elizabeth Diller states a propos Diller + Scofidio's winning the competition for the New Media Institute in Manhattan: "Some see new media and architecture on different sides of the fence. Our contention is that we can no

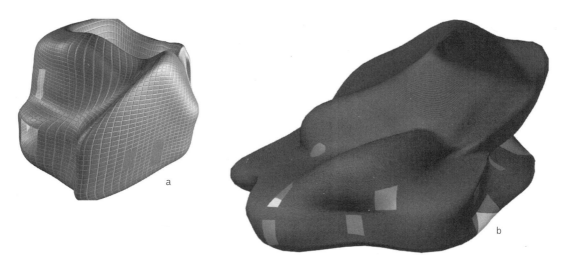

Figure 4.7a and 4.7b. Kolatan/Mac Donald Studio, *Hot Tub House* (a) and *Golf Course House* (b). Courtesy of the architects.

longer think architecture outside of computing."[40] Digital technology has not only introduced completely new parameters into the creation of spaces, but has posed a radical shift in the material, technology, and communications involved in the construction industry. Frank Gehry's buildings, for example, the Guggenheim Museum in Bilbão, "are made possible through the use of complex aeronautical software such as CATIA, which is used in the design and fabrication of aircraft."[41]

It is worth mentioning that the art and architecture theorist Hal Foster criticizes Gehry's "gestural aesthetic" in part precisely for its "technical facility of CATIA."[42] To put it in the context of this book, Gehry has, according to Foster, "gotten too much under the skin" of his buildings, creating "exterior surfaces that rarely match up with interior spaces."[43] For Foster, the disconnect between skin and structure generates two problems: "First, it can lead to spaces that are not surprising (as in the earlier houses) so much as mystifying (as in Bilbão or Seattle)—a strained disorientation that is frequently mistaken for an Architectural Sublime."[44] Whether or not we adhere to Foster's criticism of Gehry's cultural centers as "sites of spectacular spectatorship," what is important for current questions of architecture is to acknowledge two important changes in its capacity as cultural discourse. One is the fact—pointed out by Foster—that architecture's position within the arts has changed decisively since the initial debates about postmodernism and architecture in the 1970s, opening the discipline of pure forms to the problems posed by other cultural disciplines such as art and fashion.[45] The other decisive change is the introduction of digital design into the realm of architecture during the last decades. This change has transformed a visual discipline into a sense-oriented discipline.

The shift from visuality to tactility was facilitated by the electronic paradigm, which, according to architect Peter Eisenman, resonates the "baroque visual experience in its strongly tactile, or haptic quality, which prevents it from turning into the absolute ocular centrism of its Cartesian perspectivalist rival."[46] In other words, in the era of electronic media, architecture proposes a *baroque gaze* displacing the anthropocentric subjective vision. With the help of electronic media, architecture overcomes its rationalizing vision, producing a variety of viewpoints that—like in the Möbius *gender-strip*—take into consideration both the interior and exterior perspectives (whether real or virtual). Eisenman also uses Deleuze's notion of the fold as an alternative to the gridded space of the Cartesian order to explain how the traditional space of vision is changed through electronic media: "Unlike the space of classical vision, the idea of folded space denies framing in favor of a temporal modulation. The fold no longer privileges planimetric projection; instead there is a variable curvature."[47] Through the notion of the fold, buildings no longer are subordinate to or separate from their environmental fabric, but continue within it, merge with it, or even better, they *are* their environment. By this, Eisenman concludes, "a quality of the unseen" is added to vision, producing an interactive environment that perceives, that "looks back" at the viewer.[48]

Eisenman wonders why the paradigm shift from mechanical to electronic, which has taken place since World War II had not affected architecture earlier. His answer to this question has to do with "architecture's failure" to address the problem of vision because it remained within the concept of the subject and the four walls. "But these four walls no longer need to be expressive of the mechanical paradigm. Rather, they could deal with the possibility of these other discourses, the other affective senses of sound, touch, and of that light lying within the darkness."[49]

Sense-oriented architecture has clearly lit the flame of that light lying in darkness in various recent architectural projects that incorporate users' activities. The *Liquid Crystal Glass House* in Malibu, Calif., (1999) by Michael Silver (figure 4.8), for instance, uses a system of interconnected and interactive liquid crystal triangular glass panels functioning as the surface of this elongated house.

Figure 4.8. Michael Silver, *Liquid Crystal Glass House,* 1999. Courtesy of the architect.

These "responsive, constantly adapting electronic surfaces" literally transform the individual needs of the inhabitants into the disposition of the building.[50] In this *liquid architecture*[51] Silver proposes a fluid transparency, as he states: "like a palimpsest, the surfaces of the house register its user's activities."[52]

In his project description, Silver stresses the aliveness and unpredictability of the *Liquid Crystal Glass House:* "The inherent unpredictability of this system also runs the risk of being disruptive, making the design both unlivable and alien. To establish a balance between functionality and surprise, the (client controlled) scripting routines . . . are used to set up default zones that both frame and override the uncontrollable patterns produced by specific cellular automaton rules. . . . The project therefore creates a constantly changing feedback and feed forward loop sustaining four-dimensional interactions that relate in endless and unpredictable ways." [53]

Michael Silver's liquid architecture paradoxically resembles simultaneously a wild animal and a little child, as the house's interaction with its users is potentially dangerous, while still dependent entirely on their input: "The only way to know how the windows will behave is to set them in motion."[54]

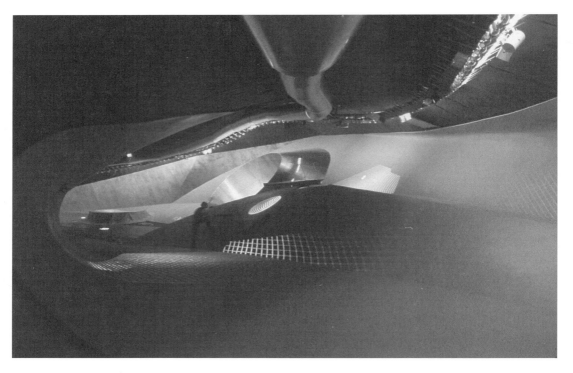

Figure 4.9. NOX, Water Pavilion *H₂Oexpo,* 1993–1997. Courtesy of the architects.

Similarly, the water pavilion *H₂Oexpo* (1993–1997), in the Netherlands by Dutch architects Kas Oosterhuis and Lars Spuybroek (NOX), is an input-driven building establishing an interaction with its users (figure 4.9):

The central idea of the project is to emerse the body in an underwater experience (the experience of the liquidity of water, but above all the experience of the body surrounded by moving matter), working on the principle of the wheelchair, a skateboard, roller-blades, or the wheel in general, namely the concept of a motor geometry or a prosthetic mobility provided by an object-carrier (in this instance, the pavilion itself) which becomes part of the action. The idea is based on the logic that attributes (or recognizes) the body's natural tendency to *incorporate* anything that might be useful to integrate or extend its own motor system.[55]

In this freshwater pavilion—a building that houses an exhibition about water on the former construction island Neeltje Jans—the sheer physical presence of the visitors activates the software built into the pavilion. Walking back and forth triggers sensors and projections on one's body. Every visitor's act, therefore, has far-reaching consequences: the more people, the more activity and the faster the light pulsates through the building. The architects see their pavilion as a dynamic system with a biorhythm, a sculptural building that behaves like a living organism. External factors play a role in the behavior of the building. A weather station outside registers data on salinity; processors translate these into commands that slow down or speed up the light and sound inside. They also influence the color of the light. The continuous interplay between people and building is due to the absence of clearly definable floors and walls and the non-distinction between horizontal and vertical—between floors, walls, and ceilings. Mist blows around one's ears, a geyser erupts, water gleams and splatters all around, and the air is filled with waves of electric sound. In this environment people lose their balance and fall. Another example of liquid architecture, *H₂Oexpo* is a testing ground for the study of interactivity in a three-dimensional environment where form and content are intimately related and blur into each other.[56]

In NOX's recent project (figure 4.10a), *Son-O-House* (2000–2004), we can detect an interesting development toward what Mark Hansen recently described as "second order interactivity."[57] Hansen points out that *Son-O-House* no longer is a first-order interactive new media project—as was the case of the fresh-water pavilion, which was based on a stimulus-response module. Rather, action is here guided by *perception in action* and therefore extends both the human and the machinic autopoetic capacity. In this "house where sound lives"[58] the viewer-participant not only influences the sounds in the installation directly, as in first-order interactivity; but the recordings of sounds (composed by Edwin van der Heide) and movements of people in home situations continually determine the composition of the structure itself.

Human movement, in fact, is the very basis for the sensorial input, which a computer translates into *kinetograms,* or three-dimensional abstractions of movement. These kinetograms (figure 4.10b) register three scales of relative movement corresponding to bodies, limbs, and extremities. The kinetograms are then mapped onto abstract paper elements—the paper is either uncut (body), cut in half (limbs), or cut in half again (hand or feet) —which are then stapled together resulting in a "porous three-dimensional structure."[59] This complex is then digitalized and remodeled into its final form, a "house-that-is-not-a-house."[60] The fragmented, flattened surface structure that results is the basis or,

Figure 4.10a. NOX, *Son-O-House*. Courtesy of the architects.

better, the skeleton of their *Son-O-House* (the outer surface of the building is made of flat strips of expanded stainless steel). In fact, the exterior structure of the house has collapsed into its interior, but not in the sense of a classic postmodern see-through structure in which we are made aware of a building's process of creation (for example, the Centre Pompidou in Paris). Rather, the *Son-O-House* has reversed entirely the traditional architectural *parcours* from action to construction to perception to sensation (Semper).[61] This house has departed from pure *sensation,* and sensation is the basis for the sound installation, as visitors' movements are continuously detected by sensors and stored in a database, which affects the composition itself. Not only does this house "see itself" through its excessive recording devices, but it also perceives and reconstructs itself constantly as a *lived experience body* and on the basis of recordings of bodies in *situations.*

Figure 4.10b. NOX, Kinetograms for *Son-O-House*. Courtesy of the architects.

Another celebrated and recently exhibited (May 15–October 15, 2002) example of materialized interactivity in architecture is the *Blur Building*, once again by Diller + Scofidio (figure 4.11). *Blur* is a holistic body concept realized in a "media building that hovers mysteriously over the lake."[62] Technically speaking, the building—developed by the Extasia team for the Swiss Expo 2002 in Yverdons-Les-Bains on Lake Neuchâtel, Switzerland—consists nearly entirely of water like the human body. *Blur* is a cloud of mist formed by 12,500

Figure 4.11. Diller + Scofidio, *Blur Raincoat Glow,* 2002. Courtesy of Diller + Scofidio.

spray nozzles producing a fog system: "Lake water is filtered, then shot through a dense array of high-pressure fog nozzles and regulated by a computer control system."[63] Not only is *Blur* "smart weather," in that the building changes its appearance depending on the (unpredictable) weather of the day. It is also, as Mark Hansen points out, "space that has been made wearable,"[64] not least with the help of the designated "braincoat" with which one experiences the building (figure 4.12): "As visitors pass one another, their coats will compare profiles and change color indicating the degree of attraction or repulsion, much like an involuntary blush—red for affinity, green for antipathy. The system allows interaction among 400 visitors at any time."[65]

The architectural innovation of *Blur* lies not only in the fact that this is no longer a *building*—it is rather a *pure atmosphere,* as Diller + Scofidio themselves emphasize—but also in the fact that this "habitable medium"[66] no longer emphasizes vision, but rather the proprioceptive *bodily* experience of inhabiting space. In other words, Diller + Scofidio reevaluate and relativize the dominance

Figure 4.12. Diller + Scofidio, *Blur View on Ramp*, 2002. Photograph by Beat Widmer. Courtesy of Diller + Scofidio.

of vision in architecture by providing an "immersive environment in which the world is put out of focus so that our visual dependency can be put into focus."[67] As Eisenman describes it in relation to the architecture of the fold in the era of electronic media, *Blur* is an environment that perceives and "looks back" at the user.

Diller + Scofidio chose the instability of the weather for *Blur* because the weather is one of the examples of our cultural obsession with control, and of the anxiety resulting from not being able to overpower our environments. The quintessence of the *Blur* bubble is to present weather not only as a natural process, but also as a cultural phenomenon: "At stake is how we interact with each other through weather, not only as a shared obsession but also as a process of global communication."[68]

Interactivity through participation, and the resulting chance factor, are the main issues of such first-order interactivity projects as *Liquid Crystal Glass House* and *H₂Oexpo,* as well as the second-order interactivity affecting the building's genotype in such projects as *Son-O-House* and the *Blur,* with which the architects show us to different degrees our (still) restricted ability to control nature. At the same time they emphasize the very new technologies involved in these buildings-in-process, or "buildings becoming buildings."[69] It is this contradictory blurring of technological euphoria and dysphoria that captures the current architectural zeitgeist.[70]

What all of these projects have in common is not only interaction (mostly with water), but also two basic ideas: one is the chance factor built around the presence of individuals and their particular interaction with the buildings; the other is the idea of pure mediation and presence in completely demediatized "natural" settings. But in the case of the buildings there is also another dimension: their interactivity makes these buildings seem alive, their environment perceptive, as Eisenman had it. And what could be more convincing of their authenticity than that? Chance and mediation seem to be the determining factors to have taken the place of the body as raw material performances in the spirit of 1960s wounds. Now, we are confronted with organic bodies outside the realm of the human, where objects—and in the case of architecture, buildings—are coming to life.

The collapse of distinctions between building and environment, inside and outside, etc., has been revolutionized immensely by new media; the fold has become one of the key metaphors for the realm of new media as such. The digital image offers itself to the dissolution of limits in that it does not create an inside, but that it uses the outside frame of the screen as a mirror for the inside. This virtual inside is an unknown universe that no longer is limited by obstacles from the mechanical real, but offers new possibilities of using spaces, for example, digital fly-throughs with avatars that take on subject positions only possible in virtuality. Or, to return to Eisenman's vision, virtuality is a condition of oscillation between opposites in real space.

The Virtual Guggenheim Museum (1999–2001) by Asymptote architects Hani Rashid and Lise Anne Couture (figures 4.13a and 4.13b) is an example of a virtual environment that is "fueled by the basic human desire to probe the unknown."[71] This Internet-based museum houses digital and Internet art, which encompasses a number of virtual user experiences in the viewing and surveying of recent electronic acquisitions as well as other Guggenheims. The museum is a navigable, multidimensional, architectural experience controlled and activated by online visitors. It is designed as a "prototype museum for the future with a strategy of combining the museum's mission with the state of the art digital technologies."[72] As Rashid reports about the Guggenheim Virtual Museum, the intention was to create a multidimensional architectural body that is fluid and dynamic, offering an adequate space for the experience of digital media art.[73] This experience, though, goes far beyond the usual museum tour, using virtuality to speak the language of the featured media art. One does not lose time by walking through real museum spaces, but moves in the speed of a click from one platform or cyber-wall to another. The transition from one space to the other is seamless; there is no need for doors or security systems. The Virtual

Guggenheim lets the user interact with the artwork, creating a collective conscience between the space and user.

Media artists Aziz + Cucher's latest series of media installations, *Synaptic Bliss* (figure 4.14), is another attempt at merging the subject with media, or making us interact with new media. Their attempt at this fusion, however, is of a symbolic nature. There is no immersive interactivity at play as in *Son-O-House* or *Blur*; rather, *Synaptic Bliss* is a "metaphorical attempt to represent cycles of growth and decay, different rhythms that find audiovisual expression."[74] What is of interest in Aziz + Cucher's latest work not only is the fact that instead of the body's interior (see their installation series *Interiors* as discussed in chapter 3) the artists now explore in greater detail the border and limit of natural environments, but also to what extent their work deconstructs the difference between external and internal images.

As in the examples of liquid architecture, water is an important metaphor in Aziz + Cucher's work. Moreover, as with some of the other architects and artists discussed in this chapter, Aziz + Cucher also refer in their work to transarchitect and philosopher Marcos Novak:

Cyberspace calls us to consider the difference between animism and animation, and animation and metamorphosis. Animism suggests that entities have a "spirit" that guides their behavior. Animation adds the capability of change in location, through time. Metamorphosis is change in form, through time or space. More broadly, metamorphosis implies changes in one aspect of an entity as a function of other aspects, continuously or discontinuously. I use the term liquid to mean animistic, animated, metamorphic, as well as crossing categorical boundaries, applying the cognitively supercharged operations of poetic thinking.[75]

Synaptic Bliss offers further insight into the question concerning image, mediality, and body, as raised at the beginning of this chapter. It adds to this question the context that even without immersive, interactive new media strategies, the images can be intended to invoke *feelings of immersion:*

This series of work is very sensorial, almost psychedelic; it attempts to bring the viewer into an ecstatic awareness of their bodies in their surrounding environment as a process of infinite interconnection (hence "Synaptic") which in our understanding also brings a feeling of joy ("Bliss") as opposed to one of confusion in the inability to separate one's self from the outside.[76]

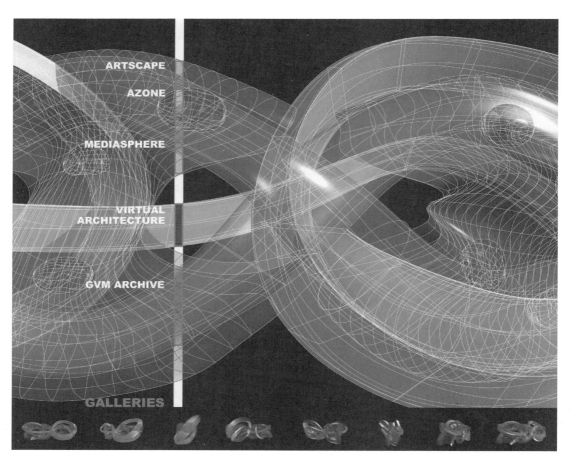

Figures 4.13a and 4.13b. Asymptote: Hani Rashid and Lise Anne Couture, *The Guggenheim Virtual Museum,* Navigational Study and Virtual Atrum; New York, New York, 1999–2001. Courtesy of Asymptote.

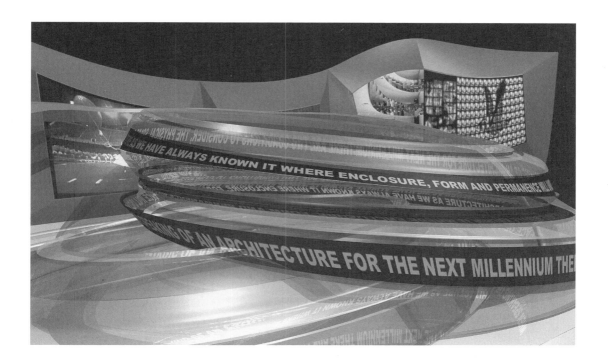

This psychedelic ecstasy of the inseparability of inside and outside addresses issues of the *image de corps,* that is, issues concerning the body as perceptive apparatus, which were central to Bergson's corpocentrism as discussed in chapter 1. It is in light of this observation that I venture a conclusion about these new media art–driven architectural installations: it is not exclusively the question of interactivity that reveals the body as mediation, as in *Son-O-House, Blur,* and other examples. Rather, as so brilliantly shown in *Synaptic Bliss,* imagination, vision, and images already are there to entertain the body's mediatic nature, as also suggested in Hans Belting's anthropology of the image.

The new media–driven architectural examples also have made evident something else: how previously distinct disciplines are linked within the common language of the digital image and its ability to transcode[77] information about bodies, buildings, or anything else into the binary code to be fitted into the order of the computer screen. For Hansen, this constitutes a clear indication that the digital image no longer can be thought only on the level of "surface appearance," but that with it "the entire process by which information is made

Figure 4.14. Aziz + Cucher, *Synaptic Bliss,* 2004. View of installation, Villette Numérique Paris. Courtesy of the artists.

perceivable through embodied experience"[78] comes into semantic play. The consequences of the inclusion of the process in the product are yet to be determined. What is clear, however, is that they are of drastic nature. As pointed out by Tim Lenoir and Casey Alt in their reflections on intersections in bioinformatics and contemporary architecture, as a result of digital image a variety of fields and disciplines "either have been or are being remade from the outside by electronic media."[79]

In chapter 2 I mention the two-sidedness of new media, in that they belong to the realm of visuality (as well as that of the other senses, as seen in some of these architectural examples), but at the same time are driven by a machinic logic. However, this logic is only active when the apparent *loss* of the body in the digital realm is brought to surface—as is the case with so many of the new media art examples under analysis in the next section.

The Corporealization of the Image in New Media Art

> In the beginning, the human subject is closer to the form of the
> other than to the emergence of his own tendency. He is originally
> an inchoate collection of desires—there you have the true sense of
> the expression *fragmented* body—and the initial synthesis of the *ego*
> is essentially an *alter ego;* it is alienated.[80]
>
> —JACQUES LACAN, *THE SEMINAR OF JACQUES LACAN, BOOK III, THE
> PSYCHOSES*

With the above quote I shall now return to the discussion of Lacan's fractal body
image discussed in chapter 1, which is fundamental to the understanding of any
kind of media art, particularly *new media* art because of its excess of construed
viewing positions. In the *Mirror Stage* Lacan posits that the construction of identity goes hand in hand with the perception of the bodily self through a deceptive image that is either framed through somebody else's gaze (the mother), or
through the frame of a medium. With the emphasis on mediation, it is a necessary and logical consequence that new media will be highly invested in questions of identity and constructivism, and, as a result, in the role of the frame,
which is missing in the digital realm.

The frame is in fact one of the keys to new media art criticism. In his discussion of Jeffrey Shaw's digital environments (for example, *Place—a user's manual,*
1995; *Place—Ruhr,* 2000), Hansen describes the artist's trajectory as a "movement from the technical frame (the image) to a confrontation with its constitutive condition of possibility, the (human) framing function."[81] This movement
is crucial for our current concerns, as well, as it moves the role of the frame from
the external image into the internal (empty) space of the human body, a truly
Lacanian move. As Donald MacKay phrased it in 1969, it is the very framing
that *constitutes* and *creates* information, and more importantly, "information remains meaningless in the absence of a (human) framer and that framing cannot
be reduced to a generic observational function, but encompasses everything that
goes to make up the biological and cultural specificity of that *singular* receiver."[82]
In Umberto Eco's theory of semiotics from 1975 the "cultural specificity of the
singular receiver" was called "encyclopedia;" hence, the open reference system
that a given receiver holds. In Eco's pragmatist theory of enunciation this is one
of the most important issues, as it points to the fact that the encyclopedia is by
definition an open system. Consequently, any given message or text is an open

system, too—open to receive the codes and subcodes from any receiver's cultural encyclopedia.[83]

The importance of the frame and the body as framer has been pointed out by Deleuze in the context of his investigation on cinema (*Cinema 1,* 1983, and *Cinema 2,* 1985). In his reading of Bergson's *Matière et mémoire* (see chapter 1), Deleuze describes the process of perception as a substraction of certain images from the flow of images that are indifferent to the perceiver. He compares this operation to the act of framing: "It is an operation which is exactly described as *framing:* certain actions undergone are isolated by the frame and hence, . . . they are forestalled, anticipated."[84] Hansen's Bergsonian thesis—that the human body qua center of indetermination functions as a direct *filter* of information and *creator* of image—explains the corporeal focus within new media art, as stated at the end of chapter 2. However, as Hansen points out, it is not least of all thanks to the ontology of the realm of new media that the body can function as a filter framing the originally bodyless digital information, and, unlike in Deleuze's theory of the movement image, that the very operation of framing brings us back to the body itself. To describe the movement inherent to new media art even more concretely, the images produced by the perceiving body are framed and "caught" by the screen or mirror and then redirected back to the body. Hansen, therefore, argues for the necessary correlation between the aesthetics of new media and embodiment. He declares new media art to be under the impression of what he calls the "'Bergsonist vocation of framing the digital image"[85] in this "shift from the visual to the affective, haptic, and proprioceptive registers."[86]

At this point it becomes necessary to better define the digital image, as well as differentiate it from and relate it to, the virtual. Hansen's definition of the digital image stands in the Bergsonian-Deleuzian tradition:

the so-called digital image explodes the stability of the technical image in any of its concrete theorizations. Following its digitization, the image can no longer be understood as a fixed and objective viewpoint on "reality" . . . since it is now defined precisely through its almost complete flexibility and addressability, its numerical basis, and its constitutive "virtuality."[87]

At the same time, this definition stands in contrast to the German media theorist Friedrich Kittler's notion of the "technical medium" of digitality, the effect of the "decoupling of information and communication that began with telegraphy and reached its zenith with the digital computer."[88] The assumption here is the gradual disembodiment of information, which occurred throughout the twentieth century in three waves of cybernetic configurations: homeostasis, reflexivity, and virtuality.[89] Hansen's notion of the digital image deconstructs previous theories of the disembodiment of information in the age of electronic media in that for him new media are an experience that "explodes the technical image" and brings it back to the body, an experience that is—more than ever—in desperate need of actual bodies and notions of embodiment.

On the basis of the examples in chapters 2 through 4, I would like to call this shift in the era of new media a shift toward the *corporealization of the image*—in other words, far from witnessing a gradual disembodiment of information and images, the age of new media constitutes the current moment in a process of embodiment or corporealization. This shift was made possible by the oscillation between a fragmented and holistic body concept in a history of the body that has been tending toward increased mediation ever since early modernity (as we see in chapter 1). What remains to be determined, however, is whether new media are really *new,* and whether there is indeed a paradigm shift at stake in the age of digital information. This question has been addressed widely and differently in current media theoretical discussions, and a detailed report would exceed our present interest in new media art. I want to stress, however, that the answer to this question depends on what exactly is under examination: the communication process between user and medium, the medium itself, or the effects and products of the medium. As far as the process of communication goes, Lev Manovich points out that new media are nothing other than an old concern with illusionism, in which each historical period "offers some new 'features' that are perceived by audiences as an 'improvement' over the previous period (for example, the evolution of cinema from silent to sound to color)."[90] Similarly, Oliver Grau defined virtuality as the human relationship to images—a human strategy of immersion, which is all but new.[91] Mike Sandbothe addresses the question of new or old with a pragmatist critique of the hybrid or "transmedial" medium of the Internet, in which he does not see any radical novelty per se, but "a digital netting of already known media."[92] The McLuhan scholar Derrick de Kerckhove, however, sees television as the last step in the evolution of frontal and theoretical media. In his media theory, the tactile, participatory, interactive strategies of new media do indeed constitute an ontological shift in that they are considered revitalizations of the communication strategies between users in and outside of the realm of new media.[93]

The relationship between old and new media has been theorized at length in the media theories of Marshal McLuhan (*Understanding Media: The Extension of Man,* 1964) and Friedrich Kittler (*Aufschreibesysteme 1800–1900,* 1985), among others. It is largely thanks to these theories that the late twentieth century stood under the impression of a media materialist approach, which is at the basis of *Getting Under the Skin* as well as the various processes employed in the production of new media art or architecture. There is, however, a major question that remains, namely, whether new media has moved us beyond the analogue cinematic image—the classic form of expression of the modern era—or whether it has immersed us even further into the moving image logic of cinema.[94] For Manovich, the cinema is and remains the dominant cultural form of the twentieth century, playing a fundamental role in the cultural configuration of new media. The paradox he points to is that although all imaging is becoming computer-based the dominance of cinematic imagery is becoming even stronger. Somewhat in contrast to Manovich, Hansen sees the need to "break with the cinematic metaphor."[95] He dismisses Manovich's claim that the manual component of the *making* of the digital image constitutes an epistemological shift, arguing that Manovich ignores the manual dimensions of the precinematic regime (for example, cranking the handles of Eadweard Muybridge's zoopraxiscope). What matters to my own media-theoretical approach, however, is not to find a final answer to the question of the status of the cinematic image within the new media age, but is that the process-oriented new media practice features the body more than ever as *operator.*

Contrary to this view stands Vivian Sobchack's argument that "the electronical is phenomenologically experienced not as a discrete, intentional, and bodily centered projection in space but rather as simultaneous, dispersed, and insubstantial transmission across a network."[96] In the electronic paradigm, in which *referentiality* has become *intertextuality,* Sobchack sees no future for the body, for which she has reserved the encounter with the cinematic code as the only authentic phenomenological experience. I argue, however, that despite the fact that the spectator of electronic art may be invested in the "surface," as she argues, and precisely because of his or her "flattened investment" in, for instance, deep surface architecture, body and medium reemerge as one *flesh.*

More relevant to the approach taken in *Getting Under the Skin,* that is, of a body theory in which the body is thought as constitutive mediation, is Hans Belting's anthropology of images. Belting argues that the digital media reintroduce the body analogy via denial, and replace the body's absence with what he calls *iconic presence.* Like Roland Barthes for whom the photographic image was a return from the dead (*La chambre claire,* 1980), for Belting images "live from the paradox that they perform the presence of an absence or vice versa."[97] Belting emphasizes the new media's capacity to "pursue the mimesis of our own imagination," as was the case in Aziz + Cucher's *Synaptic Bliss:* "Digital images inspire mental images, much as they are inspired by mental images and their flux."[98]

Whether new or old, the constitution of the digital image is somewhat problematic, as pointed out by John Johnston, who in his article *Machinic Vision* has raised the question whether we can still talk about *images* when "the image itself becomes just one form that information can take, and if perception can no longer be defined in terms of the relationship between images."[99] It is here that the body comes into play as an image in the Bergsonian sense that perceives by substracting from the multiplicity of images from its environment (the virtual) in order to *actualize* information. In this "shift from an ontology of images to an ontology of information,"[100] the questions concerning perception move far beyond the coding and decoding processes; rather, the perceiver's filtering body is needed to frame the bodyless image information: "The body, in short, has become the crucial mediator—indeed, the 'convertor' (Ruyer)—*between information and form (image):* its supplemental sensorimotor intervention coincides with the process through which the image (what I am calling the digital image) is created."[101] The body as mediator, however, is only one side of this throughgoing relationship between body and medium. It is the medium that appears as corporeal in Johnston's era of machinic vision—a truly Deleuzian era. Once we consider the constitutive power of *framing,* and hence the corporealization of the image, it becomes clear that the image no longer is one representative of a single *actual* world, but merely is one actualization of a *virtual* world of infinite possibilities.

For Grosz, the virtual is not a separate entity from the real; rather, the outside is a *virtual* condition of the inside, or as Hansen puts it, the virtual is "a *quality* of human life, 'that capacity, so fundamental to human existence, to be in excess of one's actual state.'"[102] Despite that it is not easy to reconcile the Deleuzian, neoBergsonian, and feminist accounts of virtuality and the body with psychoanalysis, it is hard not to read Hansen's last quote as an invitation for a psychoanalytical explanation of virtuality. Psychoanalysis has been interested in cyberspace for the fact that the idea of the ego, or "ego-envelope" (Anzieu) perfectly fits the virtual arena of cyberspace in that the ego is one of many possible

realizations of the virtual. This explains the psychoanalysis interest in cyberspace as a ground for the quest of identity, in which the screen functions as the mirror image, a "prosthetic supplement for the subject's forgoing dispersal/failure, for the lack of co-ordination and unity."[103] Web avatars and graphical skins, as discussed in chapter 3, have contributed decisively to the possibilities of the quest of identity in "cyber-identity-games." With the possibility of creating a virtual persona through Multi User Dungeon (MUDs), and other virtual reality (VR) environments, the "screen-persona" can even adopt more importance than the "real-life-persona."[104] Avatars and other computer agents stage this importance, providing us with new faces and new facets in the new world of the screen. In a Lacanian analysis of "Cyberspace, Or, the Unbearable Closure of Being," Slavoj Žižek describes avatars as incorporations of "ego-envelopes" that mediatize the ego, protecting it from both the "real" inside, and the "real" outside.[105] Or as Sandy Stone has it, cybernetic space can be put on like a garment, which for her means to "put on the female."[106]

What emerges from the neophenomenological and the psychoanalytical accounts of cyberspace is that this is not a *nonspace,* but on the contrary an actualization of a potentiality of life, and in that sense it has the quality of the virtual, as that which is *becoming.* As Grosz writes: "there can be no liberation from the body, or from space, or from the real . . . . The cybernetic focus on the body is precisely a mode of singling out and intensifying certain regions of the body, its stimulation to maximal degrees."[107] Throughout this book, the various analyses of bodily configurations at the turn of the millennium can be seen as revelations of these intensified regions of the body; having been singled out within the various strategies of getting under the skin, these bodily strata are now serving as new extended spaces and metaphors for new spaces, which have been incorporated into various realms from popular culture and advertisement to medical visualizations of the body's interior—to the performing arts, postorganic architecture, and new media art.

In new media art since the 1990s, cyberspace functions as an experimental arena where themes like "controlled randomness,"[108] which emerged in the avant-garde movements of the early twentieth century, are staged. Digital art is very much in debt to questions developed by the previous art movements of Dada, Fluxus, and conceptual art: "The importance of these movements for digital art resides in their emphasis on formal instructions and in their focus on concept, event, and audience participation, as opposed to unified material objects."[109]

There are innumerable examples of interactive new media art.[110] In the following, I discuss in detail two new media art pieces from the realm of digital narrative environments. First is Sharon Daniel's interactive website and computer installation *Narrative Contingencies* (2000): [111]

A database of images and texts with a web-based interface, it engages audiences both by inviting them to contribute personal artifacts and stories, and by allowing them to generate random results, constructing a narrative from chance combinations of words, sounds, and images. Visitors can make their own contributions to this evolving artwork using the computers, camera, scanner, and printer in the gallery.[112]

Narrative Contingencies expresses most emblematically the 1990s-extensions manner of using the logic of new media in art installations. The project presents us with a break down of several boundaries of codes. There is no longer a difference between words, images, and sounds, and hence the codes of data float into each other delivering random access to the respective codes of communication. The artist and creator of the project no longer is detached from the viewer; in fact, meaning can only be constructed in the concrete interaction, specifically by giving an input of a word, object, or sound. The position of subjectivity is therefore distorted, and the installation seems to tell us: *You can only grasp me while interacting with me. In the next nanosecond it could be already all different.* The emphasis does not lie on the product, but on the process. The artwork is evolving into a sort of nonplace like an airport, or the World Wide Web, that a lot of people go through without ever stopping or staying for good. There is absolutely no control over the different instances of this narrative-chance generator. The outcome is unpredictable, and therefore often surprisingly funny.

Similarly, the Canadian sound and video installation artist David Rokeby uses the arbitrary chance factor in the denomination process in one of his projects, *The Giver of Names* (1990–present). As Rokeby's website describes, the installation is a reflection on the process of semiosis:

The Giver of Names is quite simply a computer system that gives objects names. The installation includes an empty pedestal, a video camera, a computer system and a small video projection. The camera observes the top of the pedestal. The installation space is full of "stuff" . . . objects of many sorts. The gallery visitor can choose an object or set of objects from those in the space, or anything they might have with them, and place them on the pedestal. When an object is placed on the pedestal, the computer grabs an image. It then performs many levels of image processing (outline analysis, division into separate objects or parts, colour analysis, texture analysis, etc.) These processes are visible on the life-size video projection above the pedestal. In the projection, the objects make the transition from real to imaged to increasingly abstracted as the system tries to make sense of them.[113]

The Giver of Names (figure 4.15) reflects on the process of semiosis by making visible the possibilities of machine vision (as opposed to human perception): A video camera captures a digital still of an object that a participant places on a pedestal. After a series of processes takes place using databases of words and phrases, the computer linked to the camera begins to formulate descriptions of the particular object.

Narrative Contingencies and *The Giver of Names* are literate systems emphasizing the randomness and the complexity of the construction of meaning when they create a narrative. The output often looks like a Dadaist poem:

seeing - Inside this pool of books
naked words
tap dance like a nude descending a staircase.
Under watchful eyes,
shots ring out, the pool drains, and you start over again.[114]

As Christiane Paul points out, similar to these computer installations, "dadaist poetry aestheticized the construction of poems out of random variations of words and lines, using formal instructions to create an artifice that resulted from an interplay of randomness and control."[115] What is at stake and being questioned in these recent computer installations, however, is the process of sense per se. It no longer is just a reflection on the possibilities of the collage, such as the incorporation of the frame. Rather, at stake here is the core issue of communication itself, a return to the essential question: "how is meaning constructed?" By emphasizing the "idea of rules being a process for creating art,"[116] which resonates in the use of the mathematical algorithm at the basis of any computer program, these installations question any possible aspect involved in the construction of meaning—from creation to reception, to the incorporation of the environment, to the possibilities of blurring all codes of communication involved. Their self-criticism and autoreflexivity, however, does not make these

Figure 4.15. David Rokeby, *The Giver of Names,* 1990–present. Courtesy of the artist.

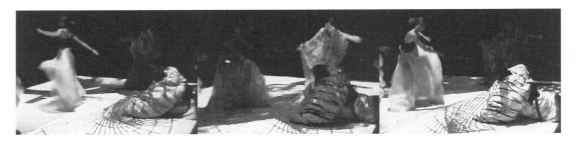

Figure 4.16. Sha Xin Wei, still of dancers in a *TGarden* responsive media space in V2 Rotterdam, 2001. Courtesy of the artist.

artifacts easier to read. On the contrary, it is not really their *readability* that they are about. These digital narrative environments point to the instability of meaning, but acknowledge at the same time that we are already much too immersed in this logic for it to be likely to abandon it.

In the following, I mention selected examples of new media art in which (similar to the architectural examples from the previous section) haptic space—both internal to and produced by the viewer's affective body—has replaced visual space.[117]

In collaboration with the artists research groups Sponge[118] and fOAM,[119] media artist Xin Wei Sha produced the *TGarden* experiments (2001), an interactive dance performance and a true example of haptic space (figure 4.16). *TGarden* is a space in which bodies and media become the same.[120] The affective viewer-participants' experience is described as follows:

You choose one of a set of fantastical costumes made of white fabric that can register projected images. You are led into a small space draped in black curtains and are then dressed by an attendant . . . . You are told to listen, move, and attend to what is happening as you move. You are released from the dressing chamber into a room roughly 20 by 20 by 20 feet, in which there are one to four other people also dressed in diverse fantastical costumes. The costumes serve as phenomenological experiments: one is a transparent skin that clothes you in a heavy armor, another increases your volume but keeps your weight unchanged. In any case, each costume defamiliarizes your body so you may more readily improvise gestures. The room is filled with a humming, slowly varying, textured tone, occasionally shot through with explosive streaking sounds. In some cycles these explosions are triggered by a dynamic of accumulating charge and release. In other cycles, a dense aural texture thickens the ambience but also makes it harder to individuate your own contribution to the sound field. The floor is painted with moving shapes and lines and textures cast from a video projector 20 feet directly overhead. As you move you see that your shadow is in turn shadowed by graphics projected on the floor, patterns, wings that echo and respond to your movement. As you pass other people, sometimes the shadows overlap and mix and sometimes they explode into dust. Sometimes as a person passes near you, your shadow detaches and jumps across the floor to her. She steals your shadow and drags it along by accident the first couple of times but then takes it intentionally as everyone joins the impromptu game. Sometimes you exchange and re-exchange shadows. As you lift your own arms, you may notice very subtle changes in the field of sound, perhaps a sinusoidal "signature" whistle.[121]

Chapter 2 demonstrates that the logic of chance inherent to these computer installations is a logic inherited from the avant-garde, from Dadaist performances to happening art.[122] As Michael Kirby points out, though, even Marcel Duchamps' ready-mades were in part constructed through this very logic of chance:

Marcel Duchamp dropped three threads, each exactly one meter long, onto three sheets of glass from a height of one meter. Fastening them down, he used the sinuous lines arrived at by chance (that is, gravity, etc.) to make three measuring sticks, the varying curved edges of which are each exactly one meter in length. The six pieces are called Trois Stoppages-Etalon or Three Standard Needle Weavings (1913/14).[123]

Just like in the *TGarden* experiments, the *chance event* has become a common metaphor in modern dance, too. A metaphor, as the choreographer Johannes Birringer explains, that might stand for the unconscious:

If you produced and programmed the motion paths in the whole parameter, and then collaborated with a dancer, the resulting dance would be a new composite (chance event); it would be unfolding, immediate, and yet would interlink present/presence and storage (past/memory) in a way that appeared to well up as if from the unconscious, from someplace other than the self, in some indeterminate and unforeseeable way.[124]

It becomes quite clear in this choreographic description that the posthuman subject in question performs as "a complex network of signified differences, postponements, and unrootednesses in space," in other words a "network of symbolic discourses and representations of its cultural environment."[125] These symbolic discourses are clearly represented by the digital chance logic of an unforeseeable distribution of data, an order that like in some antivirus programs needs to be defragmented from time to time. The differences, postponements, and unrootednesses in space, however, can be interpreted as representing a logic of the unconscious, a field of experience most important to current concerns, for it is the only guarantee or proof of the "real,"[126] which is the ultimate goal, and in itself the only proof of the desired first-person experience. The quest for the ultimate proof of the "real" and for the authenticity of the first-person experience is of course no news, but has to be seen in the context and as one of the leitmotifs of modern art. Ever since the avant-gardes, this desire has been pursued and vastly represented. However, it has become one of postmodernity's trademarks.

In *The Return of the Real,* Hal Foster points out how the strategies of the real can be traced to several art movements of the 1960s—the "minimalist genealogy of the neo-avant-garde," pop art, superrealism (photorealism), appropriation art, and others—and how it has since become one of postmodernity's trademarks.[127] Foster reminds us of Roland Barthes' interpretation of pop art: Barthes saw in this new expression (mainly in Andy Warhol's work) a "desymbolization of the object and a release of the image from any deep meaning into simulacral surface."[128] The "return of the real," in other words, can be seen as a strategy of flattening out the art-object (whether digitally or not), or better, pushing it onto the surface of the screen. The "real," of course, can also be read in a psychoanalytical way: we are therefore entering the dangerous sphere of the *real* of death (not only of the author) and of psychosis in general.

The unconscious can be said to "resemble" the digital in some ways, which is why, for example, the web calls for such metaphors as a "split self." Žižek described avatars as incorporations of "ego-envelopes," proving the necessity of the masquerade throughout life, which—as we have seen in many artistic projects discussed in this book—continuously hide an empty space or a nonspace. Splitting the self—to put it in Žižekian terms—is the realization that there was not any self in the very beginning, and that the self exists only as a split entity.

In this regard it is worth mentioning one of feminist media artist Mary Flanagan's digital art pieces *{collection}* (figure 4.17).[129] This project, says Flanagan, serves as an example of how women artists in the era of 1990s extensions "are turning the tables on the construction of the subject." The purpose in Flanagan's beneficial computer virus, originally called *{phage},* is to "think of the computer in a nonhierarchical way."[130] In this networked computer application that creates a visible, virtual, collective unconscious "the computerized mem-

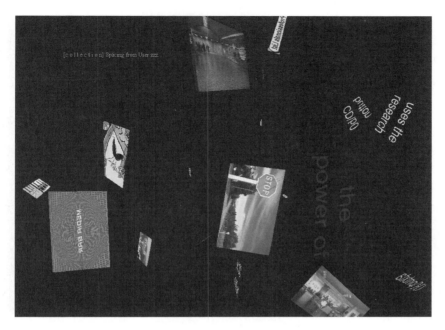

Chapter 4

Figure 4.17. Mary Flanagan, *[collection]*, 2002. Courtesy of the artist.

ory takes on a life of its own."[131] The project *{collection}* scours hard drives of the computers that have the downloadable program installed collecting bits and pieces of user's data—sentences from emails, graphics, web browser cached images, sound files, etc.—creating this material into a moving, three-dimensional continuously shifting map.[132] In *{collection}* Flanagan emphasizes the discussed issues, the chance generator, and the similarity of the unconscious to the computer. The artist states that *{collection}* is reminiscent of, and visualizes the process of, memory.[133]

The emphasis on visualizing the process of memory brings with it a focus on randomness and unpredictability, and consequently a critique of control. In fact, the beneficent computer virus is intended to exhibit autonomy in its selection and display of media and computer. Flanagan uses the computer logic here to display a cyber-feminist prospective: "Through its nonhierarchical organization and its divorce of creative control from the user to the machine, *{phage}* is an attempt to alter the epistemology by creating a *feminist map of the machine*."[134]

The unconscious is also of interest to the interactive DECONcert by James Fung and Steve Mann, "in which audience members actively (and unconsciously) choreograph a collective cyborg consciousness by contributing their own brain-wave patterns."[135] In this digital performance piece the audience translates their brain waves, recorded through leading-edge EEG technology, into the realm of music. The unique outcome of this brain-wave configuration was performed at Toronto's Deconism Gallery on March 21, 2003.

From the new flatness of recent architecture to the corporealization of the image in new media art, the examples and underlying theory of chapter 4 demonstrate a move toward embodiment. The image has gotten rid of its frame, and has been instead redirected onto the body itself. Body discourse is, in this sense, necessarily a media discourse in that the body, pushing through its frame, has revealed itself layer by layer as comprising the media that purport to represent it. The strategies of getting under the skin have given individual layers their own (inter)face, empowering them to circulate as flattened fragmented body parts in the realm of cyberspace. However, I point to an epistemological shift between chapters 3 and 4: whereas the examples from popular culture in chapter 3 engage in a struggling discourse that suffers a nostalgic drag in getting rid of the bodily interiors, the new media architecture and art examples in chapter 4 have gotten rid of the body, merging the flesh of technology with that of the interacting viewer-participant. The medium that signifies the body, its representation, no longer is any different from the raw material of the body of the installation itself. Without mediation the body is nothing; moreover, mediation already is what the body always was in its various historical and cultural strata.

It is important to note that there is a number of media artists—especially biologically oriented artists—at work today who are most critical about the fascination of virtual and interactive body recombinations. The *emerging media*[136] artist Paul Vanouse, for instance, dedicates his work to questions of biotechnology and genomics as currently emerging media forms. His *Relative Velocity Inscription Device* (2002), for instance, is a live scientific experiment, using the DNA of his own multiracial family of Jamaican descent, that explores the relationship between early twentieth-century eugenics and late twentieth-century human genomics. The experiment takes the form of an interactive, multimedia installation, containing a computer-regulated, biological separation gel through which four family members' DNA samples slowly travel. Each DNA sample contains one of the six genes generally accepted as influencing skin color. The family members' skin color genes are raced against one other in a sequence of experiments (one for each of the six genes). In Vanouse's *Relative Velocity Inscription Device* he develops a "racist map of the machine," similar to Flanagan's "feminist map." Through randomness and live performance, the category of race is being deconstructed as relative in this playful interaction between a family's gene pool.[137]

In chapter 1, Barbaras reminded us of a crucial quote in the *Phénoménologie de la perception* in which Merleau-Ponty declares that the body "'*has* its world or understands its world without having to pass through representations;' it '*is* the potentiality of the world.'"[138] To return to Merleau-Ponty's thought, we can see how in these new media-based art examples the Cartesian presumption of the thinking subject as a secure point of departure against the objects in the world is severely undermined; the body—"the fabric into which all objects are woven"[139]—is thus not a mere intermediary, an "in-between" the subject and the world, but rather the always already-mediated unity that effectively undermines the existence of these very categories. In other words, the holistic discovery of the body as constitutive mediation has converged with an age of mediatic proliferation, such that what we are witnessing in the apparent continuing fragmentation of the body is the work of mediation itself *as* the body. It is for this reason that there can be no history of the body that is not at the same time a study of the various media that constitute embodiment as such.

Conclusion: Body Discourse as Media Discourse

The body is no longer a corporeal idolatrous object; it has become an intangible subject of fascination. We dance around the high-tech pilaster construing this almost tangible phantasm. Representation is, and always was, the domain of both our embodied and disembodied yearnings. It is in the friction of this conjunction that we experience the euphoric dislocation of our present condition. Like Duchamp's "inframince," this is an insubstantial zone of disillusion where, after all is said and done, there remains only an imperceptible yet ubiquitous plenitude of being. . . . A new aesthetic comes to the fore. The art-work is more and more embodied in the interface, in the articulation of a space of meeting between the art-work and the viewer, and even in the articulation of space where the art-work as an artifact seems to disappear altogether and only communication between viewers remains.[140]

—JEFFREY SHAW, "THE DIS-EMBODIED RE-EMBODIED BODY"

The Medium Is the Body

With this insight, the media artist Jeffrey Shaw pronounces a new aesthetic era of embodied art; this aesthetic has serious implications not only on the viewer's involvement in the artwork but, as I illustrate throughout this book, the implications are much more deeply rooted. The corporealized image, which has emerged out of the discussed new media art practices and deep-surface–driven architecture, has revolutionized both theories of mediality and corporeality, reconciling them into one discipline. Body art, in other words, no longer can be seen as one form of media art, but rather as the necessary expression within the realm of new media.

In the discussion of Eisenman's architectural theory, we see that electronic media have added "a quality of the unseen" to vision, producing an environment that perceives and "looks back" at the viewer. In a next step of this argument on vision, Eisenman notes that with "the quality of the unseen" the anthropocentric subject is displaced. What interests him here is not the dispersion of subjectivity (into cyberspace) as much as the fact that an unbroken continuity between interior and exterior—metaphorized with the fold—changes traditional vision. Eisenman adds, with the trope of folding vision "from *e*ffective to *a*ffective space"[141] to a realm that is more than reason, meaning and function.

The argument of affective media is also at the heart of Hansen's new media philosophy, in which departing from Bergson's principle he argues that there can be no perception without affection. It is through this art form that according to Hansen "new modalities through which the body can filter—and indeed give form to—the flux of information"[142] are currently developed, dramatically changing both notions of mediality and corporeality.

In chapter 4's examples of new media art and architecture, we see how the logic of new media has infiltrated the contemporary body concept, and how the body as frame, in turn, has become coeval with mediation. Architecture, traditionally conceived of as the craft of building a dwelling for the human body, now reflects a new understanding of that body—no longer as a separate, exterior structure to house a bodily interiority, but as a continued or extended embodiment of that body's essence as it has been grasped by the discourses analyzed throughout this book—as primordial mediation.

But how do the examples of new media art and performance art in the realm of 1990s extensions relate to the architectural examples of new flatness and deep surface? Besides the rhetorical figures of randomness, chance, authorlessness, and the collapse between the inside and the outside, there seems to be at least one more common thread: all the examples of new flatness, deep surfaces, and new media art show that the current body discourse has "gotten rid" of the body insofar as the medium has become corporealized itself, and has therefore taken the place of the actual body—as with the *Blur,* in which interactivity has constructed itself a "house." Its final layer peeled off, the body no longer is a medium for something else, standing in for a truth or a reality that lies beyond the surface. Rather, the surface has collapsed, merging inside and outside, refusing to relegate itself to the subservience of one last mediation. The medium, in other words, has become the body.

Getting Under the Skin is the attempt to trace and analyze the various steps the body has taken—both historically and literally—to "push through the fourth wall" and eventually emerge as mediation. As new technologies have allowed for the opening of the body and its dispersal into fragments of information, these technologies have in turn served as strategies for understanding and ultimately controlling the body, which artists, architects, and others have deployed in the realization of new bodily configurations. What the outcome of this process may mean in the long run certainly is not yet determined.

Most important for the conclusion of *Getting Under the Skin* is that media no longer can be understood as McLuhen's "extensions of man;" rather, what recent new media art and architectural practices show is that the *subject-centered* body has been left behind insofar as the digital image has corporealized itself—as it has pushed through the frame of materiality or "exploded the frame," as Hansen has it.[143] In this understanding there is no body as "raw material," which would imply that there is something like an original body, a body that is prior to inscription and semanticization. But no, the current body under the influence of media technologies can merge and bend; and, by inhabiting it, we—the viewer-participants—can become part not only of its genotype, but also of its phenotype, as many of the examples in chapter 4 show (for example, *Son-O-House, TGarden*). What is at stake in these examples is a holistic body notion that has been fed or informed by a fragmented body; this is a body whose pieces have never been more penetrated and whose data have never been better collected than now in their being rendered into digital bits. But the output of this process does not assume a unified subject that achieves its "wholeness" only through the interrelation of the various body parts. The holism in question in these media art and architecture installations is of a different kind. It is a holism that authorizes every bit and every piece of the fragmented body to take over the body as a whole, to serve as interface. In late-twentieth-century popular culture the body and all its organs no longer simply serve as a medium of expression, as a semiotic layer toward the outer world. Rather, the body and its parts themselves have adopted the characteristics of a medium, wherein lies the return to a holistic body concept. On the basis of this, I suggest that we ask is this in fact anymore a *body,* that is, a *human body,* that is being released as whole through these body installations? The answer is no, as these installations are examples of how the body of twentieth-century concerns, in all the discussed realms from psychoanalysis to phenomenology and cognitive science, has been replaced by issues regarding mediality itself.

Notes

Preface

1. Bernadette Wegenstein, *The Representation of AIDS in the European Media* (Vienna: Vienna University Press, 1998).

2. See chapter 3 for an in-depth discussion of von Hagens's "anatomy art."

Chapter 1

1. Antonin Artaud, "To Have Done with the Judgment of God, A Radio Play" (1947), in *Selected Writings,* ed. Susan Sontag (New York: Farrar, Straus, and Giroux, 1976), 565.

2. Bernard Andrieu, *Le corps dispersé: Histoire du corps au XXe siècle* (Paris: L'Harmattan, 1993), 9; my trans.

3. The *Nouvelle Histoire* grew to a large extent as a reaction against the positivistic approach to history of the late nineteenth century. At the beginning of the twentieth century, French historians enlarged and enriched the historical discipline with writings of various kinds from archeological to oral documents. Criticizing the notion of "historical event," the methods of the new historians focused on delivering a "problematic and not automatic" concept of history (Jacques Le Goff, "L'histoire nouvelle," in *La Nouvelle Histoire,* ed. and dir. Jacques Le Goff, Roger Chartier, and Jacques Revel; [Paris: CEPL, 1978], 218); the present was to be understood through the past, and the past through the present. An important concept, coined by historian Fernand Braudel (1958), was that of "la longue durée." This temporal concept entailed that, despite history's rapid change,

historical deep structures can only be seized over time because the changes to economical and social systems can be evaluated only long after a system has been implemented.

4. In 1929, Marc Bloch and Lucien Febvre founded the legendary journal *Annales d'histoire économique et sociale* to accompany and illustrate the achievements of the new historians.

5. Qtd. in Jacques Revel, *Histories: French Constructions of the Past,* ed. Jacques Revel and Lynn Hunt (New York: The New Press, 1995), 18.

6. Ibid., 241.

7. Bryan S. Turner, *The Body and Society: Explorations in Social Theory,* second ed. (London: Sage, 1996), 7–8.

8. Michel Feher with Ramona Naddaff and Nadia Tazi, *Fragments for a History of the Human Body,* I–III (Cambridge, MA: The MIT Press [Zone], 1989).

9. Feher, part I, 11.

10. Feher, part I, 13.

11. Feher, part III, 11.

12. Feher, part I, 15.

13. See my discussion of Thomas Laqueur, note 25.

14. Chris Eliasmith, ed., "Dictionary of Philosophy of Mind," [electronic database]. Available from http://www.artsci.wustl.edu/~philos/MindDict/. I refer to holism throughout this book in the context of its meaning as *interrelation,* that is, of all body parts, without which the body would not be able to achieve its *wholeness.* This term comes from analytic philosophy, particularly W. V. Quine's logics (From a Logical Point of View, 1953), in which he stated that claims about the world are confirmed not individually, but only in conjunction with theories of which they are a part, that is, holistically.

15. Turner, *The Body and Society.* See, especially, the enriched introduction by Bryan Turner.

16. In this regard it is worth mentioning the phenomenon of reality television and its revolutionary appearance in the late 1980s as a political-economic response to the economic restructuring of U.S. television; in particular, such promoters of current Western

beauty ideals as the so-called "body makeover" shows, such as *Extreme Makeover, I Want a Famous Face,* and *The Swan.* See my *Reality Made Over: The Culture of Reality Television Makeover Shows,* under review.

17. Anthony Giddens, *The Transformation of Intimacy: Sexuality, Love, and Eroticism in Modern Societies* (Cambridge, England: Polity, 1992).

18. Norbert Elias, *The Civilizing Process* (New York: Urizen Books, 1978–1982).

19. Giddens, *The Consequences of Modernity* (Stanford: Stanford University Press, 1990).

20. See my dissertation, *Die Darstellung von AIDS in den Medien: semiolinguistische Analyse und Interpretation* (Vienna: Vienna University Press, 1998), based on the medialization of AIDS in Europe in the 1990s (starting with the French *Journée du Sida* in 1994).

21. Françoise Baranne, *Le couloir: Une infirmière au pays du sida* (Paris: Gallimard, 1994); my trans.

22. I want to add that—preceding Giddens—Michel Foucault had already taken the biopolitical factor into consideration in his study of the history of sexuality, *Histoire de la sexualité* I–III (1976–1984). "Biopower" is, according to Foucault, a force deployed by governments operative within a scale ranging between the optimization of life and the regulation of mortality. It is one of the consequences of the passage from a *disciplinary* society to a society of *control,* wherein "life has become an object of power." Michel Foucault, "Les mailles du pouvoir," in *Dits et Écrits* (Paris: Gallimard, 1994), 194; qtd. in Michael Hardt and Antonio Negri, *Empire* (Cambridge, MA: Harvard University Press, 2000), 24.

23. Barbara Duden, *The Woman Beneath the Skin: a Doctor's Patients in Eighteenth-Century Germany,* Thomas Dunlap, trans. (Cambridge, MA: Harvard University Press, 1991), 4.

24. Vesalius, for instance, dissected a uterus that looked like an inverted penis; see Vesalius' *De Humanis Corporis Fabrica* (1543).

25. Emphasis in original. Thomas Laqueur, "Amor Veneris, vel Dulcedo Appeletur," in *Fragments of a History of the Human Body,* Part Three, ed. Michel Feher (New York: Zone, 1989), 94; see also Thomas Laqueur, *Making Sex: Body and Gender from the Greeks to Freud* (Cambridge, MA: Harvard University Press, 1990).

26. Jean-Luc Nancy, "Corpus," in *Thinking Bodies,* ed. Juliet MacCannell Flower and Laura Zakarin (Stanford, CA: Stanford University Press, 1994), 31. French original, *Corpus* (Paris: Éditions Métailié, 1992).

27. Ibid., 29. I want to clarify, however, that Nancy does not refer to alterity in a psychoanalytical sense of one's own fractal body image here, but to body as other. For the psychoanalytical account of the body, see note 81 on Lacan.

28. See Galen, *On the Usefulness of the Parts of the Body,* vol. I and II, trans. and ed. Margaret Tallmadge May (Ithaca, NY: Cornell University Press, 1968).

29. Ibid., 49.

30. Jonathan Sawday, *The Body Emblazoned* (New York: Routledge, 1995), 212.

31. David Hillman and Carla Mazzio, ed., "Introduction," in *The Body in Parts: Fantasies of Corporeality in Early Modern Europe* (New York: Routledge, 1997), xii–xiii.

32. Ernst Cassirer, *The Individual and the Cosmos in Renaissance Philosophy* (Philadelphia: University of Pennsylvania Press, 1963), 3; qtd. ibid., xiii.

33. Hillman and Mazzio, *The Body,* xiii–xiv.

34. Ibid.

35. See William Egginton's thesis that modernity is to be defined in terms of a "theatrical" spatiality that enables the human subject to perceive the world in the form of a screen on which the viewer projects him or herself; his or her body may be displayed and contemplated as an object simultaneous with the act of contemplation itself. William Egginton, *How the World Became a Stage: Presence, Theatricality, and the Question of Modernity* (Albany: SUNY Press, 2002).

36. Jay David Bolter and Richard Grusin, *Remediation: Understanding New Media* (Cambridge, MA: The MIT Press, 1999), 34.

37. See Claudia Benthien's introduction to her American edition of *Skin: On the Cultural Border Between Self and the World* (New York: Columbia University Press, 1999), viii; for a summary of Benthien's history of skin, see my chapter 3, "How Faces Have Become Obsolete."

38. A prime example of this is the recently established Allen Institute for Brain Science in Seattle, Wash., founded in 2004 with the help of the Bill and Melinda Gates foundation, and Microsoft cofounder, Paul Allen, who donated $100 million for brain research.

39. The booming literature in the current philosophy of mind proves the importance and controversy of today's brain research. See Arnold H. Modell's *Imagination and the Meaningful Brain* (Cambridge, MA: The MIT Press, 2003); or Lawrence A. Shapiro's *The Mind Incarnate* (Cambridge, MA: The MIT Press, 2004).

40. Jean-François Lyotard, "Can Thought Go on Without a Body?," in *Materialities of Communication,* ed. Hans Ulrich Gumbrecht and Pfeiffer K. Ludwig (Stanford: Stanford University Press, 1994), 286–300.

41. Ibid., 300.

42. Alan M. Turing, "Computing Machinery and Intelligence" (1950) in Douglas R. Hofstadter and Daniel C. Denett, ed., *The Mind's I: Fantasies and Reflections on Self and Soul* (New York: Bantam Books, 1981).

43. Ibid., 53–54.

44. Turing himself was, needless to say, not emphasizing the gender-theoretical aspect I am bringing to light here; rather, sexual difference served him merely as an analogy for difference per se.

45. Judith Halberstam and Ira Livingston have claimed that the "posthuman condition is upon us" in Western culture at the turn of the new millennium. See Halberstam and Livingstone, *Posthuman Bodies* (Bloomington: Indiana University Press, 1995), vii.

46. N. Katherine Hayles, *How We Became Posthuman: Virtual Bodies in Cybernetics, Literature, and Informatics* (Chicago: University of Chicago Press, 1999), 2–3.

47. Ibid., 3.

48. The term *cyber* stems etymologically from Ancient Greek κυβερνητησ meaning "steersman." Cybernetics is the theory or study of communication and control in living organisms or machines. The technical term *cybernetics* itself had first been used in the late 1940s by the computer scientist Norbert Wiener (*The Human Use of Human Beings: Cybernetics and Society* [New York: Doubleday, 1954]), who tried to find functional analogies between the human and the computer. The *cyborg,* hence, is a living organism that is human and at the same time partly like a machine, or has integrated machinic parts into his or her flesh. The OED (1989) defines a *cyborg* as a blend of cybernetic and organism: "A person whose physical tolerances or capabilities are extended beyond normal human

limitations by a machine or other external agency that modifies the body's functioning; an interpreted man-machine system." The term *cyborg,* however, was first used by the *New York Times* on May 22, 1960: "A cyborg is essentially a man-machine system in which the control mechanisms of the human portion are modified externally by drugs or regulatory devices so that the being can live in an environment different from the normal one." Since the 1960s we have been inundated with cyborg definitions. Of the most critical is that given by feminist biologist and cultural theorist Donna Haraway, who extends the cyborg idea into the realm of literature, biology, and philosophy. In *The Cyborg Handbook* edited by Chris Hables Gray in 1995, we find historical definitions of current interpretations of the cyborg from its origins in space to its use in the military, as well as its genealogy from medicine to entertainment. It is only in recent years that the field of body criticism has replaced the term *cyborg* with the term *posthuman.*

49. See chapter 4 for a critical discussion of the disembodied digital image.

50. Jean Baudrillard, "The Ecstasy of Communication," in *The Anti-Aesthetic: Essays on Postmodern Culture,* ed. Hal Foster (Port Townsend, WA: Bay Press, 1983), 129.

51. Arthur Kroker and Mariluise Kroker, "Theses on the Disappearing Body in the Hyper-Modern Condition," in *Body Invaders: Panic Sex in America* (New York: St Martin's Press, 1987). Austrian media theorist and artist Peter Weibel has argued similarly in his various writings on the history of the image. According to Weibel, a distributive logic has been established as a result of the digital image's mobility and multiplication: the image has been expedited from a society of proximity (Walter Benjamin's "aura") to a society of distance, in which its disappearance is cause for celebration. (See, for instance, *Vom Verschwinden der Ferne. Telekommunikation und Kunst,* 1990.)

52. See the section headed "Nature versus Nurture" for a detailed analysis of these issues.

53. Michel Foucault, *The Order of Things* (New York: Pantheon, 1970), 387; French original 1966.

54. The cyberpunk genre was inaugurated by William Gibson's novel *Neuromancer* (1984), and is identifiable in both fiction and film (from David Cronenberg's *Videodrome* [1983] to such mainstream Hollywood film productions as *The Matrix* series [1999–2003]).

55. See chapter 3.

56. Warren McCulloch, *Embodiments of Mind* (Cambridge, MA: The MIT Press, 1965), 72.

57. Ibid., 307. I should not fail to add that McCulloch's list of "things" that man desires figures food next to women and beds.

58. Ibid., 72–73.

59. Public lecture delivered at the Fifth Conference on Artificial Intelligence in Naram, Japan (1996), qtd. in Hayles, *How We Became Posthuman* (Chicago, IL: University of Chicago Press, 1999), 244. See also my discussion of the Visible Human Project in chapter 3, "How Faces Have Become Obsolete," and particularly Catherine Waldby's critique of the body as "data ghost" in current medical views of the body.

60. Stefan Helmreich, *Silicon Second Nature: Culturing Artificial Life in a Digital World* (Berkeley, CA: University of California Press, 1998).

61. George Lakoff and Mark Johnson, *Philosophy in the Flesh: The Embodied Mind and Its Challenge to Western Thought* (New York: Basic Books, 1999), 4.

62. Herbert Dryfus, *What Computers Can't Do: the Limits of Artificial Intelligence* (New York: Harper, 1979), 236.

63. Donna Haraway, "A Cyborg Manifesto: Science, Technology, and Socialist-Feminism in the Late Twentieth Century," in *Simians, Cyborgs and Women: The Reinvention of Nature* (New York: Routledge, 1991), 150.

64. Haraway, *Modest_Witness@Second_Millenium.FemaleMan©_Meets_Oncomouse™: Feminism and Technoscience* (New York: Routledge, 1997), 12. For a variety of approaches to the cyborg see *The Cyborg Handbook* (1995), ed. Chris Hables Gray, where one finds historical definitions of current interpretations of the cyborg from its origins in space to its use in the military, as well as its genealogy from medicine to entertainment.

65. Robert Pepperell, *The Posthuman Condition: Consciousness Beyond the Brain* (Bristol, UK: Intellect Books), 1.

66. Interestingly enough, Björk has recently produced a remediated album, *Medulla* (2004), in which she uses only human voices as instruments, which sound at times as if they were not just electronically enhanced but rather electronically produced. This liberal exchange between two productive domains, the human (what Björk calls "blood and earth") and the technological (which is remediated in this musical performance), merges here into what can be called a posthuman sound zone.

67. Frank Hoffman, "Lee Bul: cyborgs and karaoke: a traveling exhibition now at the New Museum in New York highlights the recent karaoke-based work of a Korean artist known for her high-tech feminism and 'global' fusions of culture," in *Art in America,* May 2002.

68. Hayles, *How We Became Posthuman,* 290–291.

69. For an overview of approaches to the female body within recent feminist theory, see the reader *Feminist Theory and the Body,* ed. Janet Price and Margaret Shildrick (London: Routledge, 1999). Some of these approaches will be discussed below.

70. Elizabeth Grosz, *Architecture from the Outside: Essays on Virtual and Real Spaces* (Cambridge, MA: The MIT Press, 2001), 28.

71. Grosz, "Psychoanalysis and the Imaginary Body," in *Feminist Subjects, Multimedia: Cultural Methodologies,* ed. Penny Florence and Dee Reynolds (Manchester: Manchester University Press, 1995), 183.

72. Ibid., 184, 193.

73. Grosz, "Introduction: Refiguring Bodies," *Volatile Bodies: Toward a Corporeal Feminism* (Bloomington: Indiana University Press, 1994), 5.

74. Ann J. Cahill, *Rethinking Rape* (Ithaca: Cornell University Press, 2001), 52.

75. Grosz, *Volatile Bodies,* 5.

76. For a recent contribution utilizing this approach, see Bernice Hausman's *Mother's Milk: Breastfeeding Controversies in American Culture* (London: Routledge, 2003).

77. Duden, *Disembodying Women: Perspectives on Pregnancy and the Unborn* (Cambridge, MA: Harvard University Press, 1993), 56; German original 1991. Aristotle quote from *Generations of Animals,* II, IV, 739b, 21–25, trans. A. L. Peck (Cambridge, MA: Harvard University Press, 1942).

78. Grosz, *Volatile Bodies,* 15.

79. Ibid., 17.

80. Ibid.

81. Jacques Lacan, *Le séminaire Livre XX: Encore* (Paris: Seuil, 1975), 36.

82. Julia Kristeva, *Histoires d'amour* (Paris: Denoël, 1983); *Tales of Love,* trans. Léon Roudiez (New York: Columbia University Press, 1987), 295.

83. Toril Moi, *What is a Woman? And Other Essays* (Oxford: Oxford University Press, 1999), 4–5.

84. Simone de Beauvoir, *The Second Sex,* trans. H. M. Parshley (New York: Vintage Books, 1989), 34.

85. Moi, *What is a Woman?,* 63.

86. See Gilles Deleuze, *Expressionism in Philosophy: Spinoza* (New York: Zone Books, 1990).

87. Such a notion of difference as antecedent to the elements it distinguishes has been at the heart of the philosophical project spanning the thought of Martin Heidegger, Jacques Derrida, and Gilles Deleuze.

88. Grosz, *Volatile Bodies,* 10.

89. Moira Gatens, "Towards a Feminist Philosophy of the Body," in *Crossing Boundaries: Feminisms and the Critique of Knowledge,* ed. Barbara Caine, E. A. Grosz, and Marie de Lepervanche (Sydney: Allen and Unwin, 1988), 68–69; qtd. in Grosz *Volatile Bodies,* 12. For an in-depth study of Spinoza's philosophy, see Moira Gatens and Genevieve Lloyd, *Collective Imaginings: Spinoza, Past and Present* (London: Routledge, 1999).

90. In chapter 4, The Medium Is the Body, I will investigate to what extent digitality was crucial for this move as well.

91. *Surplus* means, in other words, that feminine gender is by default gendered, and that its inscription is therefore always a surplus. See Egginton, *Perversity and Ethics,* chapter 4, in which he argues for an understanding of sexual difference as determined by the distinction between other-regarding and other-inhabiting.

92. Grosz, *Volatile Bodies,* 18.

93. Luce Irigaray, *Ce sex qui n'en est pas un* (Paris: Minuit, 1977), 133; my trans. Before Irigaray, feminist theorist Monique Wittig had already pointed to the fact that we can only speak of one gender, that is, the feminine, for the masculine is not the masculine

but the general. See Monique Wittig, "The Point of View: Universal or Particular?" in *Feminist Issues,* vol. 3, no. 2, fall 1983.

94. Grosz, *Volatile Bodies,* 19.

95. Judith Butler, *Gender Trouble: Feminism and the Subversion of Identity* (New York: Routledge, 1990), 7.

96. Grosz, "Psychoanalysis," 193. It is worth mentioning that in her *Cyborg Manifesto* (1991), Donna Haraway has also used the term *fluid* to describe the cyborg as quintessentially ethereal.

97. Ibid., 195.

98. Cahill, *Rethinking Rape,* 81.

99. See my section "Flatness and Architecture" in chapter 4 for a more detailed philosophical investigation into spatial notion of inside versus outside.

100. Grosz, *Volatile Bodies,* 209–210.

101. Nietzsche, *The Gay Science,* trans. Walter Kaufmann (New York: Random House, 1974), 35.

102. Ibid.

103. The following paragraphs are indebted to Eric Blondel's excellent summary of Nietzsche's body concept in his chapter "The Body and Metaphors," in *Nietzsche: The Body and Culture* (Stanford: Stanford University Press, 1991), 201–238; French original 1986.

104. Andrieu, *Le corps dispersé,* 43; my trans.

105. Blondel, "The Body and Metaphors," 10.

106. Ibid., 206.

107. Ibid., 207.

108. Ibid., 238.

109. Didier Anzieu, *Le Moi-peau* (Paris: DUNOD, 1995); for an exemplified discussion of Anzieu's concept, see chapter 3.

110. However, the importance of recognition by the other was, of course, already a key notion in Hegel's *Phenomenology of Spirit* in 1807.

111. Freud, qtd. in Grosz, "Psychoanalysis," 185.

112. Delivered as a lecture in 1936; first French publication 1949; Lacan, "The Mirror Stage as Formation of the Function of the I as Revealed in Psychoanalytic Experience," in *Écrits. A selection* (New York: W. W. Norton, 1977); trans. of *Écrits,* 1966, 1–7.

113. Grosz, "Psychoanalysis," 188.

114. Sigmund Freud, "Das Ich und das Es," in *Studienausgabe. Psychologische Schriften* (Frankfurt am Main: S. Fischer, 1975), 294; English footnote (added in 1927 to the English trans.).

115. François Dagognet, *Faces, Surfaces, Interfaces* (Paris: Librairies Philosophique J. Vrin, 1982), 49. Other contemporary accounts of an anthropology of the body are presented in the work of David Le Breton: *Anthroplogie du Corps et Modernité* (Paris: Press Universitaires de France, 1990); *L'adieu au corps* (Paris: Éditions Métailié, 1999). In his most recent book *La peau et la trace: sur les blessures de soi* (Paris: Éditions Métailié, 2003), Le Breton deals with today's piercing and tattooing practices, among other body marking traditions. These body markers serve as benefactors of identity and can be read sociologically as a battle against sufferance.

116. Elizabeth Grosz, *Volatile Bodies,* 209–210, 40.

117. Dagognet, *La peau découverte* (Le Plessis-Robinson: Collection Les Empêcheurs de Penser en Ronde, 1993), 51s.

118. Steven Connor, *The Book of Skin* (Ithaca, NY: Cornell University Press, 2004).

119. Ibid., 65.

120. Anzieu, *Le Moi-peau* (Paris: DUNOD, 1995).

121. Ibid., 13.

122. Lacan, "The Mirror Stage."

123. Otto Rank, *Der Doppelgänger: eine psychoanalytische Studie* (Wien: Turia & Kant, 1993); reprint of 1925 ed.

124. In *Trauer und Melancholie* (1915), Freud uses the metaphor of the lost objects' shadow that falls onto man and triggers the emotion of mourning.

125. Grosz, "Psychoanalysis," 190. See the insightful reading of anorexia nervosa in the legendary 1950s case of Ellen West (the pseudonymous anorexic subject of analyst Ludwig Binswanger) by Gail Weiss in "The Abject Border of the Body Image," in *Body Images: Embodiment as Intercorporeality* (London: Routledge, 1999), 87–102. Weiss reads West's illness as a "lack of fluidity and/or multiplicity" (102) of her body images, an attempt to be too coherent (and a refusal of destabilization), her *idée fixée* of getting fat that makes West suffer from anorexia, and makes her leave her body image behind, as she ultimately opts for suicide.

126. Henri Bergson, *Matière et mémoire,* 1896.

127. Bergson qtd. in Andrieu, *Le corps disperse,* 60; my trans.

128. Ibid., 62.

129. Ibid., 64.

130. Ibid., 65.

131. It is worth mentioning that for G. W. F. Hegel, phenomenology had yet another meaning, namely the metaphysical representation of human conscience from sensual naivety, ethics, art, religion, science, and philosophy to the state of absolute knowledge.

132. Ibid., 198; my trans. We should also mention the Czech phenomenologist Jan Patočka who was influenced by Edmund Husserl, his teacher, and later also by Martin Heidegger. Patočka's "a-subjective phenomenology" is not a mere academic endeavor that theorizes the *Leibkörper,* but a practical and highly political philosophy that attempts to realize a relation to the lived world (*Lebenswelt*). Ilja Srubar, preface, *Jan Patočka: die Bewegung der menschlichen Existenz* (Stuttgart: Klett-Cotta, 1991), 29. Patočka, who gave his life to the battle against Czech Communism, was cofounder with Václav Havel of the Charter 77, an anti-Marxist movement in former Czechoslovakia.

133. As Francisco J. Varela, Evan Thompson, and Eleanor Rosch point out in their introduction to *The Embodied Mind* (Cambridge, MA: The MIT Press, 1991), during the times of Merleau-Ponty in the 1940s and 1950s, "the potential sciences of mind were fragmented into disparate, noncommunicating disciplines: neurology, psychoanalysis, and behaviorist experimental psychology" (vvi). They note that it was not until the emergence of cognitive science in the 1970s that cognitive psychology, linguistics, artificial intelligence, and philosophy could be included in the study of mind.

134. Merleau-Ponty, *The Prose of the World,* trans. John O'Neill (Evanston: Northwestern University Press, 1973), 78; qtd. in Weiss, *Body Images,* 10.

135. Andrieu, *Le corps disperse,* 272.

136. Ibid., 274

137. Weiss, *Body Images,* 5; the same argument was made by Nancy in *Corpus.*

138. I am grateful to Stuart Murray (University of Toronto) for bringing this to my attention.

139. Merleau-Ponty, *Merleau-Ponty à la Sorbonne. Résumé de cours 1949–1952* (Grenoble: Cynara, 1988), 319, qtd. in Andrieu, *Le corps disperse,* 295; my trans.

140. Weiss, *Body Images,* 13.

141. Ibid.

142. Ibid., 15. It is worth mentioning at this point that Weiss reads Merleau-Ponty not only against Lacan, but also against Paul Schilder, whose *The Image and Appearance of the Human Body: Studies in the Constructive Energies of the Psyche* (1935), as Weiss reminds us, was the first full-length study of the body image.

143. Ibid., 21.

144. Stuart Murray, entry on "Maurice Merleau-Ponty," in *Dictionary of Literary Biography: Twentieth-Century European Cultural Theorists,* second series, vol. 296, ed. Paul Hansom (Columbia, SC: Bruccoli Clark Layman, 2004): 308.

145. Renaud Barbaras, *Le désir et la distance* (1999); *Le tournant de l'expérience* (1998); *Merleau-Ponty* (1997); *La perception* (1994); *De l'être du phénomène: l'ontologie de*

Merleau-Ponty (1991) (English translation: *The Being of the Phenomenon: Merleau-Ponty's Ontology* [Bloomington: Indiana University Press, 2004]). In what can be called a "post-phenomenological" French tradition (where "post" would stand for "after phenomenology's heyday"), of crucial importance is Michel Henri's *Philosophie et phénoménology du corps* (1965); Jean-Luc Marion's *Étant donné: essai d'une phénoménologie de la donation* (1997); or Dominique Janicaud's *La phénoménologie éclatée* (1998), to mention only a few influential works in this tradition. I am indebted to Kenneth Surin (Duke University) for pointing out the impact of "post-phenomenology" in this regard.

146. Barbaras, *The Being of the Phenomenon,* 7. This formulation is evidently offbeat for body art and body installations in the twentieth century, which is discussed in chapter 2.

147. Merleau-Ponty, *Phenomenology of Perception,* trans. Colin Smith (London: Routledge, 1962), 235. I want to give the full citation of this famous quote: "[My body is the fabric into which all objects are woven,] and it is, at least in relation to the perceived world, the general instrument of my 'comprehension.'"

148. Murray, email message to author, 5 February 2005.

149. Merleau-Ponty, *Phenomenology of Perception,* 51. As Barbaras points out, this problem is known as the problem of intentionality in Husserl.

150. Leonard Lawlor and Ted Toadvine, translators' introduction to Barbaras, *The Being of the Phenomenon,* see note 137.

151. Martin Heidegger, "Letter on Humanism," trans. Frank. A. Capuzzi, in Heidegger, *Pathmarks,* ed. William McNeill (Cambridge, UK: Cambridge University Press, 1998), 239. (German original, 1949).

152. Ibid., 242.

153. Ibid., 247.

154. Ibid., 249.

155. Martin Heidegger, *Being and Time,* trans. Joan Stambaugh (Albany, NY: SUNY Press, 1996), 140. The ellipsis (in the original) is Heidegger's way of saying "anything."

156. Heidegger is inspired by Nietzsche's *Twilight of the Idols,* Section IV, "How the 'Real World' Finally Became a Fable": "The real world attainable for the wise man,

the pious man, the virtuous man—he lives in it, *he is it,*" trans. Duncan Large (Oxford: Oxford University Press, 1998), 20.

157. Heidegger, *Nietzsche, Volume 1: The Will to Power,* trans. David Farrell Krell (San Francisco: Harper Collins Paperback, 1991), 98–99. (German original, 1961).

158. Steven Connor, *The Book of Skin,* 49.

Chapter 2

1. Bill Viola in an interview with Nicholas Zurbrugg, *Art Performance Media: 31 Interviews,* ed. Nicholas Zurbrugg (Minneapolis: University of Minnesota Press, 2004), 332.

2. The historical accordance of electronic media with postmodernism goes back to the third movement, described by Fredric Jameson, of the three decisive historical moments of "technological revolution within capital itself." This third moment takes place in the 1940s (the other moments being the 1840s with the cultural logic of realism expressed in photography, and the 1890s with the emergence of modernism and its most prominent technological instantiation in the cinema), and its center-less logic of networked subjectivity, as well as its desire for simultaneity results from the phenomenological *immateriality* of new media. In political-economical terms, it is a logic that reflects the workings of multinational capitalism. See Fredric Jameson, "Postmodernism, or The Cultural Logic of Late Capitalism," in *New Left Review* 146 (July-Aug.): 53–94.

3. An earlier version of this chapter has appears as, "If you won't SHOOT me, at least DELETE me! Performance Art from 1960s Wounds to 1990s Extensions," in *Data Made Flesh: Embodying Information,* ed. Robert Mitchell and Phillip Thurtle (London: Routledge, 2003).

4. Jay David Bolter and Richard Grusin, *Remediation: Understanding New Media* (Cambridge, MA: The MIT Press, 1999), 5.

5. William J. Mitchell, *The Reconfigured Eye: Visual Truth in the Post-Photographic Era* (Cambridge, MA: The MIT Press, 1994), 8; qtd. in Bolter and Grusin, *Remediation,* 31. It should be added that N. Katherine Hayles also recognizes the emphasis on the process in the Second Wave of Cybernetics in the 1960s where the theme of reflexivity replaces the theme of homeostasis and prepares for the era of virtuality (Hayles, *How We Became Posthuman,* 141).

6. "What: Mob Scene. Who: Strangers. Point: None," Berlin Journal by Otto Pohl, in the *New York Times,* August 4, 2003: A4.

7. Similar actions have been pursued by the Tactical Art Coalition of the CRITICAL ART ENSEMBLE, such as the action "Halifax Begs Your Pardon!" (2002). In this critique of tourism, the artists interact with both Haligonians and Halifax-tourists, "bringing out occurrences/histories, opinions, and meanings that have been dispossessed, silenced, or ignored." http://www.critical-art.net/tactical_media/halifax/index.html

8. *Brus Muehl Nitsch Schwarzkogler: Writings of the Vienna Actionists,* ed. and trans. Malcolm Green in collaboration with the artists (London: Atlas Press, 1999), 35.

9. For the apparently not-so-small body dismorphic movement of apotemnophilia (love for amputation), there exists an Internet discussion listserv "amputee-by-choice," in which amputee wannabes can exchange information. See Carl Elliott, "A new way to be mad," in *The Atlantic Monthly* (December, 2000): 71–84.

10. *Brus Muehl Nitsch Schwarzkogler: Writings of the Vienna Actionists,* 237.

11. See the exhibition Die verletzte Diva. Hysterie, Körper, Technik in der Kunst des 20. Jahrhunderts, Munich, March–May, 2000. For another recent example, see Elisabeth Bronfen and Barbara Straumann, *Die Diva. Eine Geschichte der Bewunderung* (Schirmer/ Mosel, 2002).

12. Paul Virilio, the French media philosopher, in an interview with Andreas Ruby, qtd. in *The Virtual Dimension,* ed. John Beckmann (New York: Princeton Architectural Press, 1998), 180.

13. Kathy O'Dell, *Contract with the Skin: Masochism, Performance Art, and the 1970s* (Minneapolis: University of Minnesota Press, 1988).

14. Ibid., 9.

15. Ibid., 12. Speaking of self-mutilation, it is worth mentioning the French film *Dans ma peau* (2002) by Marina de Van as a recent example of investigating the painful inhabitation of the (female) skin.

16. William Egginton, "Reality is Bleeding: A Brief History of Film From the 16th Century," in *Configurations* 9, no. 3 (fall 2001). The term *reality-bleed* comes from David Cronenberg's cyberpunk thriller *eXistenZ* (1999).

17. Lev Manovich, *The Language of New Media* (Cambridge, MA: The MIT Press, 2001), 45.

18. *"Pixels* are *picture elements,* the dots that electronically paint the letters on to the computer screen," qtd. in Richard A. Lanham, *The Electronic Word: Democracy, Technology, and the Arts* (Chicago: The University of Chicago Press, 1993), 3.

19. The French, *colle,* means paste or glue. Sabine von Fischer, in her "The Shock of Collage," explains, "The term 'collage' appeared between 1915 and 1920 in France to describe a new technique applied in Surrealist and Cubist painting where different materials were glued (collé) to form a composition of not evidently connected images or surfaces," in *TransReal,* no. 7 (November 2000), 86.

20. Historically, "tableaux vivants" are related to real-body representations imitating famous art pieces, mainly painting and sculpture. This form of expression in its modern form began in the Goethe-era of late-eighteenth- and early-nineteenth-century romanticism and ever since has been a lively constituent of modern art's imitating the imitations of imitations—including the incorporation of icons from the mass media (Cindy Sherman, Yasumasa Morimura, Pierre & Gilles, to name just a few artists). See the recent exhibit at the Vienna Kunsthalle, "Tableaux Vivants. Lebende Bilder und Attitüden in Fotografie, Film und Video," Vienna, 2002.

21. Hans Ulrich Gumbrecht, in "Postmoderne," *Reallexikon der deutschen Literaturwissenschaft,* vol. 3, Berlin De Gruyter (2003), 136–140.

22. Fedele Azaro, *Futurismo. I grandi temi 1909–1944,* ed. Enrico Crispolti and Franco Sborgi (Genova: Mazzotta, 1998), 122–123; my trans. For an extended discussion of the futurist trope of velocity, see Jeffrey T. Schnapp's anthropology of speed, "Crash (Speed as Engine of Individuation)," *Modernism/Modernity,* vol. 6, no. 1, 1999.

23. Philip Auslander, *Liveness: Performance in a Mediatized Culture* (London: Routledge, 1999), 57.

24. Cage taught Kaprow at the New School in New York from 1956–1958.

25. Qtd. in Michael Kirby, "Happenings: An Introduction," in *Happenings and Other Acts,* ed. Mariellen R. Sandford (New York: Routledge, 1995); first published in Michael Kirby, *Happenings Anthology* (New York: Dutton, 1965), 19.

26. *Manifesto tecnico della lettatura futurista,* and *Distruzione della sintassi—Immaginazione senza fili—Parole in libertà;* my trans.

27. Marinetti created the negatively connoted neologism *passatismo* to criticize old and established literary ideals of the classic Florentine style, that is, the *Tre Corone* Dante, Petrarca, and Boccaccio.

28. Clement Greenberg, "Collage," in *Art and Culture: Critical Essays* (Boston: Beacon Press, 1965).

29. Kirby, *Happenings,* 11–12.

30. Hans Belting, "Image, Medium, Body," in *Critical Inquiry* (Winter 2005), 304. I will return to the issue of the anthropology of images for the discussion of new media art and architecture in chapter 4.

31. Kirby, *Happenings,* 11.

32. Kirby, *Happenings,* 15. I would like to add the French lettrist movement to the list of twentieth-century art forms that emphasize processing and simultaneity, which it does in a style that has been called "visual poetry" for its fluid letter forms and various calligraphic techniques (for example, the manifesto of lettrist poetry by Isidore Isou, *Introduction à une Nouvelle Poésie et une Nouvelle Musique,* 1947).

33. Text from video *Chris Burden: A Video Portrait,* prod. Peter Kirby and Dan Zimbaldi, dir. and ed. Peter Kirby, coproduction of the Newport Harbor Art Museum (Media Art Services and Zona Productions: Newport Harbor Art Museum, 1989).

34. "Breaking into reality" is a result of a reality-bleed that did not just start with the avant-garde, but arose at the same time as the culture of representation, namely, with the origins of modern theater in early modern Europe; see William Egginton, *How the World Became a Stage: Presence, Theatricality, and the Question of Modernity* (Albany: SUNY Press, 2003).

35. For a complete list of futurist theater plays, see my "Marinetti and the Futurist Theatre," in *Dictionary of Literary Biography,* vol. "Twentieth Century Italian Theatre," ed. Rocco Capozzi and Donato Santeramo (Columbia, SC: Bruccoli Clark Layman, 2004), forthcoming.

36. In his famous novel *Nadja* (1928), the surrealist André Breton, who evolved directly from the culture of Dadaism, concludes: "La beauté sera CONVULSIVE ou ne sera pas." ("Beauty will be CONVULSIVE, or it will not be.")

37. The word *Merz* that Schwitters used in all these titles stems from the German *Kommerz*. The artist had used the word for the first time in a collage, and since then added it to any artwork.

38. Motherwall, *The Dada Painters and Poets* (New York: George Wittenborn Inc., 1951), 62–63; qtd. in Kirby, *Happenings Anthology,* 12.

39. The house was entirely destroyed during World War II, but was reconstructed for the exhibition at the Kunsthaus in Zurich, "Der Hang zum Gesamtkunstwerk," in 1983.

40. A redefinition of space also affected the realm of modern dance: "The emphasis in modern dance in general has been away from the two-dimensional picture-frame approach of classical dancing and into a dynamic three-dimensional use of space that might be related to the dominant tendency in Happenings to reject the traditional stage, but most modern dance retained the matrix" (Kirby 24).

41. Jean Baudrillard, "Simulacra and Simulations," in *Selected Writings,* ed. Mark Poster (Stanford: Stanford University Press, 1988), 172s.

42. Kirby, *Happenings,* 22.

43. Recall from chapter 1 that as a poet Nietzsche had already "invented" a new language prior to Artaud that would be capable of expressing reality and life at the same time; see Blondel, "The Body and Metaphors," 203.

44. Artaud, *The Theater and Its Double* (New York: Grove Press, 1958), 114.

45. Derrida, "Le théatre de la cruauté et la clôture de la représentation," in *Écriture et Différence* (Paris: Seuil, 1967), 343; my trans.

46. Ibid., 363.

47. Kaprow, "Excerpts from *Assemblages, Environments & Happenings,*" in *Happenings and Other Acts,* 235. For a detailed discussion of Kaprow see the section on "The Syntax of Performance."

48. Schwitters, Catalogue of exhibition at the Centre Georges Pompidou (Paris: Édition du Centre Pompidou, 1994), 77.

49. *Aktionismus. Aktionsmalerei Wien 1960–65,* ed. Peter Noever (Wien: Österreichisches Museum für Angewandte Kunst, 1989), 62.

50. Kristine Stiles, "Unverfälschte Freude: Internationale Kunstaktionen," in *Out of Actions: Aktionismus, Body Art & Performances 1949–1979,* Catalogue to *Out of Actions* exhibit at the Austrian Museum of Applied Arts, Vienna, June-September, 1998 (Osfildern, Germany: Cantz, 1998), 290; my trans.

51. "Panorama 1: Painting in Motion (Draft)," in *Brus Muehl Nitsch Schwarzkogler: Writings of the Vienna Actionists,* 199. For more detailed information on Schwarzkogler, see *Rudolf Schwarzkogler,* ed. Eva Badura-Triska and Hubert Klocker (Wien: Museum moderner Kunst Stiftung Ludwig, 1992).

52. Muehl and Brus founded the institute for Direct Art in 1966.

53. Text of *Invitation for the Second Total Action* by Brus and Muehl (Vienna, Galerie Dvorak, June 24, 1966); qtd. in *Brus Muehl Nitsch Schwarzkogler: Writings of the Vienna Actionists,* 41.

54. *Performance* and *competence* correspond with Ferdinand de Saussure's concepts of *parole* and *langue.*

55. David Crystal, "Speech act," in *An Encyclopedic Dictionary of Language and Languages* (Oxford, UK: Blackwell, 1992).

56. J. L. Austin, *How to Do Things With Words* (Cambridge, MA: Harvard University Press, 1975); first ed. 1962.

57. For example, Valie Export, Cindy Sherman, Mariko Mori, Yasumasa Morimura, Pierre & Gilles, Andres Serrano as seen at the exhibition, "Appearance" at the Galleria d'Arte Moderna in Bologna, January-March, 2000.

58. *Brus Muehl Nitsch Schwarzkogler: Writings of the Vienna Actionists,* 41.

59. Frazer Ward, "Some Relations between Conceptual and Performance Art," in *Art Journal,* vol. 56, no. 4, winter 1997.

60. Kaprow, *Essays on the Blurring of Art and Life* (Berkeley, CA: University of California Press, 1993), 59s.

61. Ibid., 59.

62. Ibid., 62–63

63. Ibid., 65.

64. Ibid., 62.

65. Ibid., 63–64

66. Of course, the use of nonprofessionals is a common factor in any realism, for example, in the Italian film movement of *Neorealismo.*

67. *Camera Lucida: Reflections on Photography,* trans. Richard Howard (New York: Hill and Wang, 1981).

68. In *Trauer und Melancholie* (1915), Sigmund Freud uses the metaphor of the lost objects' shadow that falls onto man triggering the emotion of mourning.

69. In the video about Chris Burden's actions, we can see interviews with the rare witnesses of his performances, who turn out to be his friends and colleagues.

70. Text from video: *Chris Burden: A Video Portrait.* Produced on the occasion of the exhibition Chris Burden: A Twenty Year Survey organized by Anne Ayres, associate curator, and Paul Schimmel, chief curator. Executive Producer: Newport Harbor Art Museum, Ellen Breitman, curator of education. Producers: Peter Kirby and Dan Zimbaldi. Director and Editor: Peter Kirby. 1989.

71. Kaprow, *Happenings and Other Acts,* 230.

72. See, in particular, the section in chapter 4, "The Corporealization of the Image in New Media Art."

73. Kaprow, *Happenings and Other Acts,* 234.

74. This new logic is also anticipating the format of the reality show, so prominent today.

75. Roswitha Mueller, *Valie Export: Fragments of the Imagination* (Indianapolis: Indiana University Press, 1994), 34.

76. Paul Schimmel, "Der Sprung in die Leere. Performance und das Objekt," in Stiles, *Out of Actions,* 84.

77. Mueller, *Valie Export,* xix.

78. Amelia Jones, *Body Art: Performing the Subject* (Minneapolis: University of Minnesota Press, 1998), 1. As Jane Blocker points out in her *What the Body Cost* (Minneapolis: University of Minnesota Press, 2004), "the acceptance of the body in art came at a price, that the shift from the pure object of high modernism to performance had both liberating and deeply reactionary effects" (14).

79. Barbara Rose, "Orlan: Is it Art? Orlan and the Transgressive Act," *Art in America,* vol. 81, no. 2 (February 1993), 83–125. For a more recent and in-depth analysis of Orlan's art, see the contributions by Fred Botting, Scott Wilson, Orlan, and Rachel Armstrong in "Part Three: Self-Hybridation," in *The Cyborg Experiments: The Extensions of the Body in the Media Age,* ed. Joanna Zylinska (London: Continuum Press, 2002).

80. Laura Mulvey, "Visual Pleasure and Narrative Cinema," in *Visual and other Pleasures* (Bloomington: Indiana University Press, 1989).

81. Mueller, *Valie Export,* 17–18.

82. For Lacan, the symbolic *je* has the function of suturing together fragments of the imaginary body.

83. In her interpretation of Holly Hughes's performance *Clit Notes* (1994), B. J. Wray reads the staging of the female genitalia as an *aesthetics of lack:* "The parodic performances of lack in these pieces foreground the complex relationship between 'real' lesbian bodies and their entry into a phallic representational economy." B. J. Wray, "Performing Clits and Other Lesbian Tricks," in *Performing the Body/Performing the Text,* 190.

84. Jones, *Body Art,* 227.

85. The term *discourse* has to be specified, in that almost all disciplines of the humanities operate with it, from linguistics to sociology. In my current use of *discourse* I refer to the semiotic notion of a *text* that is produced by a specific media-genre. Each genre has its own possibilities of creating the *Énoncé,* and the respective *Énonciateur* and *Énonci-*

ataire, that is, the utterance, the uttering subject, and the receiving subject, in the way(s) that is pertinent to the genre itself (see Algirdas Greimas/Joseph Courtés, *Sémiotique: dictionnaire raisonné de la théorie du langage,* Paris: Hachette, 1993, 125). A digital webpage, for instance, has multiple *Énonciateurs* and *Énonciataires,* which makes it a typically postmodern medium. By multiplying the uttering and receiving subjects, the stress shifts to the utterance itself.

86. Amelia Jones and Andrew Stephenson, *Performing the Body/Performing the Text* (London: Routledge, 1999), 3.

87. Ibid., 198.

88. Ibid.

89. Ibid.

90. Ibid., 235.

91. Jacques Derrida, "Videor," *Resolutions: Contemporary Video Practices,* ed. Michael Renov and Erika Suderburg (Minneapolis: University of Minnesota Press, 1996), 74; qtd. in Jones, Body Art, 200.

92. Bolter and Grusin, *Remediation,* 34.

93. Interview with MUD (Multi User Dungeon) user, in Sherry Turkle, *Life on the Screen: Identity in the Age of Internet* (New York: Simon & Schuster, 1995), 13.

94. Auslander, *Liveness,* 32.

95. "The fact of television," in *Daedalus,* vol. 111, no. 4 (1982), 86; qtd. in Auslander, *Liveness,* 44.

96. Ibid., 40.

97. Ibid., 9.

98. Ibid., 53.

99. Hal Foster, *The Return of the Real* (Cambridge, MA: The MIT Press, 1996), 127.

100. Slavoj Žižek, *The Plague of Fantasies* (London: Verso, 1997), 134.

101. Oliver Grau, *Virtual Art: From Illusion to Immersion* (Cambridge, MA: The MIT Press, 2003), 5.

102. See the extensive discussion of *flesh-art* with concrete examples from popular culture in chapter 3.

103. Qtd. in Michael Rush, *New Media in Late 20th-Century Art* (New York: Thames & Hudson, 1999), 56.

104. This logic corresponds to a 2003 television ad for an Internet provider, in which the hypertext is represented as a "clickable surface," getting "deeper" and by each click, and providing "information" for every single word. It is a paranoid universe that literally cannot come to any stop, or "rest," for it proposes a hyperlink to every word or item.

105. Bolter and Grusin, *Remediation,* 45.

106. Marshall McLuhan, *Understanding Media: The Extension of Man* (Cambridge MA: The MIT Press, 1996), 8; first ed. 1964.

107. Fredric Jameson, *Postmodernism, or, the Cultural Logic of Late Capitalism* (Durham: Duke University Press, 1991).

108. Rush, *New Media,* 65–69.

109. Byron Reeves and Clifford Nass, *The Media Equation: How People Treat Computers, Television, and New Media Like Real People and Places* (New York: Cambridge University Press, 1996), 5. Film examples from the genre of cyberpunk reveal the ubiquity of the idea of treating screen-personalities as real. In *Virtuosity* (1995), for instance, we are confronted with a classic oppositional structure of a virtual world in conflict with the real world. The former cop Parker fights his battle in the real world against Sid 6.7, a virtual television talk show–master who was "born" accidentally through a reality-bleed. Sid 6.7 is the incarnation of evil. His brain is an amalgam of serial killers, he has supernatural skills, such as being able to morph into his environment: "I am made of everything. I am the future." More than that, Sid 6.7 is immortal, unless one removes his implanted computer chip, which—not surprisingly—is achieved at the very end by the hero-antagonist Parker. As to the bleeding effect between virtuality and reality: there is absolutely no difference in Sid's virtual or real danger for his environment.

110. Bolter and Grusin, *Remediation,* 42.

111. Steve Mann with Hal Niedzviecki, *Cyborg: Digital Destiny and Human Possibility in the Age of the Wearable Computer* (Toronto: Doubleday Canada, 2001), 5. See the more detailed discussion of Mann in chapters 3 and 4.

112. Warwick, the British professor of cybernetics, had a silicon chip transponder surgically implanted in his left arm in 1998. See the more detailed discussion of Warwick in chapter 3.

113. Stelarc, "Towards the Posthuman: From Psycho-body to Cyber-system," *Architectural Design* (Profile no. 118: Architects in Cyberspace) 65: 11–12 (Nov.-Dec. 1995): 91.

114. Edward Scheer has called Stelarc's provocations "rhetorical sculptures," in Zylinksa, *The Cyborg Experiments,* 85.

115. See Mark Dery's chapter on Stelarc, "Ritual Mechanics: Cybernetic Body Art," in *Escape Velocity. Cyberculture at the End of the Century* (New York: Grove Press, 1996), 151–181.

116. Mark Poster, "High-Tech Frankenstein, or Heidegger Meets Stelarc," in Zylinksa, *The Cyborg Experiments,* 28.

117. http://www.stelarc.va.com.au/movatar/.

118. In the section, "The Corporealization of Image in New Media Art," I will extend this important discussion of the return of the body in new media art with many more examples of digital art. As we shall see, the incorporation of the body was a necessary constitutive for today's digital art.

119. Scheer, "Stelarc's E-Motions," in Zylinksa, *The Cyborg Experiments,* 97.

120. This example given by Shannon Bell at Interaccess Gallery, Toronto, March 2003, who called Stelarc's *Prosthetic Head* "the sweetest thing."

121. Flyer at Interaccess Gallery, Toronto, March 2003.

122. We shall discuss the implications of this movement within other new media art practices in depth in the section The Corporealization of the Image in New Media Art (chapter 4).

123. Mueller, *Valie Export,* 219

124. Interview with Roswitha Mueller, ibid., 215.

125. Qtd. in Kathy O'Dell, *Contact,* 17.

126. Mark Poster, *The Mode of Information: Poststructuralism and Social Context* (Chicago: University of Chicago Press, 1990), 16; qtd. in Jones, *Body Art,* 203.

127. See chapter 1 for the entire quote from *Volatile Bodies,* 209–210.

128. Mark Hansen, *New Philosophy for New Media* (Cambridge, MA: The MIT Press, 2004). See chapter 4 of this book for an in-depth account of Hansen's new media theory.

Chapter 3

1. Sigmund Freud, *Civilization and Its Discontents,* trans. and ed. James Strackey (New York: Norton, 1961), 43.

2. An earlier version of this chapter has appeared as, "Getting Under the Skin, or, How Faces Have Become Obsolete," in *Configurations,* special issue *Makeover: Writing the Body into the Posthuman Technoscape. Part I Embracing the Posthuman,* ed. Timothy Lenoir, no. 10.2 (spring 2002).

3. Gilles Deleuze and Félix Guattari, "November 28, 1947: How Do You Make Yourself a Body without Organs?," in *A Thousand Plateaus: Capitalism and Schizophrenia,* ed. and trans. Brian Massumi (Minneapolis: University of Minnesota Press, 1987).

4. Ibid., 149–166.

5. For example, the flattened meat slices of the Visible Human Project, which is discussed in the section Techniques of Fragmentation.

6. The exhibit Body Worlds has toured worldwide. As of May 2003, more than 11 million people have seen the public display of von Hagens's Anatomy Art. The German weekly *Der Spiegel* recently revealed the down-and-dirty business of "Mr. Death" (Gunther von Hagens) who illegally purchased executed bodies from Chinese and other countries (*Der Spiegel,* April 2004): 36.

7. Lisa Cartwright, "The Real Life of Biomedical Body Images" in *Digital Anatomy*, ed. Christina Lammer (Vienna: Turia and Kant, 2001), 31.

8. Ibid., 33.

9. http://www.nlm.nih.gov/research/visible/visible_human.html.

10. The "Book of Man" is the term used by Walter Bodmer and Robin McKie for the DNA that delivers the instructions according to which all humans are made. See Bodmer and McKie, *The Book of Man: The Human Genome Project and the Quest to Discover our Genetic Heritage* (Oxford: Oxford University Press, 1995).

11. Rabinow 1996, qtd. in Catherine Waldby, *The Visible Human Project: Informatic Bodies and Posthuman Medicine* (New York: Routledge, 2000), 37.

12. Claude Shannon and Warren Weaver, *The Mathematical Theory of Communication* (Urbana: University of Illinois Press, 1949).

13. Catherine Waldby, "The Visible Human Project as a Technology of Anatomical Inscription" in *Digital Anatomy*, 37.

14. Ibid., 55.

15. Ibid., 59.

16. Richard A. Robb, "Virtual (Computed) Endoscopy: Development and Evaluation Using the Visible Human Datasets," presented at the Visible Human Project Conference, October 7–8, 1996, National Library of Medicine, National Institutes of Health, Bethesda, MD. http://www.nlm.nih.gov/research/visible/vhp_conf/robb/robb_pap.htm.

17. As José van Dijk points out in her recent essay: "Bodyworlds: The Art of Plastinated Cadavers" in *Configurations* 9:1 (2001), von Hagens elevates the plastinates to a higher level than the simulations of body models: "The plastinated sculptures, however, are as much 'imitation' of bodies as are body models, and they sometimes look less 'real' (more like plastic) than eighteenth-century wax figures" (109).

18. See the German horror film, *Anatomie*, by Stefan Ruzowitzky (2000), in which the Anatomy Institute of Heidelberg is depicted as the reloading point for a secret fraternity that is experimenting with new anatomical procedures on living bodies.

19. Exhibition video, 2000.

20. Waldby, *The Visible Human Project,* 2.

21. Dan Nadel and Jonathon Rosen, "Through a Scanner, Darkly: Imaging the Body," in *I.D.* (March/April, 2004): 74s.

22. *Focus* 94 (August, 2000).

23. Michael Taussig, *Defacement: Public Secrecy and the Labor of the Negative* (Stanford, CA: Stanford University Press, 1999), 3.

24. Emmanuel Lévinas, *Totality and Infinity* (Pittsburgh: Duquesne University Press, 1969); French ed., 1961, 214.

25. Ibid., 75. It is worth mentioning that Merleau-Ponty considered the entire human body a primordial power of expression, of which the human face is its epiphany.

26. Jean Epstein, "On Certain Characteristics of Photogénie" in *Bonjour Cinéma and Other Writings by Jean Epstein,* in *Afterimage* no. 10 (autumn 1982): 114.

27. Epstein, "The Spirit of Slow Motion," ibid., 121.

28. Robert Stam and Toby Miller, eds., "Apparatus Theory," *Film and Theory: An Anthology* (London: Blackwell, 2000), 403.

29. Joan Jacobs Brumberg, *The Body Project: An Intimate History of American Girls* (New York: Vintage Books, 1997), 62.

30. Thanks to Timothy Lenoir for having discussed the semiotics of this advertisement with me.

31. Ibid.

32. Deleuze and Guattari, "Year Zero: Faciality," in *A Thousand Plateaus* (Minneapolis: University of Minnesota Press, 1988), 170.

33. A quasi-ironic take on the perishability and volatility of the face in today's imagination is the Hollywood contribution *Face Off* (1997), in which an FBI agent switches faces with a criminal mastermind through "surgical procedure."

34. John Hockenberry, "This is the Story of the Most Fearless Entrepreneur Ever: The Human Brain," in *Wired Magazine* (August 2001): 102. It is, of course, not by coincidence that the computer era coined the term *interface* to describe communication between humans and machines, showing how unavoidable it is to think of human interaction in terms of an encounter between sur-faces.

35. Michel Foucault, *The Order of Things* (New York: Pantheon Books, 1970), 387.

36. Donna Haraway, *The Companion Species Manifesto: Dogs, People, and Significant Otherness* (Chicago: Prickly Paradigm Press, 2003), 4.

37. The difference between man and animal also has been attacked in Derrida's late deconstruction. Insofar as life is the movement of *différance,* for Derrida, drawing a concrete line between the living and the dead, or between man and animal, is impossible: "Beyond the edge of the *so-called* human, beyond it but by no means on a single opposing side, rather than 'the Animal' or 'Animal Life,' there is already a heterogeneous multiplicity of the living, or more precisely (since to say 'the living' is already to say too much or not enough) a multiplicity of organizations among realms that are more and more difficult to dissociate by means of the figures of the organic and inorganic, of life and/or death." From Jacques Derrida, trans. David Wills, "The Animal That Therefore I Am," in *Critical Inquiry* (winter 2002): 399.

38. See Richard Doyle, *Wetwares. Experiments in Postvital Living* (Minneapolis: Minnesota University Press, 2003), in which the author examines such phenomena as cryonics, cloning, and organ-sharing and compares them to science fictions. In *Place of the Dead Roads* (1984), for instance, William Burroughs talks about the "familiars": "a zone of interactivity between humans and animals, 'psychic companions' that blur the contours of human subjectivity" (7).

39. Interdisciplinary animal studies are booming. It is no coincidence that at the recent Science and Literature conference in Durham, N.C., (2004) there were a number of panels dedicated to this field, such as "Interdisciplinary Animals," "Darwin's *The Descent* and Animal Studies," or "Historicizing the Question of Animal." On a different note, I want to add that the current unstable status quo of xenotransplants (particularly from pig to human) leads me to believe that the reality of transspecies is not yet anywhere close.

40. Marc C. Taylor and Esa Saarinen, *Imagologies: Media Philosophy* (New York: Routledge, 1994), 1.

41. François Dagognet, *Faces, Surfaces, Interfaces;* see a brief discussion of this book in the section on psychoanalysis in chapter 1.

42. See my discussion of skin-architecture exemplifying the implosion of the very notions of inside and outside in chapter 4.

43. http://www.swatch.com/skin/2001/index.php.

44. Benthien, *Skin,* 222.

45. See chapter 4 for a more detailed and concrete analysis of teletactile new media art.

46. Derrick de Kerckove, "Propriozeption und Autonomation," in *Tasten,* Kunst und Ausstellenhalle der BRD, Schriftenreihe Forum 7, Göttingen: Seidl, 1996, 345; qtd. in Benthien, 234.

47. Information retrieved from the website of the exhibition Crossfemale: Metaphors of Femininity in the Art of the 90s (April 2001) in Pforzheim, Germany, http://www .crossfemale.de/english/kuenstler/rikli.htm.

48. Alba D'Urbano, "The Project Hautnah, or Close to the Skin," in *Photography after Photography: Memory and Representation in the Digital Age,* Hubertus von Amelunxen, Stefan Iglhaut, and Florian Rötzer, eds. (Amsterdam: GandB Arts International, 1996), 270–275; quote from 272.

49. Benthien, *Skin,* 237. A contemporary attempt to overcome the isolation of the naked self is Skinstrip Online, http://www.skinstrip.net/online/. On this web platform, people are invited to "anonymously express their naked identity using visual images of their bodies," as stated on the website.

50. D'Urbano, "The Project Hautnah," 274.

51. Jones, 202.

52. Elizabeth Diller and Ricardo Scofidio, *Flesh: Architectural Probes* (New York: Princeton Architectural Press, 1994).

53. From the cover of Diller and Scofidio, *Flesh.*

54. See the detailed discussion of the relationship of interiority and exteriority with examples from the arts and architecture in my article "The Medium Is the Body."

55. Elizabeth Grosz, *Architecture from the Outside: Essays on Virtual and Real Spaces* (Cambridge, MA: The MIT Press, 2002), 18.

56. Georges Teyssot, "The Mutant Body of Architecture" in *Flesh,* 35.

57. Aaron Betsky, "Diller + Scofidio: Under Surveillance" in *Architecture* (June 2000): 130.

58. A continued discussion of Diller + Scofidio's work appears in chapter 4.

59. Frazer Ward, "The Technologies We Deserve," *Parkett,* no. 60 (2000): 191.

60. Mark B. N. Hansen, "Affect as medium, or the 'digital-facial-image,'" in *Journal of Visual Culture,* vol. 2 (2) (London: SAGE Publications, 2003): 225.

61. The "digital-facial-image" (DFI) is what Hansen coins the new paradigm for the human interface with digital data.

62. Ibid. See chapter 4 for a detailed discussion of Hansen's argument in relation to new media art examples.

63. http://www.kevinwarwick.org.

64. Steve Mann with Hal Niedzviecki, *Cyborg: Digital Destiny and Human Possibility in the Age of the Wearable Computer* (Toronto: Doubleday Canada, 2002), 5. See also http://www.wearcomp.org.

65. Interview with Steve Mann by Joseph Wilson, "Cyber sensation: Cyber-guru Steve Mann opens Digifest," in *NOW* (Toronto, May 13–19, 2004): 35.

66. Eugénie Lemoine-Luccioni, *La Robe* (Paris: Seuil, 1983).

67. She is also alluding to Lacan's distinction between having and being a phallus.

68. Marie-Luise Angerer, *body options. körper.spuren.medien.bilder* (Vienna: Turia and Kant, 2000). A similar point is made by Jane Blocker in her *What the Body Cost.* Blocker understands the body as a "condition of not knowing, which results in the conflict between what we undeniably are and yet remain distanced from" (7).

69. Ibid., 91.

70. Ibid.

71. Jacques-Alain Miller further developed the concept of *extimité* in his article "Extimité," in *Lacanian Theory of Discourse: Subject, Structure, and Society,* Mark Barcher, Marshall Alcorn Jr., Ronald J. Cortell, and Françoise Massardier-Kennedy (New York: New York University Press, 1994), 74–87.

72. Joan Copjec, *Read My Desire: Lacan against the Historicists* (Cambridge, MA: The MIT Press, 1994), 128.

73. Ibid., 129.

74. The collaboration between Holzer and Lang started in the Art and Fashion Biennale in Florence (1996), and continued with an exhibit at the Vienna Kunsthalle from October 9, 1998, to January 17, 1999, called Louise Bourgeois.Jenny Holzer.Helmut Lang. The connecting link between the two artists and the designer is—as pointed out by Sabine Folie and Gerald Matt in their introductory remarks to the exhibition catalogue—that their work moves "upon a terrain alongside of which key terms like inside, the body, the self, the thoughts against the outside, the dress, the perception by others and the meaning of words have been prominently positioned." Folie and Matt, "Morphologies of Recollection" in *Louise Bourgeois.Jenny Holzer.Helmut Lang,* ed. Folie (Vienna: Kunsthalle Wien, 1998), 81.

75. Holzer, *The Survival Series,* 1983–1985.

76. Penelope Green interviewing a marketer of cosmetics, "A Miracle a Minute: Skin Cream Heaven," *New York Times,* style section, 56, April 30, 2000. http://qvery.nytime .com/search/article?res=F70814FB3D5DOC738FDDADO894D8404482

77. KnoWear, 132 West 22nd Street, 8th Floor, New York, NY, 10011.

78. Carla Ross Allen in an interview with the author.

79. Ibid.

80. Artaud, "Van Gogh, the Man Suicided by Society" in *Artaud Anthology,* ed. Jack Hirschman (San Francisco: City Lights Books, 1965), 158.

81. Nietzsche, *The Genealogy of Morals,* trans. Walter Kaufmann and RJ Hollingdale (New York: Vintage Books, 1967), 57.

82. Nietzsche, *The Will to Power,* 276, in Blondel, *Nietzsche,* 215.

83. Blondel, *Nietzsche,* 238.

84. Nietzsche, *The Will to Power,* 425, in Blondel, *Nietzsche,* 238.

85. Ibid., 135. To understand this statement in context, we need to know that Artaud refers to van Gogh's suicide in 1890, the very same year van Gogh had been in psychiatric treatment under Dr. Gachet in Auvers. Artaud interprets this suicide as "unnecessary" and "avoidable," had the doctor had more understanding and insight into the spirit of the genial artist.

86. Ibid.

87. Ibid., 144.

88. Ibid., 161.

89. Angerer, *body options,* 137.

90. Grosz, *Volatile Bodies,* 187.

91. Haraway, "A Cyborg Manifesto: Science, Technology, and Socialist-Feminism in the Late Twentieth Century" in *Simians, Cyborgs, and Women: The Reinvention of Nature* (New York: Routledge, 1991).

92. Ibid., 178.

93. Deleuze and Guattari, "November 28, 1947: How Do You Make Yourself a Body Without Organs?," 164–165.

94. Ibid., 161.

95. Ibid., 150.

96. Artaud, *Selected Writings,* 571.

97. Weber as qtd. in Angerer, *body options,* 141.

98. Deleuze and Guattari, *A Thousand Plateaus,* 156.

99. Ibid., 153.

100. Ibid., 165.

101. Angerer, *body options,* 177.

102. Gilles Deleuze and Félix Guattari, *Anti-Oedipus: Capitalism and Schizophrenia* (Minneapolis: Minnesota University Press, 1983), 12.

Chapter 4

1. Manuel de Landa, *A Thousand Years of Nonlinear History* (New York: Swerve Editions, 2000), 274

2. Portions of this chapter will appear in *Intermedialities,* Hugh Silverman, ed. (London: Continuum Press), 2006.

3. Hans Belting, "Image, Medium, Body: A New Approach to Iconology," in *Critical Inquiry* (winter 2005): 304.

4. Ibid., 305.

5. "Images intervene between the world and us. Rather than representing the world, they obstruct it and cause us to live with them." Vilém Flusser, *Für eine Philosophie der Fotografie* (Göttingen: European Photography, 1989), 9–10; qtd. in Belting, *Image, Medium, Body,* 317.

6. De Landa, *Nonlinear History,* 268.

7. This assumption is closely related to Marshal McLuhan's and Friedrich Kittler's "media-materialism," which so importantly switched the emphasis from the contents or messages of media to their material configurations.

8. I want to add, however, that this new body notion has not at all reached current representations about the female body in popular culture, as so shockingly proven by the

Canadian phone and Internet company Bell in a recent ad. While Bell's campaign and controversial payoff formulation "We are all connected" had been criticized by many theorists (for example, Wendy Chun, *Control and Freedom: Power and Paranoia in the Age of Fiberoptics* [Cambridge, MA: The MIT Press, 2005]), their recent ad for their Internet service features a female body in a "science book" with the parts of the page displaying her sexual organs cut out. The payoff reads: "You'll do anything to protect your kids from inappropriate content. So will we."

9. "Jacques Derrida: invitation to a discussion," *Columbia Documents of Architecture,* 1992, 13; qtd. in Jean La Marche, "The Space of the Surface," in *Environment and Planning* 33 (2001): 2217.

10. Elizabeth Grosz, *Architecture from the Outside: Essays on Virtual and Real Spaces* (Cambridge, MA: The MIT Press, 2001).

11. Alicia Imperiale, *New Flatness: Surface Tension in Digital Architecture* (Basel: Birkhäuser, 2000).

12. Jean Baudrillard, "The Ecstasy of Communication," in *The Anti-Aesthetic: Essays on Postmodern Culture,* ed. Hal Foster (Seattle: Bay Press, 1983), 132.

13. Grosz, *Architecture from the Outside,* 66.

14. *DOMUS,* no. 822 (January 2000): 14–19.

15. For his insight here, I must thank Maya instructor Jesse Fabian, Department of Media Study, University at Buffalo, 2003.

16. http://www.archilab.org/public/2000/catalog/kolata/kolataen.htm.

17. *Domus,* no. 822, 12.

18. Ibid.

19. Greg Lynn, "Multiplicitous and Inorganic Bodies," in *Folds, Bodies & Blobs: Collected Essays* (Brussels: La Lettre Volee, 1998), 44.

20. Alicia Imperiale, *New Flatness: Surface Tension in Digital Architecture* (Basel: Brirkhäuser, 2000), 17.

21. Jameson, *Postmodernism, or the Cultural Logic of Late Capitalism,* qtd. in Imperiale, ibid.

22. Richard A. Robb, "Virtual (Computed) Endoscopy: Development and Evaluation Using the Visible Human Datasets," presented at the *Visible Human Project Conference,* October 7–8, 1996, National Library of Medicine, National Institutes of Health, Bethesda, M.D. http://www.nlm.nih.gov/research/visible/vhp_conf/robb/robb_pap.htm.

23. Waldby, *The Visible Human Project,* 55.

24. Ibid., 59.

25. Imperiale, *New Flatness,* 20.

26. Ibid.

27. Ibid., 22; the term *tattooed concrete skin,* qtd. in Imperiale, is borrowed from Sarah Amelar.

28. In his introduction to Dan Graham's *Two-Way Mirror Power* (Cambridge, MA: The MIT Press, 1999), Jeff Wall describes the artist as follows: "Dan Graham is or has been a sculptor and a photographer, an essayist and a performer, an architect, a curator, a gallerist, a teacher, and an archivist" (x).

29. Graham, *Two-Way Mirror Power,* 174.

30. I am borrowing this title from Imperiale, *New Flatness,* 50.

31. Lev Manovich, *Language of New Media,* 55.

32. Pierre Lévy, Cyberculture, trans. Robert Bononno (Minneapolis: University of Minnesota Press, 2001), 61.

33. Manovich, *Language of New Media,* 60.

34. Ibid., 61.

35. Ibid., 31–34.

36. Jameson, *Postmodernism, or, the Cultural Logic of Late Capitalism,* 117.

37. Deleuze, *The Fold: Leibniz and the Baroque* (Minneapolis: University of Minnesota Press, 1993), 11.

38. Ibid., 3.

39. Ibid., 6.

40. "An Avant-Garde Design For a New-Media Center" by Julie V. Iovine, *New York Times,* The Arts, Section E, page 1, column 4, March 21, 2002.

41. Imperiale, *New Flatness,* 35–38.

42. Hal Foster, *Design and Crime* (London: Verso, 2002), 40.

43. Ibid., 37.

44. Ibid., 38.

45. Ibid., 27.

46. Martin Jay, "Scopic Regimes of Modernity," in *Vision and Visuality, Discussions in Contemporary Culture,* ed. Hal Foster (New York: The New Press, 1998), 3–29; qtd. in Peter Eisenman, "Visions Unfolding: Architecture in the Age of Electronic Media," in Luca Galofaro, *Digital Eisenman: An Office of the Electronic Era* (Basel: Birkhäuser, 1999), 85.

47. Eisenman, *Visions Unfolding,* 87.

48. This idea comes from Lacan's *Les quatre concepts fondamentaux de la psychanalyse* (*The Four Fundamental Concepts of Psychoanalysis*), 1964.

49. Eisenman, *Visions Unfolding,* 89.

50. http://www.newmuseum.org/now_cur_super_ficial.php.

51. Term invented by the cyber-architect Markos Novak, who proposes the notions of *transarchitecture* and *hypersurfaces:* "Liquid architecture is an architecture that breathes, pulses, leaps as one form and lands as another . . . it is an architecture without doors and hallways, where the next room is always where I need it to be and what I need it to be." See http://www.mat.ucsb.edu/~marcos/Centrifuge_Site/MainFrameSet.html.

Notes

52. Qtd. in Imperiale, *New Flatness,* 56.

53. Michael Silver, project description obtained from architect, June 2004.

54. Ibid.

55. Maria Luisa Palumbo, *New Wombs: Electronic Bodies and Architectural Disorders* (Basel: Brirkhäuser, 2000), 70.

56. Ineke Schwarz, "A Testing Ground for Interactivity, The Water Pavilion by Lars Spuybroek and Kas Oosterhuis," *archis* (September, 1997). http://www.archis.org

57. Mark Hansen and others: *aRt&D:* Research and Development in Art (Rotterdam: V2_Institute, 2005).

58. Lars Spuybroek, *NOX. Machining Architecture* (New York: Thames & Hudson, 2004), 174.

59. Ibid.

60. Marcus Leinweber from NOX in an email interview with the author.

61. Lars Spuybroek, *NOX,* 179.

62. "Diller + Scofidio Blur Building," in *TransReal,* 50.

63. Ibid.

64. Mark Hansen, "Wearable Space," in *Configurations,* special issue *Makeover: Writing the Body into the Posthuman Technoscape: Part I Embracing the Posthuman,* ed. Timothy Lenoir, no. 10.2 (spring 2002).

65. http://www.arcspace.com/architects/DillerScofidio/blur_building/.

66. Diller + Scofidio, Blur: The Making of Nothing (New York: Harry Abrams 2002), 162, qtd. in Hansen, "Wearable Space," 330.

67. Ibid., 329.

68. "Diller + Scofidio Blur Building," in *TransReal,* 55.

69. Herbert Muschamp, "Instant Inspirations: Just Add Water," in the Weekend Section of the *New York Times* (April 6, 2001): B34. This article announces the Architecture + Water exhibit at the Van Alen Institute in New York (April–September 2001), featuring five liquid-architecture buildings. Interestingly, it is often water that represents the real in its fusion with the digital.

70. This contradiction is reflected in the spirit of the web artist Lisa Jevbratt, who has a nostalgic vision of herself hooked to one of the last computers in a dark, postweb and postnuclear *Blade Runner* environment, as the artist stated in a talk on her media art in the conference series "Data-Enhancement" at the University at Buffalo on March 26, 2001.

71. http://www.asymptote.net/.

72. *DOMUS,* no. 822, "Asymptote Architecture: Guggenheim Virtual Museum," 30.

73. Interview with Max Böhnel in the German online architecture magazine *Telepolis* (October 31, 2000); http://www.heise.de/tp/deutsch/special/arch/3581/1.html.

74. Aziz + Cucher in an interview with the author, February 16, 2005.

75. Marcus Novak, "Liquid Architectures in Cyberspace," qtd. in Aziz + Cucher, project description for *Synaptic Bliss* delivered to the author.

76. Project description for *Synaptic Bliss* delivered to the author.

77. New media's programmability, and specifically their ability to transcode, is what Manovich considers the "most substantial consequence of the computerization of media." Manovich, *Language of New Media,* 45.

78. Hansen, *New Philosophy for New Media,* 10.

79. Tim Lenoir and Casey Alt, "Flow, Process, Fold: Intersections in Bioinformatics and Contemporary Architecture," in Antoine Picon and Alessandra Ponte, ed., *Science, Metaphor, and Architecture* (Princeton: Princeton University Press, 2002).

80. Jacques Lacan, *The Seminar of Jacques Lacan,* Book III, *The Psychoses* (New York: Norton, 1992), 39.

81. Hansen, *New Philosophy for New Media,* 84. This trajectory, as Hansen informs the reader, corresponds to Raymond Ruyer's treatise of cybernetics from 1954, *La Cyberné-tique et l'origine de l'information.*

82. Donald MacKay, *Information, Mechanism, and Meaning* (Cambridge, MA: The MIT Press, 1969), 54; qtd. in Hansen, *New Philosophy for New Media,* 80.

83. Umberto Eco, *Trattato di semiotica generale* (Milano: Bompiani, 1991), 196.

84. Deleuze, *Cinema 2,* trans. Hugh Tomlinson and Barbara Habberjam (Minneapolis: The University of Minnesota Press, 1997), 62. It is important to note that Deleuze's trajectory, however, is not to move from the frame back to the body, but rather from the body to the frame, progressively disembodying the center of indetermination. (Hansen, *New Philosophy for New Media,* 6.)

85. Hansen, *New Philosophy for New Media,* 11.

86. Tim Lenoir, "Haptic Vision: Computation, Media, and Embodiment in Mark Hansen's New Phenomenology," foreword to *New Philosophy for New Media,* xxiv.

87. Hansen, *New Philosophy for New Media,* 8.

88. Ibid., 76.

89. Hayles, *How We Became Posthuman,* discussed in chapter 2, "(Dis)embodiment and Artificial Intelligence/Artificial Life."

90. Lev Manovich, *Langugae of New Media,* 181.

91. See the in-depth discussion of Grau's history of virtuality in chapter 2.

92. Mike Sandbothe, *Pragmatische Medienphilosophie* (Göttingen: Velbrück Wissenschaft, 2001), 152.

93. Derrick de Kerckhove, "Touch versus Vision: Ästhetik neuer Technologien," in *Die Aktualität des Ästhetischen,* ed. Wolfgang Welsch (Munich: Fink, 1993); 137–168.

94. Moreover, as William Egginton argues, the specific representational form of cinema owes more to its epistemological configuration as a form of theatrical spatiality than to

its particular technological elements. See "Reality is Bleeding: A Brief History of Film from the 16th Century," *Configurations* 9, no. 2 (2001): 207–230.

95. Hansen, *New Philosophy for New Media,* 42.

96. Vivian Sobchack, "The Scene of the Screen," in Hans Ulrich Gumbrecht and K. Ludwig Pfeiffer, *Materialities of Communication* (Stanford: Stanford University Press, 1994), 101. However, I want to mention that in her recent book *Carnal Thoughts: Embodiment and Moving Image Culture* (2004), Sobchack includes a phenomenological reading of media beyond the cinema.

97. Belting, "Body, Image, Text," 312.

98. Ibid., 309.

99. John Johnston, "Machinic Vision," *Critical Inquiry* 26 (autumn 1999): 46–47.

100. Hansen, *New Philosophy for New Media,* 123.

101. Ibid., 123.

102. Ibid., 50–51; emphasis added.

103. Slavoj Žižek, *The Plague of Fantasies* (New York: Verso, 1997), 137.

104. Sherry Turkle, *Life on the Screen: Identity in the Age of the Internet* (New York: Simon & Schuster, 1996).

105. Žižek, *The Plague of Fantasies,* 142.

106. Sandy Stone, "Will the Real Body Please Stand Up? Boundary Stories about Virtual Cultures," in Michael Benedikt, ed., *Cyberspace: First Steps* (Cambridge, MA: The MIT Press, 1991).

107. Grosz, *Volatile Bodies,* 18.

108. Christiane Paul, *Digital Art* (New York: Thames and Hudson, 2003), 15.

109. Ibid., 11.

110. For an extended list of digital art projects dealing with art, technology, and science, see the website provided by Stephen Wilson: http://userwww.sfsu.edu/~infoarts/links/wilson.artlinks2.html, or his book *Information Arts: Intersections of Art, Science, and Technology* (Cambridge, MA: The MIT Press, 2002). Sharon Daniel's installation can be accessed through *The 46th Bienniel Exhibition Media/Metaphor web-archive:* http://www.corcoran/exhibitious/previous_results.asp?Exhib_ID=89

111. Presented at the 46th Biennial Exhibition at the Corcoran Gallery of Art, Washington D.C., *Media/Metaphor* (December 9–March 5, 2001).

112. http://www.corcoran.org/biennial/DANIEL/bio.html

113. http://homepage.mac.com/davidrokeby/gon.html

114. This poem is the result of my input of the word "seeing" into the system. Note the similarity in this digital poetry with the poetry of the avant-gardes of the early twentieth century (for example, Marinetti's "Words in Freedom" qtd. in chapter 2).

115. Paul, *Digital Art,* 11.

116. Ibid.

117. Hansen, *New Philosophy for New Media,* 15.

118. http://sponge.org.

119. http://fO.am.

120. Xin Wei Sha in an interview with the author.

121. Xin Wei Sha, "The TGarden Performance Research Project," *Modern Drama,* forthcoming in 2005. University of Toronto, Graduate Centre for Study of Drama.

122. One of the best examples to illustrate the importance of chance is the name-finding of the Dada movement itself, which was apparently chosen by chance from a dictionary.

123. Michael Kirby, *Happenings,* 22.

124. Johannes Birringer, *Media and Performance Along the Border* (Baltimore: The Johns Hopkins University Press, 1998), 141.

125. Elisabeth Bronfen, "Die Vorführung der Hysterie," in *Technologien des Selbst: Zur Konstruktion des Subjekts* (Frankfurt am Main und Basel: Hochschule für Gestaltung Offenbach und Stroemfeld Verlag, 2000), 78; my trans.

126. Just like in the science fiction thriller *Blade Runner* (1984), the "Voight Kampff Test" searches for real memories to distinguish "replicants" from humans. In more recent science fiction, the proof for being cyborgs, or nonhumans of some kind (including clones), has become more visible (as suggested by the trend of body inscriptions). In *The Sixth Day* (2001), for instance, clones can be distinguished from the original only physically through a red dot inside the lower eyelid.

127. Hal Foster, *The Return of the Real* (Cambridge, MA: The MIT Press, 1996), 127.

128. Roland Barthes, "That Old Thing Art," qtd. in Foster, *Return of the Real,* 128.

129. Exhibited at the 2002 Biennial at the Whitney Museum of American Art in New York City. http://www.whitney.org/2002biennial/.

130. Mary Flanagan, "Hyperbodies, Hyperknowledge: Women in Games, Women in Cyberpunk, and Strategies of Resistance," in *Reload: Rethinking Women and Cyberculture,* ed. Austin Booth and Mary Flanagan (Cambridge, MA: The MIT Press, 2002), 445.

131. Interview online with the curator of the Biennial.

132. http://www.maryflanagan.com/collection.htm.

133. Ibid.

134. Mary Flanagan, *Hyperbodies, Hyperknowledge,* 449.

135. Deconism Museum and Gallery: http://wearcam.org/deconism/cyborg_echoes_simplified_html.htm.

136. For Paul Vanouse, the moment of a medium's emergence as an art form involves intense scrutiny of its typical usage prior to artistic intervention. Vanouse's fundamental interest, however, is an even more radical understanding of emerging media. Not

only artistically contemplating the relationship of a technocultural medium (like the Net) to the arts, but rather contemplating the relationship of the technoscientific medium to the broader culture including the arts. Paul Vanouse in an email interview with the author; see also interview with Paul Vanouse, forthcoming in *Revista a mínima: Propuestas visuales y conceptuales contemporáneas.* http://www.ubicarte.com/aminima/.

137. For more details on this project see http://www.contrib.andrew.cmu.edu/~pv28/rvid.html.

138. Barbaras, *The Being of the Phenomenon,* 7.

139. Merleau-Ponty, *Phenomenology of Perception,* trans. Colin Smith (London: Routledge, 1962), 235. I want to give the full citation of this famous quote: "[My body is the fabric into which all objects are woven,] and it is, at least in relation to the perceived world, the general instrument of my 'comprehension.'"

140. Jeffrey Shaw, "The Dis-Embodied Re-Embodied Body," in *Jeffrey Shaw. A User's Manual—Jeffrey Shaw. Eine Gebrauchsanweisung: From Expanded Cinema to Virtual Reality. Vom Expanded Cinema zur Virtuellen Realität,* Anne-Marie Duguet, Heinrich Klotz, Peter Weibel, eds. (Ostfildern: Hatje Cantz, 1997), 157.

141. Eisenman, *Visions Unfolding,* 87.

142. Hansen, *New Philosophy for New Media,* 122.

143. If Hansen's central insight is that new media need a new philosophy that is specifically concerned with the body, mine has been its complementary inverse—that no theory of embodiment can be thought outside of considerations for new media.

Index